Dear Donald,
Many, many Thanks
and oodles of Blessings

Marva Y. Stith
NKA Marva
Woods
Stith,

The Author
Feb 7, 2012

$25.00

Black Star Girl

$295.00

Black Star Girl

MARVA WOODS STITH

iUniverse, Inc.
New York   Bloomington

iUniverse books may be ordered through booksellers or by contacting:

iUniverse
1663 Liberty Drive
Bloomington, IN 47403
www.iuniverse.com
1-800-Authors (1-800-288-4677)

Because of the dynamic nature of the Internet, any Web addresses or links contained in this book may have changed since publication and may no longer be valid. The views expressed in this work are solely those of the author and do not necessarily reflect the views of the publisher, and the publisher hereby disclaims any responsibility for them.

ISBN: 978-1-4401-9581-5 (sc)
ISBN: 978-1-4401-9579-2 (hc)
ISBN: 978-1-4401-9580-8 (ebook)

Library of Congress Control Number: 2009913696

Printed in the United States of America

iUniverse rev. date: 2/25/2010

African-American Pearl

A

Snowflake,

Fingerprint,

DNA,

Each unique as I must be,

African-American Pearl,

Black Star Girl,

Proud of a legacy

Endowing me with

Who I am, all I can be,

African-American Pearl,

Black Star Girl.

There's not one

Quite like me.

Marva Woods Stith

For

Jai Haley Dungey

William Hale Dungey III

Jasmine Taylor Stith

Sydney Darynne Stith

My grandchildren who give renewed energy
to my desire to live everyday making a
positive difference in the world.

For

Farah Diba Stith and John Darin Stith and his wife Patricia

My children who have patiently anticipated
this book celebrating a grandfather they never knew.

Contents

Acknowledgments

To God, with thanksgiving for the blessing of family and friends; may he always be praised through my words and my actions.

In loving memory of John and Iva Woods, who raised me to value a standard of living requiring knowledge, fortitude, self-confidence, pride, patience, service, and respect for others.

With tremendous thanks to siblings who all my life have lived in my heart and soul as encouraging friends. Remembering Kathleen and Sharon, our sisters raised with us, who died too soon. To my big brother, Johnny, twin Jim, and little brother Larry, "living somewhere in California," I could not have pulled this together without our long telephone conversations and your patience recalling details from childhood experiences on. To Cynthia, my sister who lent me her ear, letting me read portions over the telephone for her commentary. To Roy, my baby brother, who critiqued as many chapters as I sent to him, whom I learned enjoys history as much as I do thus pushed me to continue documenting "my history."

To a school no longer in existence, Williamsfield High, and the Class of '55 anticipating our fifty-fifth reunion this summer, the memories strengthen today as the experiences did then.

To Shirley Kendall Kelly, a friend from college days at AM&N whose excited interest in this project of mine enabled a modern Augusta, Arkansas, connection I never want to lose—thanks for your enthusiastic input.

To all the wonderful folk I worked with in corporate America, I was truly privileged to know you.

To Nazzarena Mazzarelli, an inspiration as one of the few women directors in the company; over the years a constructive listener and faithful friend whose encouragement fortified my determination to write about family, thank you.

To Rhina Ramirez Schiffman, a friend and helper in times past whose diligent approach to achieving in spite of adversity continues to inspire.

To those who are the Galilee United Methodist Church family and our pastor, Reverend Edmund E. Martin, whose Sunday morning sermons have encouraged this effort of mine, many blessings.

To Mr. Arthur Pannill, a dedicated pioneer in our church, your thoughtful questions and advice, brief and to the point enabled my progress with this writing exercise. Thank you, my friend.

To Evon Fulson, one of so many supportive friends, whose constant reminder of the importance of this book existing for the young people in my family has kept me motivated and on the path, thank you.

To Gussie Klotz, my neighbor and friend, and all others who knew of this project and despite its ad infinitum process continued encouraging sentiments at any opportunity. I am grateful.

Introduction

Recorded in our family Bible for future generations to deal with as they might are the words "Great-grandfather Woods—19 years old when released from slavery." Each time I read that note, it grounds me with courage and strength. I am a survivor of *slavery*. The nineteen-year-old was my father's grandfather.

It was also inspiring when my father's father, the son of that slave, left an inheritance of sixty-nine dollars for his children to share "after paying all of Papa's expenses and debts," as Uncle Joseph wrote in his August 1954 letter to my father. Considering conditions for black men during my grandfather's time, his ability to leave an estate for his sons and daughters impressed me, again, with the strength of my genes. My father's parenting would continue to inspire my personal strengths.

The 1959 edition of Arkansas State AM&N's *The Arkansawyer Yearbook* records in black-and-white print my career goal of becoming a personnel manager. I felt quite daring as I gave the interviewer the answer to his question. At the time, it was a more optimistic than realistic goal for a black person, much less a woman, to achieve. Discriminatory employment practices affecting minorities and women were a fact of life, intimidating such an accomplishment. Prepared to graduate with some 250 classmates from the predominantly black college in Pine Bluff, Arkansas, I was ready for the challenge.

Earlier in the year, my mail box in the Student Union held the good news that I had passed the Federal Civil Service Entrance Examination (FSEE) and could be hired for a professional career in the federal government. My score was a good one. However, having completed the Business Administration program at AM&N and earned my Bachelor of Science Degree, I wanted to open doors to rewards earned succeeding in the private sector. Government wasn't my preferred path to a business career.

I had achieved my father's major goal for me. It was time to realize my own, success in a major corporation, regardless of my gender or color. I was confident. As the great-granddaughter of an African who had survived an enslaved life in America, my genes include those of generations of folk with determination and courage. That slave's son, my grandfather, lived a long life as a family man, a farmer, and a Baptist preacher. And most importantly, *his* son, my father John Wesley Woods, Jr., was an intentional parent.

Mr. Woods (as most people called him; I called him "Daddy") determinedly raised his black children to be honest, confident, productive adults equipped to take care of themselves. Daddy had many skills. He would help them develop theirs. My father did not have a college degree. His children would have the opportunity for the life-enhancing benefit of higher education. Daddy had a succession plan for educating each child. He would see the older children through college, and they would help the younger ones coming behind. I was the second oldest and knew my responsibility. I had to finish college and help the others. All of his life Daddy tended to his goals. I tended to mine. The outcome may not have met my father's expectations, but his lifelong plan ingrained strength of purpose that fortifies me to this day.

My father's proud, independent demeanor convinced me he descended from a line of African tribal chiefs. He was tall walking, though more of average height than tall in stature. He was a stocky, muscular, not fat, darkest dark brown man. His was a serious, square-shaped face, pleasant, and he smiled only when something was truly humorous. Evenings after work, following a supper of meat and potatoes, bread and butter, lemonade or Kool-Aid, or milk, and for sure a homemade dessert, Daddy relaxed in his form-fitted over-stuffed chair and read. He seemed addicted to current events as he scoured daily newspapers, fact-filled magazines, and nonfiction books, never novels.

On my library shelf is a first edition of *Kabloona*, by French writer, Gontran de Poncins, published in 1941. The book is a detailed account of the author's experience living with Eskimos as he journeyed twenty thousand miles in fifteen months in the Arctic. It belonged to my father and was the only story-like book I knew him to have. As a teenager, I read the epic several times, which pleased Daddy immensely. I seemed to be "learning," which he insisted his children incorporate in their activities.

My mother, Iva Eulalia Newman Woods, with loving loyalty, supported her husband's plans for each of us. She was a gentle lady, a homemaker who kept an attractive, well-organized environment for her family. Not only did she maintain a recipe box, a button box, a mending basket, and a sewing box, she also had a stationery box of pens, ink, paper, postage stamps, and other items for corresponding. Mother wrote warm, newsy, interesting letters. Her formal education ended when she finished eighth grade. Nevertheless, she was a diligent reader. She kept up with newspapers brought into the house and enjoyed magazines and poetry. Another cherished book in my library is her tattered first edition of Robert Louis Stevenson's *A Child's Garden of Verses*.

Mother was a buxom, ample woman with a beautiful round face framed by a head full of black hair so straight we gave her a periodic Toni Home Permanent for the style with body and curl she preferred. Her hair, together with a complexion more white than tan, made me smile each time I heard her adamantly profess "one day we darkies will be treated like other people." She was not dark at all.

The Adams (Mother's maternal family) and Newman family histories indicate her heritage included Cherokee and Delaware Indian. Mother's stalwart manner, independent, self-assured personality and prideful bearing, led me to believe she was the descendant of an Indian chief. That together with the African tribal chief possible in my father's bloodline was surely the force conflicting the lives of my siblings and me as we dealt with a society that found it easy to summarily disrespect even ignore our existence. Each of us lives proudly independent lives in our communities.

Although Daddy constantly said we must go to college, my prideful mother uttered the words that initiated my determination to do so. I was six years old. We were in the kitchen. I was helping fix dinner. She didn't preach or lecture as Daddy did. Quite matter-of-factly, not looking at me, she talked. At the sink, rinsing cold water through the potatoes she had just peeled, she sort of mused, "I've always thought each generation should do better than the one before." I didn't say a word; I immediately accepted her premise. It made sense. No more just thinking about going to college. I would do it. My father graduated from high school but not college. Silently I vowed to get my four-year degree and fulfill the expectations of both parents.

My father's constant imperative "Go to college; get your degree," a mantra of many black parents in his time, was quickly followed with a motivational declaration directly referencing the unlawful and lawful unfair treatment endured by blacks in those days. "Whatever they do to you or against you, no one can take that piece of paper away." He would add, "Things will change, and you must be ready for different opportunities."

Aunts, uncles, and friends, bombarded with Daddy's articulate declarations for educating his children, shook their heads dismissively and admonished him to "just take care of them now." They had a point. Our family kept growing and struggled financially. Daddy's entrepreneurial mind set fostered a stubborn determination to reject better paying jobs as a laborer, or in a steel mill, or other factory. Daddy refused the confinement of what he termed stagnating, boring work.

My self-reliant father experienced numerous setbacks, yet he had his three oldest children in college at one time. And thanks to my father's goal-tending parenting, I thrived after a business experience that could have acutely derailed a less prepared individual.

Daddy died in 1960. He was fifty-eight years old. It was his heart. Mother was forty-nine. He passed just days before their twenty-fifth wedding anniversary.

Not much of John Woods's life was easy; still there was pride, love, fun, and triumphs—thus these stories of challenge and accomplishment, his and mine.

Marva Woods Stith

Chapter 1

The Beginning I Know

In the Appalachian foothills, not far from the Ohio–West Virginia state line in Fleming, Ohio, on a fair June day in 1911, a girl child was born to Jesse and Bertha Adams Newman. It was their second daughter, and they named her Iva Eulalia. She would be the last of their four children. Baby Iva was destined to become my mother.

That summer, in rural Augusta, Arkansas, lived a wise, resourceful nine-year-old named John Wesley Woods, Jr. He was destined to become my father.

John, baby brother to sisters Modes and Odessa and big brother Joseph, was the fourth child born to the union of John Wesley Woods, Sr., and Mary Stewart Woods.

From first knowledge my roots go back to the African continent and the torturing slave trade that forced my people away from heritage and family, I've been fascinated by what I don't know about my ancestors. Only because my father told me so, I know great-grandfather Woods was nineteen years old when released from slavery. My father's birth certificate shows his dad, the son of that slave, was born in Mississippi in 1873. My father was born in Tupelo, Arkansas, in 1902. Hopefully, one day my offspring will learn more about our past.

Daddy told me his mother, also born in Mississippi, died when he was very young. It was a sad fact he credited with propelling him into a constructive adult life.

His father remarried, and the family added two sons, Roger and Robert and two daughters, Ermalee and Cleadria. John Woods, Sr., was a farmer, most likely a sharecropper. I never knew. I did know Grandpa Woods didn't own the land, which inspired my father's goal to become a landowner. John's stepmother, a diligent housewife and mother, took good care of her large family. Still, I grew up hearing my father's stories of a childhood experiencing motherly neglect. His busy stepmother gave more attention to her youngest, cooking, cleaning, washing, ironing, and mending. My daddy said he was never hungry or dirty, but that wasn't enough. He didn't like being raggedy or unkempt. It was a disappointment to reach into the clothes basket and pull out trousers or shirt—torn, a button missing, belt loops hanging, seams ripped apart, or pant leg needing the hem dropped for the growing boy. Taking the garment to his stepmother, she pushed him away with, "there's the needle and thread, fix it yourself." He did. Mending progressed to sewing, making something new out of something old. He began to cut and stitch fabric into clothing—mostly shirts. He also began cutting and trimming his own hair when he wanted it done. His hard-working dad and mother praised him, and he kept improving.

Daddy may have been playing baseball when Mother was born, it being a summer day and he loved baseball. More likely he was helping with the farming—hoeing, weeding, watering, and feeding stock. My dad admitted he had fun as a kid—after his chores were done—playing baseball, and other games and reading. Still, his strongest memory seemed how he picked up life skills doing what his stepmother didn't have time for. Such was the basis, years later, of his lectures on worthwhile, continuing rewards for children who learn self-reliance at a young age. He earned money when mothers sent their children to him for hair cuts. Grown men even paid "that Woods boy" who regularly cut their hair. I'm sure the productive habits Daddy developed as a child became the performance foundation for his entire life, and particularly as our family's goal-setting, self-sufficient patriarch.

John W. Woods, Jr., graduated from Augusta Arkansas' colored high school and continued his education at Branch Normal College,[1] a predecessor of the state's colored Agriculture, Mechanical and Normal School (AM&N) in Pine Bluff, Arkansas. His studies early in the 1920s at the two-year school included barbering and tailoring. He didn't finish his second year. Later, when I was in high school, Mother shocked me revealing that as a young man, Daddy had married and divorced long before she met him.

Although I never heard the astounding news from Daddy, people who knew him in his early years corroborated Mother's words. Those old acquaintances talked of him being in love, leaving Arkansas, and going to find work in St. Louis, Missouri. He only told us he found work in St. Louis in a factory and didn't like the work. It wasn't like anything he had ever done before. He vowed to make a living either tailoring or cutting hair as he did "on the side." He spoke incessantly of one day having his own business, thus planting a seed to germinate, grow, and blossom into his future, and mine. Someone listened to his passion and passed on the enthusiasm to another who had something to offer the young adult black man who would become my daddy.

A customer's relative who lived in Zanesville, Ohio, was a businessman who owned a vacant shop and was looking for a barber, a trustworthy proprietor. John Wesley Woods, Jr., had never heard of Zanesville. Still, envisioning an opportunity, he made the contact and traveled to explore the possibility in the town surely five hundred miles or more distant from St. Louis, in east central Ohio.

It was the late '20s, early '30s, and Mr. Napoleon Love owned a building where, in the rear, with its private back-door entrance, he ran a thriving juke joint with food, music, drinking, and dancing. Fronting the thriving, noisy business, under the same roof, was a fully equipped barber shop waiting to open and welcome customers as soon as a barber could be found.

John Woods liked the setup. He recognized potential for building a good business.

Nap Love liked John Woods, who presented himself as a hard-working gentleman, demonstrated himself to be a skilled barber, and came recommended by family. Mr. Love rented the barber shop to the stranger from St. Louis.

Soon customers referred others to the new shop located on 2nd Street beyond one end of Zanesville's famous "Y" Bridge at the convergence of the Muskingum and Licking Rivers. (For some time, the bridge was noted in *Ripley's Believe It or Not* as the only bridge in the world you could cross and still be on the same side of the river.) John Woods's clientele enjoyed invigorating discussions prompted by his avid reading and a mind inquisitive for the point of view of others. The new barber in town ran the profitable business his landlord anticipated.

* * * * * * * * * *

Iva Newman met John Woods in 1934 when she came to his barbershop for a haircut. Mother initially visited the shop because she liked a girlfriend's stylish new haircut. Mother returned because she liked the barber.

I once had a cherished photo of my father posed in the open doorway of his shop, the striped barber pole positioned over his right shoulder affixed near the door frame. He looked like a man in charge of an already promising life, in a crisp turned-up long-sleeved white dress shirt and sharply creased dark slacks, exuding confidence galore. No wonder my mother was interested in such a handsome, well-to-do looking man—a dream catch for any single woman. The twinkle in my dad's eye and turn to his head seemed to say, "We should get to know each other."

Daddy's fascination with baseball continued into adulthood. Mother's occasional interest in the game brought them together a second time. One perfect day, Mother and her girlfriends from down in the country came to town to watch a baseball game at the stadium. The Zanesville Black Stars, the local Negro sand-lot team was playing. John Woods was there. They saw each other.

Daddy, never lacking conversation, focused on getting to know the beautiful, chubby doll-like young woman who was to become my mother.

Mother learned the interesting black man who flirted with her was not just a barber. He was one of the owners of the Zanesville Black Stars.

"Yes," Mother told him, "I come to town all the time." And she did. She worked as a housekeeper for a white family who lived on "the Terrace," an affluent section of town with large rambling homes and green, spacious lawns.

He learned she had a day off each week and suggested she stop by the shop her next day off so he could trim her hair. She did.

My father being a barber was definitely the linchpin to the permanent coupling of my parents. Having her hair trimmed became a regular habit. When I was a child, I overheard Mother and her best friend, Edith, laugh about how Mother's hair kept getting shorter and shorter and her grin grew broader and broader.

Mother lived down in Washington County's Barnett Ridge, Ohio, with her widowed father. Grandpa Newman recorded in his family Bible 1874 as his year of birth and his wife, the grandmother I never knew, Bertha Adams Newman, was born in 1878. She died in 1918, leaving my mother motherless from a young age.

Iva Newman was twenty-three years old when she met my dad and well into marrying age. Still, her father; her brothers, Arkley and Cleo; and sister, Cora, disapproved of the baby of the family's interest in an "older man." And he was a black man. In those days, black meant color, not race. On first sight, Mother and her family with their fair or light skin, fine glossy hair, and chiseled facial features might be seen as other than Negro as could many colored families in Zanesville at the time—the Barnetts, the Mayles, the Adams, and the Stevens, to name a few. Being dark skinned was seen by some as an undesirable feature. My father speculated his rich black skin color may have been a truer concern than age for the family of the woman he loved.

In the end, Daddy's respected reputation as a successful businessman, his first-class style, and trustworthy manner helped dispel the Newman family's spoken or unspoken dissatisfaction to him marrying my mother. They married in November 1935. Daddy was thirty-three years old. Mother was twenty-four.

Chapter 2

The Times

1935—Zanesville, Ohio Population 35,000–36,000 The African-American population is estimated to have been less than 2 percent of the town's population. Only days before Thanksgiving, in a civil ceremony, John Wesley Woods, Jr., married Iva Eulalia Newman.

My parents married with love and in anticipation of a bountiful lifetime together in a country poised to conquer turmoil on several fronts.

In Washington, DC, Congress earnestly awaited President Franklin Delano Roosevelt's signature to legislation designed to keep America out of a second world war. On August 31, 1935, President Roosevelt signed the first of four Neutrality Acts, an effort to prohibit America's involvement in "foreign" wars. The legislation did not work; America entered World War II in 1941.

America was also embroiled in the throes of an economic depression, ever after known as the Great Depression. A devastating freefall of the value of the largest to the smallest companies in the Stock Market wiped out lifetime savings and personal fortunes and caused mortgage foreclosures. Bank doors were chained against customers, employees, and owners. People were hungry; some homeless. "Brother Can You Spare a Dime?" was a serious plea.

FDR had won the presidency over Herbert Hoover, on a platform centered on bringing hard times to an end. President Roosevelt refocused the federal government's power and resources. Federal banking laws were instituted. Programs, including the Civilian Conservation Corps (CCC)[2] and Works Progress Administration (WPA),[3] were developed providing jobs, transforming the nation's infrastructure, and rebuilding the confidence of individuals and families. Four more years of tough times ahead would challenge the nation's population in every social and economic class.

Seventy years had elapsed since America's horrific Civil War ended. Fought from 1861–1865, the war inflicted loss of American lives in greater number than any war before or since. The Confederate Army of the South surrendered to the Union Army of the North. Seceded Southern states were brought back into the Union. Institutionalized slavery of Negroes in the United States of America was history. Former slaves were made full citizens of the country they or their ancestors were brought to, for the most part, from the shores of Africa, crammed and shackled in the cargo hold of slave ships. Slavery ended, but the battle over the treatment of the country's colored citizens would continue to be waged.

The end of the Civil War found Negroes, individuals and families, migrating from one community to another seeking work and the life of their choice. They traveled the south, to the west, and up east, but the greatest numbers in the years to come headed to the industrialized north in search of job opportunities anticipated in factories and other big businesses.

In the 1920s when the young black man destined to become my father started his migration northward, it wasn't a happy-go-lucky adventure for colored folk moving about to places they might settle down and earn a living. Generally, black men, women, and families were unwelcome—couldn't assimilate into the general population, whether big city or small town. Living where they were allowed, you might find them crowded into industrialized areas of cities to be burdened with finding their way to service or laboring jobs in prosperous outlying neighborhoods. Or blacks might live out on the fringe of established communities and need to make their way into town to earn a living. The prejudices of the time, discrimination and frightening mistreatment by some whites, taught colored people to conduct themselves very carefully outside the insular supportive neighborhoods where there was some sense of security.

The year my parents said their marriage vows, issues addressing the attainment of civil rights for America's colored people were active on the agenda of the Negro leadership. The National Council of Negro Women was founded. Negroes rioted in Harlem. Black college students mobilized to address the injustice of discrimination and segregation, and white folks could expect no backlash or punishment for denying a colored person a place to live, work, shop, be educated, eat, and travel.

John and Iva Woods focused on what could be; what they had resources to achieve and the promise of an improved future.

After all, the National Association for the Advancement of Colored People (NAACP) and the National Urban League had been patiently, quietly working for twenty-five years to change attitudes and the power structure that kept Negroes less than first class citizens. Negro leaders wrote about, debated, preached about, and coalesced with sympathetic whites for a workable strategy to end the unfair treatment of their people in a country whose founding fathers proclaimed "all men are created equal." They called for federal law to override restrictive state laws.

The southern region of the United States was home to the legal segregation of blacks and whites. Prominently posted signs reading *No Colored Allowed* or *Colored Enter Here* or *Colored Dressing Room* or *Colored Served Thursdays Only* kept segregation in order. Demeaning as the situation was, it did provide for enterprising colored folks to succeed in businesses serving those excluded because of their color. The so-called separate but equal society provided this aspect not seen in the northern states. The mandated segregation also enabled qualified colored people to work for their own people in positions of significant importance. Educated Negro professionals taught and filled responsible leadership positions such as principals and department heads in their colored schools. Negroes in the South took pride in professionally satisfying careers as teachers, accountants, social workers, secretaries, bookkeepers, lawyers, nurses, dentists, and doctors. And in the southern states, black-owned businesses such as clothing stores, restaurants, night clubs, theaters, funeral parlors, grocery stores, liquor stores, and dry cleaners thrived.

In the North, where my parents met and married, legal segregation and laws giving authority to the unfair treatment of African-Americans may not have prevailed but their lives and the living condition of people of color were restricted due to widespread prejudice and discrimination. In the cities, colored folk looking for a job, discriminated against because of their color, found work limited to cleaning, serving, lifting, digging, perhaps working in a factory; likely doing manual labor. Unlike in the Southern States, it was highly unlikely to find people of color clerking in stores, working in offices, or waiting tables. My siblings and I never knew of a black teacher in our public schools.

In the North, there may not have been signs posted ordering blacks to keep out or saying they must use a certain door or their shopping was restricted to certain days. However, racial prejudice was an accepted way of conducting business. In the white-owned businesses, colored customers were ignored, certainly to serve whites first. Colored customers were treated with suspicion and distrust and couldn't expect to get a drink of water or go to the bathroom. Black people were not shown the same variety and good quality merchandise. They were generally addressed with disrespect, first names only or addressing even the oldest adult as "boy" or "girl."

Due to widespread prejudice in the North, a market existed for the Negro to maintain a business serving the black population and others as well. Negroes owned retail, entertainment, and service organizations. Except for personal service entities such as beauty and barbershops, and funeral parlors, African-

American proprietors competed with the less favored white-owned store when that store's price was lower. Keeping prices competitive was a crucial problem for the black-owned business sorely dependent upon the support of their own community to prosper.

Voting, an act of immeasurable importance for America to maintain its democracy, was not a right and privilege equally available to every citizen. Each state in the Union established its own voting rights legislation. Under the law of most southern states, a person was required to meet certain conditions at the polling place, those requirements aimed to keep the colored from voting. They might be asked for documentation of good character, be required to pass a written test, or be required to pay a sum of money in order to register or vote. Thus, important political power gained through the popular vote rested with the majority group in all jurisdictions. Consequently, the economic, social, and political advancement of minorities was curtailed where legislation, existing law, zoning, sale, and purchase of property were involved. Not until federal legislation, the Voting Rights Act of 1965, was signed into law by President Lyndon B. Johnson was this bedrock of inequality in our country addressed.

My father believed the mistreatment of Negroes would come to an end. The voices of the few seeking equality for all would grow to be the voices of the majority achieving equality for Negroes. His optimism and the opportunity throughout America for Negroes to be entrepreneurs fueled my ambitious father's plans to be a successful businessman. He planned to have his own barbershop or shops, perhaps a tailoring business, and Daddy saw every reason to develop his Zanesville Black Stars into a winning, profitable baseball team. As soon as racist policies were broken that kept blacks out of the American and National Baseball Leagues, his team would be a welcomed, profit-making resource of athletic talent.

John and Iva married with plans to have a big family. (Mother claimed Daddy wanted nine children—a baseball team.)

The newlyweds moved into a little house Daddy owned on Whipple Street in Zanesville's fourth ward. Daddy's goals remained firm. One day he would not work for others but prosper being his own boss.

Chapter 3

Children and More

The couple started their family immediately. First born, son John Wesley Woods III, came into the world the following September.

Johnny was a brilliant baby. I know, because throughout my childhood I heard Mother and Daddy constantly share his magnificent accomplishments to any stationary ear. They bragged their first born sat, unsupported, at three months and took his first steps so quickly, "he never crawled." Johnny, they glowed, walked, unassisted, at nine months. He spoke his first words quite early. Potty training him was no problem; such an intelligent child.

In a photograph, my big brother poses dressed up in a white long sleeve shirt with a dark tie appropriately knotted though not at all under his chubby chin, and wearing black dress pants, short, as was the custom at the time for children in his age group. White socks above high-top white baby shoes complete his attire. Johnny's thick curly hair, neatly combed and brushed, suggests the concentrated effort it must have taken his parents to perfect. The handsome baby boy exudes the potential his early development promised—a daunting role model for the siblings yet to come share his world.

And come we did! The next year, in November, my twin brother, James Franklin and I were born. Jim was named for our maternal grandfather, James C. Newman, whom we called "Granpa" and knew to be "Jesse Newman." Jim's middle name represented our parents' tribute to America's president, Franklin Delano Roosevelt. Mother and Daddy, along with many others, revered the president's unwavering effort toward bailing the country out of the Depression and for his words and actions showing respect for colored people and their importance to the nation.

They named me "Marva," affording my lifetime opportunity to proudly recognize a beautiful black woman and a famous black sports personality as I announce, "I'm named after Marva Louis, Joe Louis's first wife."

From his days as the World Heavyweight Boxing Champion, Joe Louis became a sports personality, nonpareil. He continues to be an icon in the boxing world.

"Lee," my middle name, honors Aunt Ermalee, Daddy's baby sister. They didn't intend a lilting two names in one, like hers. I was simply—Marva. That is, unless I was in trouble, then, I heard, firmly, "*Marvalee!*"

In less than two years, the ambitious, eligible bachelor, an enterprising barber, and the demure young lady from down in the country, who did housekeeping work for rich folks living on the hill, became a family of five beautiful people. First snapshots show us outside Zanesville's Union Baptist Church. Daddy, Mother, and little Johnny pose around an impressive straw twin-baby carriage. Jim and I nestle in the carriage's fluffy bedding. Our tiny faces peer into the camera lens, seeming both bored and curious. The family in their Sunday best portrays confident prosperity.

Daddy took charge of their family; Mother lovingly followed his lead. She was proud of the man she married and quite willingly quit her job housekeeping for others. Mother cherished being a housewife and homemaker for her family. For the rest of their lives together she never worked outside the home. They valued Daddy being the family's provider.

Daddy's income from the barbershop was not enough to take care of his growing family, so he kept several jobs and income-producing ventures going on at the same time. He sold Florsheim shoes door to door and anyplace a customer opportunity was possible. Just as enthusiastically he sold life insurance for the Atlanta Life Insurance Company. For a short time he was a ticket distributor for entertainment events he booked into town.

Daddy was most passionate about his responsibilities as president and business manager of the Zanesville Black Stars. Daddy believed the team was truly "A Negro Team With Speed and Class," as proclaimed on their business stationery, and had the potential to be a success in every way. When baseball business consumed time he had promised for the family, Daddy was apologetic, but it was clear to Mother he valued the team and loved the challenge. Mother did not—no way! Anytime gate receipts didn't cover expenses, Daddy and the other owners had to go into their pockets to make up the difference. Mother would not hide her concern for their family's sacrifice.

Daddy was certain the Black Stars would one day be a consistent money maker because Zanesville was a good baseball town. Their players and those on Negro teams of the era were amazing athletes to watch. Many moved on to play in the Negro Leagues. Negro players could not make it onto the rosters of the American and National leagues, or even their farm clubs, because of their color, not their talent. Nevertheless, it was a time when baseball was the national pastime in America. Still, Daddy and their management team struggled to increase revenue to cover uniforms, equipment, transportation, and salaries for the Black Stars. Gate receipts fell short more times than not.

Finally, Daddy acquiesced to Mother's view; it was a losing venture for the no-longer- single man. He relinquished all association with his beloved baseball team.

Perhaps my father was able to make the decision due to an unavoidable priority foisted on him and his family by the City of Zanesville. The unexpected development presented a wonderful option for Mr. Woods's attention.

* * * * * * * * * *

Couched in disruptive change, good fortune smiled on the Woods household. The house on Whipple Street was in the right place at the right time. Theirs and neighboring homes were claimed by Zanesville under "eminent domain," to be demolished to build *Cooper Mill Manor*, garden apartments; moderate income housing.

The city distributed buy out offers to all the property owners. "Okay, we'll take it," they said, everyone except my dad. "Not enough," he said.

Tirelessly, he tried to convince the others to reject the amount offered. "Hold out," he encouraged. "Demand more. Our property is worth more to them than what you're being told." Instead, not wanting to risk losing anything, they accepted the city's offer. Daddy held out, went to court, and won. The story is he was paid twice that first offered, much more than the others. For sure, he received enough to finalize contracts for building his family a new home in the city up on Cliffwood Avenue.

* * * * * * * * * *

Our new house, modest by today's standards, impressed many as its construction progressed. "Did you see the house Mr. Woods is building?" they informed one another with their rhetorical question. The one-story white-shingled house with cinnamon colored roof tiles looked out over Cliffwood Avenue. Large double dormer windows looked over the front porch roof, tucked under their own cinnamon colored roof. The veranda-like porch spanned the front of our house, which was built into a sloping hill in the middle of the lot. The descending front yard was centered with a concrete walk to a half dozen steps marching down to the city sidewalk.

A spacious backyard sloped gently upward behind the house. Both front and backyards were ideal for attractive terracing sometime in the future.

However, the house was not just a residence. From first learning they were being bought out of their Whipple Street home, Daddy saw an opportunity and began making plans. Negotiating a loan from First National Bank, and then staying on top of the execution of details, large and small, with the architect and contractors, Mr. Woods was certain he had the basic necessities to secure his family's financial future. The new house had made a family-operated business a reality.

John Wesley Woods, Jr.,
my father, 1935

Two of my father's siblings,
Aunt Modes and Uncle Joseph

John Wesley Woods, Sr.,
my paternal grandfather

Iva Eulalia Newman Woods,
my mother, 1935

One of my mother's siblings
Uncle Cleo

James C. (Jesse) Newman and Bertha Adams Newman,
my maternal grandparents

Chapter 4

The New House

My father's collaboration with his architect and contractor resulted in a house of some significance at that time in Zanesville. It was in our same neighborhood of mostly black families; up the hill, over on Cliffwood Avenue. To those passing by 622 Cliffwood Avenue, it may have been as ordinary as any other house under construction. However, in 1941 it was said to be the first centrally air-conditioned private home built in town by anyone, black or white. Also, inside were a few amenities not commonplace in a family home.

Entering the front door, you stepped onto an expanse of honey golden hardwood flooring. You were immediately in the living room, with the dining room straight ahead. I remember my wide-eyed approval upon first seeing what appeared to be one huge room, barely noticing the gently curved almost room wide archway evenly separating the space.

On the living room's right wall, a few feet from the front, a door opened into a bedroom. Farther along off the dining room, a small archway carved out a hallway with a bedroom at each end and full bath and linen closet between. Behind a swinging door at the left end of the back of the dining room was an eat-in kitchen with modern appliances. Except for the kitchen and bath, the lovely hardwood floors prevailed throughout.

Built onto the dining room's far wall was a schoolroom-like blackboard complete with a chalk tray. Only it was constructed with plywood, not slate. Daddy had searched and found the appropriate finishing for the board and then the black paint that responded to chalk and erasers just as if it was slate. That blackboard was all about my father steering his children into thinking activities—preparing them for college.

We played word games and tested our arithmetic and spelling skills holding competitions entertaining the family. As we grew older, we were given pop quizzes, Daddy always the quizmaster. Mother was the encourager, a motivator quietly reminding us of Daddy's expectations. She kept chalk on hand and didn't make out a grocery list without inquiring, "Do we need chalk?" For sure, our parents were a team. Daddy was the team leader.

Jimmy liked to draw. Using both colored and white chalk, his sketches of animals and cartoonlike people were so neat we hated to erase them. Daddy began to look for similar creativity from Johnny and me. We didn't show artistic talent. We only elicited laughter for our effort. Jimmy was the artist in our family.

The board, an educational tool, was fun and work too. Before company came, particularly if invited for dinner, we had to make certain the board was cleaned, erasers and chalk put away, and chalk dust thoroughly removed from any surface. Yet we liked having the blackboard, especially when Daddy wasn't around. Then we had a great time playing tic-tac-toe.

A highly polished, usually closed maple door next to the blackboard opened to a finished stairway leading to the attic. Friends bold enough to infer the new home may already be too small were assured the house "had potential." The potential was in the attic. "Later when we finish the upstairs, we'll have more than enough room," my parents assured the concerned one. (Mother was expecting their fifth child. Sadly, at only two days old, the baby, our little sister, Vernice Maxine died. The next year Jacqueline Sue was born. Jacqueline died at eight months old with rheumatic fever.) As it was, the attic was forbidden territory. "It's dangerous. The walls and flooring are only plasterboard," Mother and Daddy warned us. "Step anywhere or lean against anything and you'll fall through and hurt yourself. Don't go up there!"

The attic was used for storage, reason enough to entice curious children to explore. They had stashed baby things and other stuff I hadn't seen from the Whipple Street house, and small suitcases of fabric samples Daddy had accumulated for the tailoring shop he might have one day. My favorite carton was filled with "wheels" of red, green, or bright orange "Admit One" tickets. They were the admission tickets distributed to the entertainment groups he once helped bring to town. Mostly, we liked to gingerly make our way through the attic and lean on the front window sills to look beyond our street into backyards a block away. Luckily for us, our forays into the forbidden territory ended without anyone stepping through the ceiling.

We had a full basement, not "finished" but concrete throughout with special features. My favorite was the playroom where we rode tricycles and wagons and soared on a swing built into the unusually high ceiling. The swing, a traditional heavy twisted rope swing with a wide wooden seat, was like one hanging from a tree in someone's yard. I had never seen nor heard of another home with a swing suspended from a basement ceiling. Kids playing with us were impressed. Their parents shook their heads incredulously. I didn't hear anyone express the sentiment, but Mother said they thought Daddy was strange, not at all harmful, but different. I often heard Mother, in support of her husband, speak glowingly of the attention he gave to the activities of his children.

Another notable aspect of the basement was an extraordinary laundry area. Huge hot and cold water pipes tracked across the ceiling and down the wall into three sets of laundry tubs and two large washing machines. Commercial ironing mangles and sorting tables lined the two walls cornering the area. Open shelving hung on the wall above each table. Storage cabinets were tucked underneath every table. In addition, two drying rooms took a lot of space; one enclosed, the other, a larger and open clothes drying area. In the enclosed room, bolted from the ceiling, were many, many parallel rows of clothes lines for hanging wet wash and two tall and wide floor-standing drying racks with prickly frames. They were used for stretching delicate lace drapes, tablecloths, and linens needing air dried. The grander-than-usual fixtures and accommodations were crucial to my father's plan. He had included in our home, the *Home Laundry*.

Advertising cards were widely distributed. Daddy promoted and assisted the family business he said was Mother's to handle. (Mother smiled skeptically when he said that.) New customers became repeat customers; their belongings returned in a few days washed, dried, folded, and ironed. Many afternoons I made my way down the basement stairway to sit quietly on the fourth step from the bottom and watch the hustle and bustle as Mother supervised and worked with the women they had hired.

Daddy continued to barber full time, and sell shoes and insurance while he helped run the laundry. "One day income from the laundry will be enough to let the other work go. We may have several laundries," he promised. The new house fulfilled my father's ambition to provide for his family with a successful business of his own.

Times Recorder file photo
This photo is from the website of a local
newspaper, the *Zanesville Times Recorder*.
It is captioned "The Zanesville Black Stars, a black semi-pro
baseball team played in Zanesville in the 1940s".

Daddy's passion for his
baseball team transferred to their
Home Laundry

John Wesley Woods III
their first child

Twins came the next year—
my brother Jim and me.

Johnny, Marva, and Jimmy
in the Putnam Hill Park

Chapter 5

1941

Our move to 622 Cliffwood Avenue, eagerly anticipated by my parents, wasn't accomplished without enduring considerable anxiety. Daddy was the catalyst for the unrest because he did as he wished, not as he was told. When following vs. leading was seen as an option to him, Daddy tended to lead. Although a descendant of slavery and thus the servitude foisted on generations of his family down through the years, my father had no problem activating the free will inherent in human nature and very present within his character. He took charge if at all possible.

The City of Zanesville wanted us to leave Whipple Street when my father was not prepared to comply. He was calm about the matter. So much so, it may have appeared he ignored their written notices to vacate. He hadn't. He had a plan for them to follow his lead. Emotionally, as well as figuratively, he pushed the official papers aside letting their existence energize him to accelerate overseeing the contractor's progress on 622 and to encourage Mother's bravery in facing men coming to our door insisting on knowing when we were getting out, vacating their property. My dad's plan called for his family to move directly to the new house, not into interim housing. Since the house wasn't finished, the city had to be stalled. Mother helped by courteously greeting city officials who came to our front door accepting their urgent messages with sincere understanding.

Late spring 1941, it was obvious the city would have its way. No more delays. The housing authority had paid for the property; it was theirs. Heavy equipment was poised to demolish the little house just as they had wrecked most of the neighborhood. Our time was up. Daddy saw we had to go the day he came home and found Mother in tears. Sobbing, she told him how the city representatives had promised to put the family out on the street. Mother's emotional message convinced my father he had lost the standoff. Our new home wasn't ready. His family had to make the first of two moves.

Daddy had hoped we wouldn't have to pack and unpack twice because we had a brand new baby. Mother gave birth to a little girl on April 21, 1941. She was named Kathleen Marie.

Naming her was not a simple exercise. Without hesitation, Daddy suggested Kathleen as a beautiful name for his daughter. Mother resisted. "Why? We don't know anyone named Kathleen. We're naming our baby after one of your old girlfriends?" she questioned her husband. "Of course not," he said, his tone casually dismissing the possibility.

Finally, after verbal deliberation sufficient to stay in my brain all these years, with pragmatic reluctance, Mother acknowledged "Kathleen" was okay. She had several rationales. First, it was a pretty name. Second, she and Daddy both admired the strong clear voice of a popular singer of the time, Kate Smith,[4] whom Daddy said looked a lot like my mother. Third, Mother said "Kathleen" was a perfect match for "Marie," Aunt Cora's middle name.

Once Daddy accepted the fact we had to move, in practically no time, our family of six vacated Whipple Street. Baby Kathleen was not yet two months old. We went as Daddy and Mother knew we could to the Archey family. Mr. Archey was Daddy's close friend and business partner and also a part owner of the Black Stars and the team's secretary and treasurer. At the time, Mr. Archey and his family were the only colored people with a home in the beautiful Brighton Boulevard area of Zanesville. For many weeks Mr. Archey had implored my father to bring us to live with them until we could get into our place. Finally Daddy agreed and moved us out to share their lovely home.

What had seemed a very spacious house those times we visited no longer felt so after we crowded in. But thanks to the Archey's generous hospitality and Mother's fabulous organization skills, we did okay making their home our home too. Mostly we time-shared the kitchen, our bath schedules, and handling the family's laundry. We were well-behaved children, and if not, well, Mother and Daddy were firm and patient, too. There were no crises, just minimal comfort and privacy for all of us. So the day Daddy announced we should pack and prepare to leave a sense of thankfulness from both the host and guest family filled the air.

Mother got busy, evidencing wordless relief with her enthusiastic approach to repacking her family's belongings. When the truck and men came to help move us, we were ready. Suddenly, we were gone, and all of us and everything we owned were in the new house.

"The contractors aren't quite through at 622, but we can move in. They've agreed they can work around us," Daddy had told us. Occupancy permits were not required as they are now.

The interior contractors were several weeks away from completing their work and would, indeed, work around us. Even though my brothers and I stayed out of their way, we just barely escaped a tragedy. I remember the panic, mostly me screaming, as Jimmy began to tumble through a hole in the living room floor. It was a large, rectangular, and rough opening for a floor register not yet secured to an air conditioning duct. Hearing my scream, Mother rushed from the kitchen. Amazingly, the heating contractor was in the basement, directly beneath the opening, catching Jimmy before he hit the concrete floor. The near disaster prompted our parents to realize even though there was much to do, looking after us had to be Mother's only task.

* * * * * * * * * *

The Home Laundry opened as soon as the contractors finished and left us to ourselves. Advertising fliers brought the first customers. Referrals continued to bring others. The first reliable customers were white families who lived on the Terrace and in prosperous neighborhoods out west of town.

In the beginning, customers dropped off and picked up their clean laundry. Customers received the advertised prompt service. Good business got better when Daddy had a telephone installed. In those days, most homes in our neighborhood did not have telephones. The family next door did, but we didn't. Customers began telephoning to arrange pick-up and delivery, which Daddy handled using a small panel truck bought just for that.

Our father continued to barber full-time and keep up his weekly debit accounts with Atlanta Life Insurance Company. And every Thursday afternoon, when the barbershop was closed, he went out to the Civilian Conservation Corps (CCC) Camp to earn extra money cutting hair.

My parents were doing just fine. Daddy's business plan was meeting his expectations.

Everything changed on Sunday, December 7, 1941, when the Japanese bombed Pearl Harbor. President Roosevelt declared the United States of America at war with Imperial Japan. Several days later Nazi Germany and Fascist Italy declared war against us.

America began immediate mobilization for the nation's full armed engagement in the conflict aptly called World War II. For more than two years, England, France, Russia, and other allies had been engaged in fierce battles on the continents of Europe, Asia, and Africa. Now America was in the fight.

Government and private resources were immediately directed toward military priorities. Manufacturing plants all over the country were converted from making consumer items such as appliances, household goods, furniture, and especially automobiles and their parts to begin making tools, tanks, machinery, weapons, and ammunition, whatever was needed for the war effort. The CCC Camps were closed. Many men quickly joined the army, navy, air force, coast guard. Able-bodied men between the ages of eighteen and thirty-five were drafted and sent without delay into one of the branches of the armed forces. Women joined the military also, were nurses, primarily; black women were likely to work in the kitchen or the laundry. The war introduced a significant change in civilian employment opportunities for women. As the men were drafted or enlisted, women were soon hired for the tasks the men left behind--in industry, on assembly lines, even in offices, and defense plants, all jobs previously known to be for men only.

Mother's employees quit to take jobs learning new skills, earning higher wages, and to help the war effort. Anyone wanting a job had better options than the laundry. Not able to hire help, Mother and Daddy couldn't continue their new business. They had to shut down the laundry. Daddy sold the equipment—washing machines, ironing mangles, and the panel truck. The telephone was taken out. The Home Laundry was out of business before a first year anniversary could be celebrated.

****

Daddy was too old for the draft plus he had five dependents to care for. Not acceptable for duty even if he tried to enlist, his contribution was limited to civilian service. He served as an air raid warden with the Civil Defense program. (Johnny said Daddy also used the time to collect insurance premiums as he patrolled his route.)

Air raid wardens went to work when deep ear penetrating sirens wailed, announcing the town was having a "blackout." It was a practice drill for everyone to perfect an immediately invisible world in case enemy planes came overhead to drop bombs on us. Every light had to be turned off. Darkness was essential. My dad walked his assigned area, making certain inside and outside lights were turned off and black window shades pulled down. If he saw the tiniest speck of light, he banged on the door to get in and help make things right. If enemy pilots were to sneak through our skies, they should not find a target for their bombs. No way would we suffer as they had in Pearl Harbor. I felt safe with my dad looking out for us.

Something did frighten me and generated bad dreams many nights. A water tower stood several blocks up our street, high on the top of Putnam Hill where Shelby Street, Cliffwood Avenue, and Matthews Street converged. The monstrous storage tank filled with tons of water appeared balanced on gigantically tall spindly steel legs perched directly above our home. Even before Pearl Harbor, I was scared to death of the water tower, its tiny red light on the very top quickly blinking on and then off to warn airplanes of the obstruction in their path high in the sky. I couldn't stop worrying, "What if?" What if disaster happened because a tiny crack in the tower's gleaming steel side went unnoticed? For sure, the first teeny sliver of liquid seeping free would quickly grow and burst into torrents of heavy cold water forcing trees, homes, cars, and people, kids especially, to their destruction in the most violent flood. I did not know how to swim. Even if I could, there was no way possible to escape the water exploding from the fractured skin of that tower. Yes, my bedtime prayer even before the war included a plea that God made sure the water tower suffered no damage and remained intact forever.

The war continued and my fear escalated. No doubt about it, the formidable tower had to be a danger for any airplane. In fact, I looked in the direction of the tower immediately upon hearing a blackout siren's scream. I had to know the red light, high on its own almost invisible antenna above the tower, had vanished. Then, not seeing the blinking warning, a new worry crept into my head. What if *friendly* aircraft inadvertently brought doomsday into my world; the light *was* out, and not seeing it, they slammed into the water tower?

I was one scared child, yet I knew I was fortunate to be in America— my fear imagination based upon the war news from Europe and other places. Bombs were not dropped on our homes and churches, libraries, hospitals, schools, and cities. My pain and misery rested in fear of someone we knew and loved being hurt or killed in the war in distant lands. There was the *anticipation* of unbearable sorrow and danger that consumed the young and old.

There was the stranger, a woman living in Cooper Mill Manor at the end of our street. People said she never answered her door; she didn't want to risk finding someone from the War Department bringing word her son was killed fighting in Europe. School kids talked about seeing her face from the little window in her front door. Others scoffed and did not even believe there was a boy from that place away in the war. Some even thought the apartment was vacant—that no one lived there. Me, I was absolutely quiet when the subject came up, for very good reason.

One morning, walking to school, all by myself, too late to be with the others, hurrying along, I glanced at the fabled front door. She was there, peering through the foot square window glass. For the smallest half second, our eyes locked. I clearly remember seeing her so-sad dark eyes. I tried to make my six-year-old eyes say, "I'm so sorry. I'm so sorry. Good Luck." It brings tears to my soul remembering that moment.

Children were involved in the war effort, encouraged to save string and pick up tinfoil to turn in to use as materials making things for the war. Antilitter campaigns were several decades in the future. Public trash containers didn't exist as they do now. Discarded trash was thrown from car windows and dropped on sidewalks. Litter was everywhere. As a first grader, on my way to and from Wilson School, head bent to the ground, my eyes searched for the tinfoil in trashed chewing gum wrappers and cigarette packages. Cigarette packages were the best source for the shiny innards. Chesterfield, Lucky Strike, Philip Morris, Camel, each empty package that had been tossed to the ground was collected, pulled apart, and the thin tinfoil carefully smoothed and shaped into a quickly growing round ball. I liked collecting the tinfoil knowing it was necessary for the defense of the country.

I never knew if my dad wanted to be in the war. I've felt he was conflicted about wanting to serve. I heard him and other men with disgust in their voices speak of the limited soldiering Negroes were permitted because discrimination against them in the military was as bad as it was in their daily lives. The segregation of whites from blacks prevailed just as it did in the Southern states. "They'll only let us cook, shine shoes, clean the latrines," my father and others mourned. Daddy always did his best to avoid being where he was disrespected, mistreated because of his race. He wouldn't be able to do a thing about it in the military. Perhaps my proud father was thankful he wasn't eligible and didn't have to be demeaned in the role he played to gain the victories dearly sought and prayed for.

Then black troops were given weapons and sent to the front lines. Eventually the Tuskegee Airmen, trained to be fighter pilots, participated in missions against the Germans. After hearing that kind of news, the men in our neighborhood were energized and hopeful about actually fighting in defense of their country.

Throughout the seemingly never-ending war, grownups said Johnny could be the first person in our family drafted to fight. The prospect was horrible. Not just because of the danger but it meant many more years of war. Johnny was just a kid, not nearly eighteen. I prayed the fighting was over, soon. After all the news suggested World War II was quite likely the war to end all wars! If it ended before Johnny and Jimmy were drafted, they might never have to be soldiers.[5]

My father gave up barbering to take a wartime job at Wright-Paterson Air Force Base in Dayton, Ohio. He did it because civilians were needed for tasks directly related to the war effort. He also appreciated the increased income for the family. At Wright-Paterson he was hired for construction work and in the process learned how to plaster as he soundproofed a propeller laboratory.

Daddy traveled to Dayton every Sunday night, staying all week, returning to us on Friday nights. We all missed him, but as Mother told anyone, "Our sacrifice is nothing compared to families with men away from home in the war."

Nighttime would come; the water tower's ominous presence threatened my life; my daddy was not home with us, and there was war all over the world. I was afraid.

Chapter 6

Over!

August 14, 1945, President Harry S. Truman announced Japan had surrendered. In the spring Italy had been liberated from Germany then some weeks later, Germany surrendered. The Japanese surrender was signed on September 2, 1945, which President Truman said was truly V-J Day.

Nevertheless, there was peace at last. The war ended long before my brothers could be drafted. The world no longer seemed colored in drab hues of grey, brown, and dirty green. Instead, the air was light and breezy; colors of bright blue, white, red, and yellow seemed to be everywhere. Music was joy filled, lilting, and voices loud in pleasure. It was a wonderful time.

A sense of ecstatic prosperity prevailed in our country. The black population had renewed hope for the beginning of improved race relations in America, better job opportunities, respectful treatment, and better all-around living conditions. After all, blacks had worked and, in the end, fought together with whites to win battle after battle and finally the war itself. Black and white America shared giddy satisfaction anticipating the return of the servicemen and women from danger.

What a relief to think of Clifford Mayle out of danger. He and Mother's best friend, Edith, were a young married couple and didn't even have children yet. Their house was two doors up the street from ours. Their backyard had a peaceful grape arbor over a narrow walkway. I used to sit in the arbor, hiding from everyone, thinking, in the cool deep shadows, vines heavy with leaves all around me. Once when the war was not going well at all, I was sorry to be nestled there hearing Mother and Edith sadly contemplate the likelihood Clifford might not return alive or in good health. I didn't sleep well that night and many nights afterward, dealing with Clifford's possible death or serious injury. Now, at last I could picture him safely in the neighborhood again.

The end of the war brought the end to all rationing. People could get what they wanted of what was available. Rationing, limiting what and how much people could buy, had been important so the armed forces would have supplies, equipment, tools, vehicles and parts, anything needed to fight the war. When rationing was in effect, our family didn't feel restricted, particularly in shopping for groceries, because there were so many of us. Each one in the family, no matter age, had his own rationing book for butter, milk, meat, fruit, vegetables, etc. Mother plaintively admitted our family's six books of stamps let her buy more than she could afford.

Soon the Sunday evening came when Daddy didn't return to Dayton. He was no longer needed at Wright-Paterson. Our father was home every day, not just weekends. Mother was content. I wasn't afraid of anything! I was seven years old, looking toward a long life ahead. The war was over.

Chapter 7

Church

I thanked God the war ended and our family was safe. I prayed for peace to continue forever, that there would be no more wars.

Perhaps from the time I could speak I spoke to God through prayer. It was natural for me to do so because Mother, early in our lives, introduced praying as a routine. She taught us the simple prayer thanking God for our food, which we said before each meal, and the prayer recited kneeling before climbing into our bed each night. The Lord's Prayer was learned in Sunday school and at home. From memorizing and reciting the three prayers, I easily gravitated to handing over to God responsibility for keeping trouble away or giving me strength to handle what life dealt. God has been a comfort, all my life.

Church was a regular experience; an important part of our family's life and my spiritual growth. Daddy was Baptist; Mother, Methodist. The family attended Union Baptist Church where Daddy participated in various activities. I clearly remember evenings, sitting, waiting in an out of the way place in a dark wood-paneled room while he attended or presided over a meeting helping with church business. At one time Daddy was the Sunday school superintendent.

Once in a church stage production, he played the devil, a portrayal so authentic it proved almost more than I could handle.

Shortly after the curtain closed on the opening night performance, that devil terrified me, appearing, it seemed, from nowhere running down the aisle to where Mother, my brothers, and I were sitting. Mother had said we were waiting for Daddy to change his clothes and take us home. As the devil glided toward us, Mother was smiling. I wasn't. The creature—his face in menacing red, black, gray, and bright white makeup, flourishing his black and blood-red-trimmed hooded cape with tall, pointy ears—kept coming closer. My young mind was thoroughly convinced it was the devil wanting us. I had watched that devil in the play, intimidating everyone on stage until he was banished through the power of good. Now the play had ended, and here he was practically in front of me. Scared to death, crying, gasping for breath, I tried to scramble away and hide behind my mother. Her comforting words (once she stopped laughing) didn't help either. "It's your father," she repeated, looking at him and then me. Several minutes elapsed before I accepted that it truly was our daddy in costume. My brothers teased me for days afterward. Daddy talked with me about the experience, making it my first lesson in the art of drama and the act of entertaining by pretending to be someone totally different than who you are.

Sunday school every Sunday and staying for church after was a family habit. With that routine, the household had a Saturday night ritual of Daddy trimming his boys' hair, Mother taking care of her girl's hair, and our shoes being cleaned and shined.

Everyone's shoes, including dress shoes for Mother and Daddy, were placed side by side on newspaper generously spread to protect the hardwood floor. My brothers used shoe brushes, squares of soft cloth, and either liquid or pomade polish to make our shoes gleam. I didn't help shine shoes because our father was a strong proponent of what was girls' work and what was boys' work. He called shining shoes boys' work. Nevertheless, I did successfully beg to be allowed to try my hand at the chore. I liked it but couldn't try making it a regular Saturday night job since that was when Mother was most likely doing my hair.

"Doing my hair" meant Mother was straightening or pressing it (either term was used). She washed it earlier in the morning using the rainwater saved from the downspout at the back of the house. She also did a final rinse of water so cold it took my breath away. (Daddy said, "After the hot and warm water washing, a good rinse with cold water will close your pores so you won't get sick with a cold.") The vinegar added to the cold water, supposedly to make "your hair nice and soft," Mother said, surely cleared my nostrils. Mostly washing hair was done on Saturday morning, sometimes Friday night. Hair had to be shampooed in time to be fully dry for straightening on Saturday evening. My hair was long, thick, soft, and very curly (nappy or kinky, we said). Mother began the process for changing it to straight hair by first applying hair oil where she had sectioned or parted the hair to reveal my scalp. She must have made and oiled more than a dozen such parts. I remember liking the process. The hair oil smelled good; it was perfumed. When my scalp had been sufficiently attended to, Mother took another small dollop of the thick hair oil, rubbed it between the palms of her hand, and massaged it throughout my full head of hair to the tip end of each strand. After doing that and finger massaging my entire scalp, the pressing or straightening would begin. She divided the hair parting it down the middle from the top of my head directly over my nose to the center of my hairline at the back of my neck. Each of those halves she divided in half from the top of my ear across to the middle of the center part. When she was through with that sectioning, she gathered and took care of very small sections of hair, perhaps no larger than the circumference of a quarter. With a hot steel comb, she combed or pressed each firmly, yet gently. The hot comb was kept at the right temperature, hot enough, but not too hot, over a flame or electric burner. It took a couple hours to do the straightening, but once the job was done, her black sturdy comb moved smoothly through my hair each morning and didn't get hung up in snarls and tangles. I loved my black shiny, straightened hair, the braids hanging down to my back, that is, until it needed to be washed again, or until I got caught in the rain without a rain scarf. A few of Mother's friends tried to dissuade her from spending so much time with my hair. "She has good hair," they said. You don't need to straighten it." Mother didn't listen to them. She said she wasn't going to put me through the pain or ruin my healthy head of hair by breaking it off as she tugged and pulled trying to comb through the kinks. So getting my hair straightened wasn't a matter of vanity; it was my mother making sure I had hair to care for when it was my responsibility to do so. I thank her for that every day.

When we were not going to Sunday school or church, the attention given to hair and shoes was moved to Sunday night. For sure, by weekend's end, we were well groomed for the upcoming week.

I didn't mind missing church, but I loved Sunday school. I took great pleasure in seeing another gold attendance star added after my name each week on the huge display board listing all who registered for classes that session. I welcomed the structure of Sunday school and walked tall and purposefully when it was my turn to take our class offering envelope to the office. When someone wasn't there to take their turn and they asked me to do it, I was one pleased kid.

I looked forward to hearing the Bible stories and collecting the colorful Sunday school cards handed out when I recited a Bible verse by memory. The cards such as Jesus praying or the stone being rolled away from his grave or Noah welcoming the animals onto the ark included the appropriate scripture. I do not remember having my own Bible, but I clamored for as many of those cards as I could get.

Being a kid with a vivid imagination, nights in my dark bedroom I frightened myself with scary thoughts. Then I recalled the lessons learned in Sunday school's Bible stories. They taught about God taking care of faithful people. The stories of Daniel in the lion's den, Job and all his troubles, and David and Goliath built and strengthened my faith. The tragedy that befell Lot's disobedient wife was a lesson that helped me too. I remembered faith and obedience was important. I believed God constantly looked after me and would see that I was okay.

Sunday school made a believer of me—not church. Church service in the sanctuary afterward was a pain. The speakers took too long. The pew seats were hard and uncomfortable, but neither of my parents tolerated fidgeting and moving about. Thus, I had a hard time staying awake. The happiest moment was walking out of church after sitting through the pastor's sermon. Little did I know, as an adult the Sunday service ritual—readings, scripture, hymns and prayers, and especially the pastor's message was what I needed to give me the fortitude and confidence to get through trials faced during the week.

Daddy insisted Sunday was a day of rest whether we went to church or not; no one was expected to work, not even do chores. Exception, Mother cooked a special Sunday dinner. Every once in a while the reverend came to our Sunday afternoon meal, but even when we were just 'family', Sunday dinner called for a lot of work. I helped Mother in the kitchen with the preparation or set the dining room table and helped clean up afterward. The women in my daddy's home certainly worked on Sunday. Mother had no problem with it. She sang and bustled about like it was a blessing to be doing so. I never said anything, but I didn't share her joy. The "day of rest" Sunday rule seemed to apply to men only.

Then one day church came to be a problem, a big problem. Daddy was not a mainstream thinker regarding the religious upbringing of his children. He would not consent to our being baptized until "they understand the decision they are making; until they know what they are doing." The earliest, he thought, at the age of twelve.

The church fathers (and mothers) were not pleased with his decision and constantly attempted to change his mind. I can remember them pleading with Mother when Daddy wasn't home. They came, Bible in hand, referencing scripture supporting their position, hoping to influence Mother to send us to classes and then be baptized. At best, they wanted her promise to try and convince her husband it was the right thing to do. "Tell him," they said, "you want the children baptized." Mother could not be moved. "His decision is our decision," she told them. Daddy said no. So it didn't happen. Sunday school was not the same wonderful pleasure it had been. I was uncomfortable, different from the other kids. On the other hand, it was kind of neat that my parents were sticking to their guns. They had become the talk of the church by refusing to go along with normal procedure. Still, I was anxious for my twelfth birthday so I could be baptized like my friends. I wasn't worried about being saved, being acceptable to God; Daddy assured me that Jesus looked after all children.

Chapter 8

Family Working Together

Summertime 1945 phased into autumn and the financial condition of John Woods's family failed to reflect the postwar prosperity hyped in news headlines. Steady, good paying jobs existed in various manufacturing plants and industry in and around Zanesville, but Daddy preferred his occupation of choice, barbering. He couldn't return to the barbershop he ran for Nap Love because the building had been sold; the shop was gone. Daddy took a barber chair in Ed Norris's shop on Linden Avenue and had plenty of good paying customers. The income, however, wasn't enough to cover the family's expenses—pay utilities and maintain a house barely five years old, and meet the monthly mortgage obligation. Providing for his family of four growing children pressured Daddy to find a means to increase his earnings. He was forced to relegate his barbering to part-time. Daddy began taking jobs in the construction trades in order to bring home sufficient pay.

Daddy's wartime experience at Wright-Patterson made the career change possible. In order to hold his civilian job at the Air Force Base, he received training and was required to join a construction workers union. Now in peacetime, Brother John W. Woods had his union card as a member of the Ohio State Building & Construction Trades Council; thus he could gainfully work in construction.

My father didn't turn down any job, gladly taking "helper" work thrown his way on a construction site. Doing what was asked of him, he was a laborer, moved dirt about, kept construction materials supplied to the builders, and cleaned up. He worked fast but also watched the "professionals" and asked questions. Soon he moved on to lay brick, put up framing, level concrete, and other tasks that allowed him to help produce the finished product. Daddy worked in most of the skill sets comprising the building trades, avoiding electrical and plumbing because neither appealed to him. His mind challenged by the contracting process and valuing the glowing critique of his work by customers and others convinced my father to go for more.

Daddy bid and won jobs as an independent contractor. He built Hubbard's Garage on Eighth Street, one of his biggest contracts in Zanesville. His contracting resulted in reducing time in the barbershop to Saturdays. Then that stopped. Time with the family was more important than the extra money one day of barbering brought in. Thus, Daddy successfully changed his career from barber to self-employment in construction.

One Sunday, after church, in time for dinner, Mr. Eli Carr visited us. He was Daddy's boyhood pal from Arkansas now living and working construction in Cleveland, Ohio. Daddy proudly spoke of his success in the construction field. The Hubbard Garage job had generated good feedback and more work, not of the same caliber, but any day it would happen he was sure. Income working for other contractors kept the family afloat. Mr. Carr bragged about his job with the company holding the Muskogee Hotel's major remodeling contract. He begged Daddy to come work with him. They needed experienced carpenters and plasterers. "We've got work even when the weather is bad," Mr. Carr said, promoting his fine situation, "union pay, steady work for a long time." Daddy liked the promise of income during inclement weather. "And you can be home with your family on weekends," Mr. Carr insisted. Those words changed Mother's passive attention to the conversation. Abruptly she emphatically gave her unsolicited vote. "No!" she said. At once the living room was quiet.

She knew the guarantee of steady employment with excellent pay was what they needed. But handling the household without her husband alongside helping manage their family was a situation she didn't need. That much she learned when he was away in Dayton. Now the family was even larger.

A second set of twins, girls, were born Christmas Eve, 1946. They were named Cynthia Eulalia and Sharon Kaye. Their first names were original. Their second names were a gift of significance; "Eulalia" being Mother's middle name and "Kaye" for Danny Kaye, one of Mother's favorite entertainers.

The new babies were not yet six months old when Mr. Carr astounded Mother with his proposal doomed to change our family routine. Cynthia and Sharon were popular additions to our family and so cute, but to me, as much work as they were fun. I helped with them, a lot. It didn't seem to me Daddy did much more than hold the babies and talk to them. But I understood Mother's agony. As Mr. Carr and my father talked, I remember Mother beginning to softly cry and then go into their bedroom. Daddy calmly, though quickly, followed after her. When my parents returned, there were no signs of tears. Daddy had gained his wife's support. Daddy told Mr. Carr to tell the people he would come to Cleveland and see about working for them.

The promise of a substantially higher, steady income was too important for the family. That fact enabled Daddy to calm Mother's concerns about him being away. Once again, Daddy was working out of town, coming home on weekends.

****

Daddy didn't come home every weekend after he began getting construction work on his own to fit into empty evenings away from us. By the time the hotel's huge remodeling was finished, Daddy had built up a contracting business in the big city. He had to stay in Cleveland to meet his contract commitments.

Mother, managing the home front, sometimes bought groceries on credit. We older ones went to Johnny Guard's Grocery Store on Shelby Street with her note asking for the credit. We returned with one or two big brown bags of items Mother had thoughtfully listed in her note. The bill was paid after Daddy came home or sent money.

When he couldn't be with us, he sent money by Western Union or special delivery mail. I remember the excitement in the house when the Western Union guy drove his car up to our house. Daddy kept a good reputation with the grocery store, paying the accumulated charges regularly. Still, Mother was prudent in using the available credit, choosing to manage without shopping, making us "get by." It wasn't unusual for us to wish for food we didn't have.

The family began to need money frequently. We did not participate in the school lunch programs at Wilson Elementary School or Grover Cleveland Junior High. Mother wanted us to come home, not hang out at school for almost an hour. We walked home each school day for a sandwich of bologna, lettuce, and mayonnaise or mustard on white Wonder bread or other lunchmeat sandwich with milk or Kool-Aid. Only once in a while did we have leftovers from supper the night before. A few times we went without lunch. Johnny, laughing about it now, recalls he and Jimmy, making their way home from school, meeting me, already returning to school, telling them no need to go home, "there wasn't anything to eat."

Many times we did not see Daddy for almost a month. He had to finish a job because a new customer was losing patience about him beginning the work he contracted to do for him. Daddy didn't have a car or a truck, so traveling within the parameters of bus schedules used valuable time he needed to keep the customers satisfied. It was his decision—a sacrifice for all of us. Everyone felt his absence. My brothers had to do without haircuts since Daddy was the only barber they ever went to—no one else. Mother's loneliness was apparent. I mainly worried about our family. After a three week absence, I wondered if we would ever be together again.

Daddy regularly wrote letters whether he had money to include or not. Mother wasn't worried. She knew she could rely on him for whatever he was paid since the last time he wrote. (In later years, as adults, my brothers vouched for his diligence, recalling when they were with him, how he went directly to the post office and at the lobby table in his grungy coveralls, wrote Mother, enclosing all he had just been paid, except a little he kept for them to live on.)

I know at home we watched for the mailman to stop at our box, anxiously looking for envelopes with Daddy's handwriting. Next, size of the envelope was important. A fat envelope meant a lot of bills hid inside. Once or twice, though, a thin letter held several fifty and a few one hundred dollar bills.

Once, a thick envelope of smaller bills got Jimmy in big trouble. After Mother read the letter out loud, letting us see the bunch of money (not how much), Jimmy slipped into Mother's bedroom, easily found Daddy's envelope on her vanity, tucked between her perfume bottle and the mirror and took "just one dollar" from those folded inside.

"She won't miss one. There are so many," he must have been thinking as he crept out of her room, slipped along the hallway, past the bathroom, through his bedroom, and then to the back door and out of the house.

It was Saturday. He found his friends and took them to the movies. They had a good time, seeing John Wayne in *She Wore a Yellow Ribbon*. His buddies surely appreciated Jim paying their way. Movies were only ten cents, but ten cents was not easy to come by.

Yes, it was a great afternoon except my brother's happy satisfied feelings were replaced with guilt. Worry over being found out and the ensuing punishment quickly blotted out his euphoria. As confidence waned that he had perpetrated the perfect transgression, he shut down, just quietly curled up under the dining room table.

Mother discovered the missing dollar bill and assumed in the excitement of handling so many bills of several denominations, she had simply miscounted. She was disappointed because she always carefully accounted for money. It had to stretch to the next time a fat or thin letter came from Daddy. It never crossed her mind one of the bills had been taken. She thought she had made a mistake.

Later that evening, her concern was Jimmy. He was not talking, not teasing nor joking around, just lying under the table, saying, "nothing's wrong," but acting otherwise. It all began to fall apart for my twin brother. Mother asked him if he was hungry. He said he wasn't. She asked him if he had a sore throat. He said he didn't. He insisted his tummy didn't hurt. Mother was not hearing what she needed to stop caring about her son's health. She made him present his forehead for her usual scientific test for high fever, a light touch to his brow with the back of her hand. Nope, he didn't have a fever. The rest of us became involved. We were curious about Jimmy's weird behavior. Then Johnny "squealed" on his brother.

We learned what Johnny had found out from C.H., "Cloudy Hugh," a good friend of both my brothers. Jimmy had told C.H., swearing him to secrecy, about how he got the money to take them to the movie. We were shocked. I remember how relieved Mother was to know she didn't make a mistake in counting the cash she was entrusted with. Jimmy's malfeasance restored my mother's money managing confidence. As for Jimmy, well, he recalls that escapade earned him the worst whipping of his life.

My Brothers Worked Too

Johnny and Jimmy from eight and nine years old worked regularly, doing chores and getting paid for working for others.

Jim had a paper route, delivering the *Times-Recorder* every morning and making his collections on Saturday. If he didn't catch a customer at home or they couldn't pay "til later in the week," he went back on a weeknight. There wasn't a telephone to call ahead. Mother did not want her kids out after sunset, so weeknight collecting worried her. She insisted Johnny had to go with him. Those boys liked that about the paper route—being out at night.

Jimmy's worry was when a customer didn't pay after several visits. In order to keep the customer, he paid the bill out of his pocket. Then it was even more important for him to collect and get his money back. Collecting became so tough he couldn't afford to keep the paper route.

Jimmy moved on to earn spending money working for our neighbor, Caddy Mayle, on his truck. Caddy hauled things for people, and Jim helped with the lifting, carrying, loading, and unloading.

Johnny shined shoes down at the court house. He said he loved that job. Not only was he paid every week, with the tips he made each day he also bought custard-like ice cream at the court house snack counter. That alone made it one of the best places he ever worked.

Pete Curtis, who hired Johnny, owned the popular shoe shine business. His two sons, Albert and Carl, also worked for their dad, shining shoes along side Johnny. Albert and Carl knew the big tippers and waited around to do their shoes and left the no-tippers for Johnny to take care of. When Johnny figured out their scheme, he also avoided the no-tippers. Mr. Curtis took my brother aside and told him he had to give good service to all who came in for a shine, whether he thought they were generous or not. "You are paid to shine everyone's shoes." Anyway, Johnny dutifully said, "Yes, Mr. Curtis," even though he didn't hear his boss giving the same talk to his sons. Johnny just hurried to a big tipper ahead of Albert and Carl. Eventually all three of them ignored the nontippers. Johnny got fired. He was sad. At the age of ten or eleven, he learned his first lesson in the painful power of nepotism practiced in the workplace.

Neither of my brothers kept their paying jobs for very long. Still, they were not lazy kids. In fact, none of us were. We didn't have the time to learn how to be lazy. Each of us had meaningful chores to do. Daddy believed a strong work ethic instilled in children as early as possible developed character necessary for a worthwhile life.

* * * * * * * * * *

When I was a little girl, I may have wanted to hang out and *play* with my brothers, but no way did I want to help them with their jobs around the house. Their chores were difficult, dirty, and dangerous.

Cutting the grass should not have been treacherous, but we didn't own a lawn mower. A mower would not have worked in our backyard anyway. Landscapers had not been hired after the contractors finished and we claimed our new home. The yard, prolifically overrun with weeds, resembled a deserted construction site. Daddy did some work with the raggedy terrain too rough for a lawn mover. My brothers used a sickle, bending from the waist, swish, swish, swishing every clump of grass. It scared me. Daddy taught them how to take big swipes with the sharp sickle and avoid slicing their legs in the process. Leaning on a four- to five-foot walking stick held about waist high with their left hands, their right hands holding and swinging the curved sickle cut a swath through the weeds, leaving what passed for grass covering the uneven ground. They never injured themselves or anyone else.

Then there were the heavy duty dirty tasks related to our home heating system, a wonderful coal furnace. It was a brand new furnace, top of the line, with shiny heating ducts running from its top sides across the basement ceiling to floor registers, two in every room, throughout the house. Heat was generated by burning coal that had been shoveled into the open door of the furnace's oven whenever the temperature in the house started to fall. It was Jimmy and Johnny's job to keep the furnace fed. If they weren't home, I did the despicable job. Shoveling coal into the furnace was better than being cold.

Coal was delivered as requested by truck to homes with a coal furnace. Getting the coal into the coal bin in our basement was another job in our house—for the boys only. Thank heaven! When, at minimum, a ton of coal was delivered by the coal supply company, it was no big deal for my brothers. The deliveryman attached his steel sliding board chute to the back of the truck, extending the apparatus into our basement window directly into the coal bin. Gravity was essentially the single force propelling the coal down the chute into the walled-in coal bin. When the driver finished his delivery and pulled away, all Jimmy and Johnny had to do was go to the basement, make certain the window was closed and securely locked, and gather any lumps of coal that may have rolled out of the bin and throw them onto the coal pile.

It was a different scenario when Mother called Mr. Jones for the coal. She did that when there wasn't enough money to buy a whole ton. Mr. Jones had a steel chute, but Daddy told him, "Don't use the chute. Just dump the coal outside the window. Shoveling it in will be good for my boys, keep 'em busy." Johnny and Jimmy did it a few hours on Saturday and after school until it was done.

Then there were coal deliveries from our Uncle Arkley. He was a carpenter and builder by trade and brought us coal in his truck. He didn't have a chute, so his coal had to be dumped in a heap on the ground and then shoveled into the basement. If not for this, the delivery from Mother's oldest brother was a welcome blessing because it was a gift. He refused any pay.

Coal delivery days could have been the best days for our family because we had the assurance of a comfortable, warm home for a few months, but moving coal around was such a pain to my brothers, we all suffered. They fussed and argued over which one of them was doing or not doing his part, and Mother had to continually pressure both of them to stick with the job until it was done.

Then there was the task of cleaning out the furnace and dealing with the accumulated ashes, another job for the boys, not the girls! Good! As the coal was consumed by the heat and converted into ashes, the residue dropped through the grate into the bottom of the furnace to be cleaned out before the small space was filled. Oxygen couldn't flow freely into the furnace when the ashes were allowed to accumulate and pack under the grate. Lack of oxygen inhibited the conduction of heat through the aluminum heating ducts into the floor registers—leaving us cold, not warm and toasty in our house.

Johnny and Jimmy were responsible for shoveling out the ashes on a regular basis. It was usually a Saturday morning job for them; more often when the weather was extremely cold and more coal was burned.

Some homeowners stored the ashes removed from their coal furnaces in a cinder block ash pit built in their backyard. (A local ash pit cleaning company came periodically and removed the ashes from the pit.) We were among the families that did not have an ash pit. Mother and Daddy talked about having one built, "one day."

In the meantime, my brothers loaded our ashes into a galvanized washtub and lugged it up the basement steps out into the backyard. Then the ashes were spread evenly over the snow, in whatever part of the yard Mother decided needed filler before spring. The larger chunks of ash (we called them "clinkers") not small enough to walk on were tossed in the ditch between our house and our neighbor Mr. Scott's hedgerow.

In freezing snowy weather, the finest ashes were sprinkled over icy steps and walkways, as we do rock salt today. Most everyone, with ash pit or not, used ashes to insure safe traction on pathways that had become sheets of ice. Some families spread coal ashes over icy tire tracks in the street to lessen potential for car and truck accidents. Drivers appreciated the effort. Youngsters in the neighborhood did not. Sled riding down the middle of the street was great fun, until someone ruined it all with *ashes*. On Halloween, the boys remembered and victimized the homes responsible for ruining their fun, even if the folks gave great stuff on trick-or-treat night. Their windows got a good soaping.

I Worked Too

In the seventh grade, at the beginning of the school year, I was called to the principal's office. What a surprise! My brothers may have known that experience, but it was new to me. They had been caught in some kind of trouble, perhaps throwing spitballs in class. "What did I do?" I wondered—not for long though. Right away, the principal asked if I would be interested in reading to a blind student. "We will pay you." I had been offered a job, one I wanted.

He gave me a permission slip my parents had to sign, and I worried, tried to think of reasons Mother and Daddy might say no. My parents were good at saying no to me, with an explanation for saying so. All the way home, I was nervous, even considered whether I should return the slip with their forged signature—a first time I considered something like that! Good for me, my thinking also took me to realize the consequence could give me trouble that was not worth it. And maybe they would be pleased. After all, it must have been because I was one of the best readers that I was chosen. Also, the job paid money, a dollar an hour. I didn't have to go to anyone's home. I crossed my fingers they would say yes.

Daddy quietly read the permission slip, looked up at me, and said, "You'll have to keep up with your school work." *Yes!* We had to apply for my Social Security number. Zanesville's Board of Education was my first employer, and the first paycheck I ever received was theirs for seven dollars. During a study hall period, I read homework assignments to a blind girl, actually just legally blind, who happened to be white. She could see, but not good enough to read her assignments. We were in the same grade, different rooms. I didn't know her until we met. I've remembered the two of us, both serious about studying, enjoyed our time together the entire school year. We did well in our classes, getting better than good grades.

Around the house, I had regular housekeeping chores—sweeping, mopping, waxing floors; dusting and waxing furniture, washing windows and venetian blinds, and washing dishes, washing clothes, and eventually ironing. As they came along, I learned how to take good care of my baby sisters and brothers.

I thoroughly enjoyed Mother's time and attention teaching me how to bake and cook. From a very young age, say age six or so, flaky scrumptious biscuits were my specialty. I was also a very good cake maker. Then other times, I was in the kitchen just reading to Mother from her Robert Louis Stevenson book of poetry, *A Child's Garden of Verses*.

Daddy gave me my first sewing lesson, assigning sewing projects. Once I had to make a dress for my doll, and Daddy made it clear I was to have it ready for his inspection when he got home on the weekend. I procrastinated; put off taking care of my assignment. Then it was an anxious, last-minute rush. I once stood wedged between the vanity and dresser where I could see the cab bringing Daddy home. I was furiously hand stitching the last unfinished seam of the doll's dress. My punishment when I didn't meet his deadline was a lecture, and I didn't feel at all good having failed.

Mother taught me how to embroider and hand stitch. Aunt Cora tried to teach me how to crochet and knit, but I couldn't get it, just like I could not learn how to play the piano. Daddy insisted I learn. We had a brand new black mahogany piano in our living room. He couldn't play; neither could Mother; no one in the family could. Daddy bought that piano specifically for me to one day play for everyone. I started taking lessons in the first grade. I could not order my fingers or my mind to grasp enough of the process to hold from one lesson to the next. After weeks and weeks of agonizing effort to "catch on," I successfully implored Daddy to let me quit. He met with the teacher, who couldn't give him reason to encourage my continuing. The ordeal was over.

Daddy promised (as he relented and let me stop the lessons), "One day you will wish you could play the piano." I shook my head quickly and profusely to respond in a relieved and so grateful tone, "not me, never, never." Today, admittedly, "I wish I could play the piano."

Chapter 9

The National Pasti...

Throughout my childhood and youth, I silently languished in self-pity because those brothers of mine had more fun than I who had to do "girl things"—learn piano, sew, crochet and embroidery, mend socks, sew on buttons, bake, cook, wash, and iron clothes. My play time was boring reading, doing tea parties with my dolls, dressing paper dolls, playing hopscotch, or dress up with a friend once in a while. My brothers, though many of their chores consisted of dirty, hard work seemed to have more fun in their recreational pursuits than I did.

Daddy was such a baseball fanatic he let his sons go out and play baseball all the time. And they were so happy! When their chores were done, they were gone. Before noon on a Saturday morning, there would be a knock on the door, and a neighborhood kid with a baseball glove, or a wooden Louisville Slugger bat or ball or all of the above would be standing on our front porch begging for Johnny and Jimmy to come out and play with him. In short order, with Mother's or Daddy's permission, outdoors they went. In the vernacular of a time yet to come, it seems to me those brothers of mine were always *in the streets* or *on the corner.*

Perhaps I'm not being totally fair. Even though my brothers and their peers did seem to be outdoors from high noon to past nightfall, they were not *hanging out.* They were hard at play, constantly. They played marbles. They played tag. They played hide-and-seek. But they played baseball, incessantly.

Those boys got together for pick-up ball games, or maybe even just the two of them to play "flys and grounders," or "catch." If others joined them, they might play Indian Ball—a competitive game not needing many players. It required only a pitcher, a catcher, a batter, and a couple others positioned in the field hoping the ball would be hit in their direction. Whoever got to the ball had a chance to be the batter by catching the hit ball "on the fly," that is, before it touched the ground, or they could become the batter when they retrieved the ball and threw it back to roll into the bat lying flat in front of home plate. Or if the ball had not been hit past the infield, the batter stood the bat straight up, perpendicular to home plate, and whoever retrieved the ball became the batter by tossing the ball and hitting the held bat. I liked that game. Yes, I got to play when it was only my brothers, Daddy, and a couple others in the game.

...ll was a big thing—popular in neighborhoods similar to how kids
...asketball today shooting hoops at home, on schoolyards, in parks. Then,
...s walking anywhere to and from school, home, or even doing errands had
a baseball glove on one hand, tossing a ball back and forth to each other—
playing pass. Baseball was an obsessive pastime. Kids also gathered daily in
open spaces to practice their hitting and fielding skills. Daddy encouraged it.
"Be serious about learning and playing the game, and you can be a professional
player. One day Negroes will play in the majors." He tried to keep them from
playing *softball*, warning it would ruin their throwing arms and the possibility
of a career in Major League Baseball.

Mother didn't want Daddy buying the regulation baseball equipment
Daddy insisted his sons needed—bats plus an infielder's glove for Jimmy and
a catcher's mitt for Johnny. The very few heated discussions my brothers and I
overheard between our parents Mother fussed, "We barely have enough money
for food, yet you buy those expensive gloves for the boys." Daddy listened,
responded patiently to her concerns, but did not waver. Speaking softly, he
made his case for getting the best equipment, particularly gloves.

Mother wasn't against his program. She just didn't think it so important
that they learn the game with the kind of bats and gloves the family couldn't
afford. They could learn just as well using inexpensive equipment.

Daddy tried to keep them playing with quality baseballs also. He collected
them from Mrs. Needham, a lady who lived next to the stadium and had many
errant baseballs land on her property. Daddy paid a quarter for each one she
saved for him. Still, no matter how diligently my brothers and their friends
tried to prevent it, baseballs were lost faster than they could be replaced. Daddy
accepted not being able to keep his sons supplied with first-class baseballs.
Eventually he would buy any ball he could, or they did without.

Once, when her boys had no baseball, neither did their friends and no
one could buy one, Mother got out her sewing basket and helped her baseball-
possessed men as only she could. Mother *made* them a baseball—"better than
the real thing," my brothers would brag. Once or twice she used a jack ball in
the core and then went to using golf balls. Johnny and Jimmy and their friends
retrieved the golf balls from the country club grounds on the edge of town. By
patiently winding string and tape and string and tape round and round the core
and diligently stitching the leather cover, Mother produced many a homemade
baseball for her boys. The balls were terrific while they lasted. They didn't last
long. A ball burst beyond repair after the bat connected for just so many hard
hit foul balls, home runs, and resounding base hits.

So where did they play their baseball games? That was not much of a
problem in those days. Vacant lots were cleaned off and made into baseball
diamonds by the boys, not the fathers. Actually, they marked off a baseball

diamond in our backyard, but our kitchen window, a couple basement windows, and my brother's bedroom window were susceptible to the smash and shatter of a connecting ball, so after the first broken window, it wasn't fun playing there.

Their best playing field was the one they made across the street. The boys with their grass cutting sickles converged on the weedy overgrown area behind the house across from ours. It was adjacent to a stand of trees we called "the woods." When they finished, they had a baseball diamond, complete with home plate, base paths, bases, and marked off foul lines. They established rules, such as, a home run was only a home run if you hit the ball far enough to make it around the bases and back to home plate. Best of all, there was no worry about breaking windows. None were close enough to be in danger. Each team wanted badly to win, but all the players were determined not to let the precious ball get lost. Each player had a crucial responsibility to keep his eye peeled on the ball's line of flight no matter how high and far the whacked ball soared. If the fielders couldn't find it, time-out was called, and base runners, umpires, those on the sidelines, everyone looked for the ball. If the ball wasn't found, the game was over. Usually that was the outcome, especially if it was near dusk and darkness inhibited their search.

My brothers and their friends were too young for the American Legion Leagues of the era. But no doubt the tremendous fun, spirit of fair play, and genuine competition experienced spontaneously on the made-up teams of those young boys and others in neighborhoods such as ours was the inspiration for the Little League system of today.

Chapter 10

Soap Box Derby

The Soap Box Derby was a wooden go-cart racing competition involving youngsters all over America. Entrants made their own carts to qualify for races in their town. Ultimate winners made it to Akron, Ohio's final race where that winner was crowned National Soap Box Derby Champion. Johnny and Jimmy's determination to build a cart that qualified to compete in Zanesville's race down Main Street gave them hours of freedom and fun with their friends. My father saw it as a creative and skill-developing activity "for boys." Mother was pleased to have them busy doing something nearby. If my brothers and their friends were going to have a cart ready for the qualifying judges, it had to be designed, built, tested, and ready to submit by late spring.

Those boys spent many a fall and winter day looking for materials to build the cart. They scoured empty fields, trash piles, construction sites, alleys, and especially behind grocery stores, wherever sturdy wooden crates and 2 x 12 wood planks might be found. Those were the basics necessary for the body of a go-cart they had to also paint and meticulously decorate to become the Soap Box one of them would drive in the coming summer's annual competition.

Since quality axles and wheels were crucial to their success, throughout the entire year, they were on the lookout for the best they could find. They couldn't buy them. They were too expensive. They searched for discarded wagons and baby carriages—perfect for providing the needed parts. In fact, any little girl, sister, cousin, neighbor of my brothers and their friends was lucky to never lose baby buggy wheels for the sake of a go-cart.

I was glad to hear Daddy order my brothers not to dismantle my doll carriage. "Don't take anything until you ask her and she says yes!" He was very firm with my brothers. More than once they had pretended to think a baby buggy of mine was *old*. "Marva never played with it. She didn't want it." Not true. And Daddy wasn't having it anymore.

One tearful time I discovered their clandestine ingenuity as I started on a sidewalk stroll with baby doll Dixie. I had dressed my beautiful life-sized dark brown colored doll in her prettiest outfit and grandly placed her in my practically new doll carriage. The walk turned into an abbreviated, rickety ride. Those boys had switched four perfect wheels with bent, old, unmatched ones found in their scavenge hunting. Trying to convince me they could make the wheels they didn't want, roll smoothly and be fine for me and my doll, they enthusiastically begged, "Let us keep your wheels, we might win. We'll be Soap Box Derby Champions." I was stubborn. Only when I threatened to tell Daddy did I hear words that worked for me. They promised I could ride the cart on a trial run down Cliffwood Avenue. My threats and tears stopped. That's what I wanted.

A Saturday morning a few weeks later, Mother and Daddy had gone to town to "take care of business"—meaning they went to the bank, to pay utility bills, and shop. Our parents' parting instructions to me had been "stay inside, get your work done." Restriction on my activities was expected but resented because my brothers were outside playing with their friends. Their favored treatment was unfair. Daddy's rationale was his sons were "working"—readying that year's edition of their go-cart. From the living room window I watched each time they zoomed down the street, passing our house.

Grieving because I was a girl and couldn't be part of such fun, I remembered: my brothers owed me! Now was the time. I could go, have fun, and be back in the house before Mother and Daddy came home. This was my opportunity for the promised ride.

I yelled from the front door, begging them to let me sit behind the driver, "just once, please?" Reminded of their promise to me, they finally said yes!

I flew out the door, across the porch, down the steps to the street, and excitedly trudged up the hill behind Jimmy and a couple of other boys who tugged the go-cart up to the top of the street, a little bit past Rev. Holt's house, onto the crest of the steep hill. Jimmy was going to drive it back down the hill. They all helped secure me behind my twin brother on the wooden seat. Wrapping my arms around his waist, I held on for the long ride down Cliffwood Avenue to Baker Street.

With a running push from behind by the "starters," we were on our way. I was happy and could feel my grin stiffen by the wind heavy against my face. We were zooming down the middle of the street. I was having fun with the boys! Then, all at once, the cart picked up much more speed, going fast, faster. It was creaking, wobbling, didn't seem to be rolling in a straight line at all. I was terrified. Panicked, I started screaming, stop! Stop! Jimmy paid no attention to me and confidently kept going, gripping the steering wheel and yelling, shrieking with glee—ecstatically pleased with our accelerating speed.

Attempting some power over my destiny, I tried to unloose my right arm from Jimmy's waist. At first, I couldn't. The force of the wind wouldn't let me pull my arm free. But I was determined. I would get my hand out and positioned palm down against the pavement to slow our descent into disaster. Finally in the strength generated by my terror, I overcame the unbelievable resistance of pounding wind and felt my hand push against the pavement rushing under the cart. It didn't help my predicament though. The go-cart maintained its speed, careening on until Jimmy braked it at the foot of the hill. There was no damage to their precious vehicle. Jimmy and I were in one piece. They could have called it an excellent run, except I suffered a traumatic injury.

My right hand was soundly run over and mangled by the cart's right rear wheel. I suffered horrible excruciating pain even before I saw how visibly and possibly dangerously I hurt myself. Mother and Daddy would see it. I couldn't hide it from them. My damaged hand dripped blood. Chunks of flesh were torn from several fingers. I was a kid who had been ordered to "stay in the house, get your work done." Now I was a kid in big trouble.

No bones were broken, but to this day, my right hand carries the scars from that experience. It's a wonder I don't have scars from the spanking I got for disobeying my parents.

Each summer, many a low-riding four-wheeled wooden cart was constructed by enterprising youngsters in our neighborhood, never to fly down East Main Street in Zanesville's local Soap Box Derby competition. The carts my brothers thoughtfully and enthusiastically constructed never made it through the trial runs hurtling down Cliffwood Avenue. The potential derby-winning cart from our neighborhood would be destroyed either rolling over an embankment, or coming to rest against a tree, or sideswiping unyielding concrete curbs or breaking apart due to faulty axles, wheels, or steering mechanism. It was a black/white issue as far as the boys were concerned. White youngsters had benefit of the hands-on attention and supervision of fathers, brothers, and uncles who were engineers or mechanics with training. Men in their families had the time to work with their children and they were financially able to buy store-bought parts for the carts they built. All of which served to help them hold a monopoly on qualifying for the available spaces in the derby. Black kids didn't have the same resources but were neither disgruntled nor discouraged. Most of our dads earned their income in laboring or service occupations. Most of them also worked two or more jobs. What our fathers did was dispense advice and encouragement, and it was fully appreciated, as evidenced by their sons' continually optimistic attempt each year to succeed.

My brothers and their friends never qualified for the Soap Box Derby, but from my perspective, as an excluded girl child, they had the best time trying.

Chapter 11

We Wanted a Dog

Mother said no. It was for all the usual reasons. "No dog!" We could not change her mind. After a while, we stopped begging.

Then, fate stepped in one night when the Zanesville Dodgers were playing a Class D league baseball game at the stadium, and Daddy, Johnny, and Jimmy were there. The stadium out on the west end of town was far enough but not too far for them to walk, which they had done on the particularly nice evening. The evening turned out to be a particularly, extra special, nice evening. Jimmy told the story. I had to stay home with Mother.

Daddy, ever a serious student of baseball, liked a good view of the pitcher working. So he and my brothers sat directly behind home plate. The game started, and Daddy started teaching, talking, and keeping his sons' attention toward how the coach, the catcher, and the pitcher interacted before the pitcher threw the ball. They second guessed the signals given to the pitcher, considering the attributes of the batter in the hitters' box and the batter waiting in the on-deck circle. His boys were developing good coaching strategy.

Only when the home plate umpire abruptly stopped the game did my family realize something unusual going on. Calling "time-out," standing straight, ripping off his chest protector, the umpire moved from behind home plate onto the infield. Why? It didn't seem to have anything to do with the players. Then they saw it. A long-haired, almost black puppy had wandered onto the ball field, crossed through the outfield, and ran into the infield. Jimmy said it was something to see. The puppy headed to second base, and there he sat, in the base path on the third base side of the bag. The little guy was either to afraid to move or simply determined to be the center of attention in the midst of the players. The game had to be stopped.

No one came forward to claim the puppy, now a flurry of activity. He pranced and danced, started and stopped, and darted and scurried avoiding attempts of as many as twenty arms grabbing for him. He was fully in charge of *his* game, "catch me if you can." At last, in spite of his frisky antics, he was corralled. The home plate umpire supervised his removal, making certain the small dog's point of entry was secured against a return visit. "Play ball," the umpire yelled. The puppy was not seen again. It was such a good game, Jimmy said, everyone seemed to forget the distraction of the stray puppy.

Afterward, on the way home, walking along Main to Pine Street, what do you suppose my dad and my brothers discovered? The puppy trotted behind them. Yes, although other families, too, sauntered along the sidewalk, the puppy the umpires ejected from the baseball diamond was following *my* family. Jimmy said no matter how Daddy tried to discourage that little puppy, he followed them to our house.

I know the story from here.

The next morning we had a dog. My brothers and I were unbelievably happy to find he had stayed. The long-legged puppy, with a more reddish dark brown than black, glossy coat of hair had curled up, tail wrapped around to where a shiny black nose was tucked against his sleeping body on our front porch.

Mother was not happy; she said the dog had to go. But days passed and he stayed. My brothers couldn't find anyone to take him as we begged all the while to let him be ours. After more days unsuccessfully trying to convince her we were responsible pet owners, Daddy did what they decided had to be done. He got rid of our dog. That wasn't surprising, since he and Mother seemed to agree on all the important issues. Daddy took the unwanted puppy to a man who lived far from town, out in the country.

One morning, not many days later, we heard whimpering coming from our basement. The puppy had found his way back to us. It was unbelievable that he could have come so far. And how did he get into the basement? Johnny checked around the house and excitedly reported one of the basement windows broken. How that happened was a mystery. Nevertheless, Daddy suggested, looking at us and then at Mother, "If the dog managed to safely come all that way, determined to be part of our family, we should keep him." Mother reluctantly shrugged her shoulders in resigned agreement while shaking her head in hopeless disbelief. We had a family council, and finally, we had a dog. We named him Skippy. We loved Skippy so much, but no more, it seemed, than he loved us. That summer, Skippy went everywhere we went, actually where my brothers went, because I didn't get to go that many places.

School started and our new pet loved going to school. No matter how careful we were to securely tie him to his rope on the back porch, many times he chewed or wriggled loose and came to us sometime during the day.

The teachers at Wilson Elementary School were not at all pleased with our resourceful dog's amazing ability to have a better attendance record than some children. Skippy's presence at school was unacceptable. When the children came out for recess, there he was, waiting to play, if he had not come into the classroom earlier. He did that a couple of times, looking for us. At first, wherever he appeared, the school principal had Johnny take him home, with stern instructions to fasten him up so he could not come back. That proved impossible. Then the principal took charge. She stopped sending for Johnny. She called the dogcatcher.

Mother adamantly and constantly warned, "If the dogcatcher gets Skippy, he is gone! I will not go get him, nor let anyone retrieve him from the pound. He must behave." We knew she meant what she said. You see, both Mother and Daddy believed very sincerely in children "behaving," so we knew Skippy had to meet the same standard.

Skippy was a wonderful pet, playfully cute, gentle, responsive, and loyal and smart, but he was also stubbornly incorrigible. Too frequently he managed to get to school when he knew we were there. So just as frequently, the dogcatcher was called. Fortunately, Skippy ran very fast and escaped their nets. Sometimes through the classroom window, we saw him dash across the street through the tall grass, into the roadside ditch and up, out, and over the fence where he disappeared into Woodlawn Cemetery. We heard shots fired. The dogcatcher intended to capture him using tranquilizer pellets, we were told. That scared us. Surely they caught him. Those days as soon as school dismissed, we hurried home. Thankfully, our dog was lying on the front porch, watching for us, panting, tired, but not hurt at all! Whew!

One day Skippy was chased from the school grounds and not languishing peacefully at home when we got there. That afternoon, on our way home, a teenager told us he saw our dog hit by someone shooting a gun at him. We didn't believe him.

"He fell but got up and went away," the kid told us, with some mercy. We refused to believe anything he said. Part of it must have been true, though. For, days came and went, and Skippy was gone. We were miserable.

Do you know what helped us feel somewhat better in weeks to come? It was Mother. She encouraged us to be hopeful.

"He'll be okay and find his way back. You'll get up one morning and see him sleeping on the back porch."

Remembering everything the kid said, it was possible, but it didn't happen. We never saw Skippy again. Mother consoled us with no hint in her words or her tone of voice blaming our beloved pet for the sorrowful consequence of his actions. And our mother moped about, looking as sad as we were. It was comforting to realize she had loved our dog, too.

Skippy was the first of many dogs owned and cherished by our family, especially Mother.

The house Daddy built in 1941—
I took this photo in 1991.

Another view with a hint of
my bedroom windows to the right.

What a surprise to discover
this photo of me on the front steps!
I believe I am eleven years old.

Chapter 12

Summertime

It didn't matter when the calendar reported the season change. Summertime for the Woods children began the day after school closed, not to reopen again until September. And we had fun.

Our family never went on summer vacations or out to Buckeye Lake like many of our friends did. We did go for the day to the County Fair, or to the circus or amusement shows in the fairgrounds. We also looked forward to the church picnic every August in Putnam Hill Park.

At times we went to Zanesville Stadium for special events. Daddy and my brothers saw Satchel Paige,[6] the phenomenal Negro League[7] pitcher in an exhibition baseball game in the stadium. And they witnessed the black athlete, Jesse Owens,[8] an internationally heralded track star, run in the stadium. In the 1936 Olympics held in Germany, Jesse Owens had won several events. It was years later when Johnny and Jimmy saw him in person in Zanesville's stadium, in a short sprint where he actually outran a motorcycle.

Mostly, in the summer, we just enjoyed ordinary routine at home. Without prodding from Mother or Daddy, we didn't sleep late. Our days started nearer to eight than nine each morning. Possibly it was the sharing of a bedroom and a bed with a sibling that made getting up and out a more satisfactory option than sleeping in late.

Little sister Kathleen and I were roommates. Our room, on the front southeastern corner of the house, had big double windows that looked out onto our spacious front porch. Johnny and Jimmy shared a corner room, too, the back corner, on the same side of the house. In between our bedrooms were the linen closet, the bathroom, and Mother and Daddy's bedroom next door to Kathleen and me.

I'm thinking my brothers were given the room farthest away from Mother and Daddy so our parents could ignore some of their bedtime antics. Also they knew their girls wouldn't sneak out the windows onto the front porch.

For a time our bedroom wasn't a good place for me. But no one ever knew how frightening it was after everyone had gone to bed. It was my imagination. My mind conjured up the picture of a gnome-like stranger sneaking up our front steps onto the porch, hiding behind the almost three foot tall, solid wood wall around the porch. I never imagined him coming into the house. I did imagine him looking into our room through the slats in the window blinds. For sure, I closed them tight each evening before dark. In my mind, he made our front porch his bedroom, curled up there underneath the windows. At times, if I wakened in the middle of the night, unable to sleep, I lay motionless trying to figure if it was his soft snoring that woke me. Was someone there? Truly "scared stiff," I couldn't get up and look.

But the next thing I knew my eyes opened and it was morning! I did sleep. All was well. Going about getting my day started, I didn't tell anyone. I knew it was totally my imagination, and I had to conquer the problem. After a while it was all over, never to happen again.

My plan on summer mornings with the entire day ahead was to finish the jobs Mother gave me as quickly as I could. There was nothing to be gained by lollygagging around.

Jimmy and Johnny were not production focused. They just wanted to get outdoors by any means they could make it happen.

After our breakfast of milk and cereal (Kellogg Cornflakes or Wheaties or Rice Krispies) or even eggs and toast (pancakes were for weekends only), Jimmy and Johnny got to work too, but they also "horseplayed," as Mother termed it.

Mother claimed efforts to keep them from "rassling," punching on each other and playing around as they went about their chores, wasn't worth the hassle. Then she did as *they* had planned; in frustration, she sent them on their way. But she "told Daddy," as she promised my brothers, and they were in trouble. You can bet after the consequence of Daddy's punishment, their "horseplay" subsided for a while. Our father did not believe in "sparing the rod and spoiling the child."

When it came to housekeeping, Daddy's participation consisted of being the effective absent boss. Mother was the instructor and the inspector. For Mother, housework involved hands-on work shared generously with each child. We were responsible for our bedrooms passing her unannounced inspection for order and cleanliness.

And with minimal help from Kathleen, I swept and dust mopped the living room and dining room and dusted furniture. Kathleen crawled about dusting bottom rungs of the dining room chairs along with table legs.

We both began learning how to wash dishes when we were not tall enough to reach the faucets. We stood on a stool. Eventually, doing dishes after every meal evolved into a household chore my first little sister and I shared.

The boys sometimes helped me with cleaning the bathroom or with the laundry. I folded and put away washed clothes. By the time I was eight years old, I began learning how to handle the ironing board and the iron. I learned how to iron by starting with handkerchiefs, pillowcases, backs of shirts, and other uncomplicated pieces.

Defrosting the refrigerator or washing windows or cleaning the venetian blind window shades were my special tasks, i.e., "Marva, give the blinds in the living room a good dusting today. We'll (*meaning me!*) wash them next week."

My brothers had yard work to do or floors to mop, wax, and polish or the basement to clean. On summer days, though—no matter how diligent we were, or not—by lunchtime, or before, we were usually free to entertain ourselves.

A good part of my entertainment included afternoons learning how to cook and especially how to bake. In fact, Mother suggesting, "This afternoon I'll help you fix Jell-O or make Kool-Aid ice pops or even bake a cake for dinner" motivated me to quickly finish my chores.

Reading, playing jacks, jump rope, hopscotch, tag, hide n' go seek, and with dolls, paper dolls, holding tea parties, and playing house were my playtime activities.

I liked playing baseball too. I enjoyed the competition, and the mechanics and rhythm of teamwork necessary to make the three outs in an inning that sent the opposition back out into the field. I liked batting—connecting with the pitcher's thrown ball, and catching—getting in place to secure a flyer or grounder in the outstretched glove. Throwing and running were not as fun. I seemed to lack the strength and stamina to do either confidently. My dad let me play ball with my brothers but not when a couple of their buddies also played. "It isn't ladylike," he admonished. I guess a girl would never have gotten to be on his Zanesville Black Stars baseball team, no matter how well she played.

Playing marbles was another popular pastime. The guys had marble tournaments, the winner reigning as champion until he was dethroned in the next tournament. Again I could join my brothers around the circle drawn in a dusty section of our yard, but not when their friends were in the game.

Evenings my brothers, their friends, and my sister and I did get together with as many as eight or more kids for serious games of hide n' go seek. It was the same with playing tag and catching lightning bugs. Yelling, laughing, running, and rambunctious times burnt up a lot of energy.

Nightfall and the first appearance of more than three or four flashing lightning bugs serenely floating about in the dark was the signal to stop whatever we were doing and catch the intermittently glowing flying insects. They were snatched and dropped into glass mason jars with their hi-jacked friends and relatives and some green grass and leaves for food. We intended for them to live a long time. That was why the lid was ice pick punched with oodles of air holes. Each of us had our own jar. If only we could catch enough to have a lightning bug lantern.

The Woods kids didn't own toy guns. Daddy and Mother didn't allow guns of any kind in the house—not even the cheesiest looking plastic ones.

All the boys in our neighborhood played with slingshots, which they made. They looked for a strong forked tree branch not much longer than eight to ten inches or larger in diameter than an inch or so. With their penknives, they whittled and shaped and smoothed the handle and two forks. Slits were cut into the two fork ends so a narrow ribbon of rubber, ten or so inches long, cut from tire inner tubes could be secured to each of the two ends. Then each end of the two rubber strips was attached to opposite short sides of the leather tongue pulled from a discarded shoe making a "sling" to propel rocks at targets. One hand firmly held the handle of the Y-shaped toy formerly a section of a tree branch. The other hand grasped the pocket (made from the shoe tongue) holding a small rock or piece of gravel heavy enough to fly through the air but not too big to manage its direction, and pulled the pocket back toward his shoulder as far as possible. Then aiming at the target, he let the pocketed rock free to zing to its mark. Targets were not allowed to be people, houses, vehicles, anyone's property, or birds or cats or any animal. Usually the target was an empty tin can or glass jars or bottles positioned where it was certain a speeding piece of lethal gravel didn't hit anyone. Soda pop bottles were not used for targets. They were too good a source of spending money. The boys collected and turned them in for the deposit store keepers paid for their return. Most every boy outdoors in the summer had a slingshot, he had made, dangling from his back pocket ready for target practicing or to challenge the expertise of one another. Johnny said Grandpa Newman used cherry wood to make them their best slingshot forks.

Seeing a snake was my most scary summertime excitement (a close second was the lightning and thunder accompanying thunderstorms). Snakes in our town weren't expected to be poisonous or even constrictors, but I still dreaded seeing a snake or hearing anyone did and it got away. That meant I might stumble upon the slithering sneaky thing again. Mostly the boys gleefully and immediately killed a detained snake by chopping its head off with a gardening hoe or shovel.

Catching flies and feeding them alive to spiders was fun to my brothers, too. Jimmy antagonized my sister and me if we happened to be around when he spied a spider relaxing in its web. Without fail, Jimmy caught a fly and threw it into the spider's web begging us "come see, here comes the spider, he almost has him, hurry up." It was gruesome. The spider took the squirming fly away never to be seen again.

Still, from my perspective, baseball was my brothers' favorite summertime pastime. It was unusual for them not to have a pick-up game every day or spend hours in practice hitting, throwing, and catching. Like our father, they loved baseball. They were lucky because Daddy expected them to play the game. He recognized their play as skill development leading to one day becoming professionals. That's why he took them to the stadium to watch sandlot, semi-pro, and farm team baseball games.

When they were allowed to go to games without adult supervision, I was jealous of their freedom. I was a girl; no way was it going to happen for me. None of my activities could possibly match their summertime fun.

Chapter 13

Boys Being Boys

One day Jimmy and Johnny headed to a baseball game and an afternoon with their friends that didn't turn out so well. It was a warm Saturday, before school was out for the summer. Johnny had badgered Mother for permission to go with a group of neighborhood boys, all of them ten or eleven years old. Mother never automatically said yes. This time it took her a while to finally cave in.

"Oh, go ahead," she relented, the usual lecture following, "be careful, tend to your own business, go straight there, and come directly home when the game is over!"

On their way, at Pine and Prospect Street, was a grocery store with baskets of fresh fruit propped outside against the front of the store. The proprietor's intent to entice folks coming by to stop and shop caught my brothers' interest. But they each grabbed an apple and moved quickly on, not stopping to pay. More daringly, Jimmy decided to dash back for bananas, which he did, still not shopping, just taking! With bananas in hand, he rushed to catch up with Johnny and their friends. Unaware the grocery owner was close behind him, you can imagine the fright when Mr. Zinnsmaster grabbed him. He got Johnny too and marched the two of them back to his store. He watched as they followed his orders to return the fruit to the baskets from where it was stolen.

He let my brothers go on their way after quietly talking to them for a while. "Don't take what doesn't belong to you just because you can. You want people to trust you, don't you?" he lectured, shaking his head as he disappeared into the store. The highly anticipated fun afternoon at the stadium had been ruined. My brothers were not feeling so good and didn't have the good time they planned. All they could think about was what would happen to them once Mr. Zinnsmaster relayed the incident to Daddy.

For many days, Johnny and Jimmy would worry about the punishment due for their transgression because Daddy never confronted them. As far as they knew, he must not have been told. There was another possibility; Mr. Zinnsmaster had talked to Daddy, and our father's tactic was to rehabilitate his sons by letting them stew in the juice of their anxiety. It worked. They were rather subdued and didn't give Mother any grief for quite a while.

For some reason though, several weeks later, when school was out for the year, Daddy announced he was taking his sons to Cleveland to work with him.

It was to be their first time away from home, and it might be for most of the summer. Still, Mother seemed not sad at all to have her growing boys under the watchful care of their father.

Another venture with their friends a year later, on a bright summer day, caused them a big problem. My brothers and three or four of their friends headed to the stadium for a ball game. They didn't have money for admission tickets, but they had a plan. They would sneak in by climbing over the wall close to the swimming pool. As they scrambled up the wall, one of them accidentally kicked in a window of the pool building. They hurried on, got into the stadium, and settled in and enjoyed the ballgame. The broken window was forgotten.

When the ballgame ended, one of the friends suggested they should all go on out to the fairgrounds. Royal American Shows, an amusement company, was in town. Daddy was working in Cleveland, and the boys knew if they checked in at home for Mother's permission, she would say no. They didn't ask her but just planned to be home before dark. Mother wouldn't complain or question where they had been, so off to the fairgrounds they headed.

As they made their way, playing, jostling one another on the sidewalk, a police car pulled alongside the group of five or six not yet teenaged boys. It was Art Tate, the only black policeman on Zanesville's force. Officer Tate questioned whether they had broken into the swimming pool. No, they had been to the game at the stadium. Let's see your ticket stubs? Uh.

My brothers didn't make it home before dark. They were taken to the police station. The police contacted Mother and explained her sons had been picked up, the reason they had been picked up, and then assured her they didn't do the deed; they were innocent. "You can come and take them home." Mother quickly decided her daring sons needed to learn a lesson. She told the police if it was okay with them, they could stay in jail overnight.

Jimmy recalls their incarceration as a horrible experience. He remembers jail cell bunk beds and him having to take the lower bunk. Only bars separated each cell one from the other. In the cells next to those kids were older men; he almost shudders remembering. "They must have been seventeen and eighteen years old, very scary with their attitude and talk," he recalled.

Daddy not home, working out of town, Mother handled the predicament her way. Holding onto a personal commitment of never intending to see her sons in police custody, she arranged for Reverend Holt to bring them home the next morning.

Never again did my mother or father have to face their children doing anything to bring the police into their lives.

Chapter 14

The Cleveland Experience

Summer 1947, the Cleveland Indians baseball organization signed Larry Doby.[9] He was the second black ball player, in our life time, behind Jackie Robinson, to take the field for a Major League team. Larry Doby, an exciting hitter and fielder, had starred many years playing in the Negro Leagues. He was the first black to play in the American League. Daddy's long-held conviction that Major League Baseball would open up to include blacks had become reality. He assured Johnny and Jimmy they would see Larry Doby play in Cleveland Stadium. And they did. For it was the summer of '48, my ten- and eleven-year-old brothers traveled with Daddy to live and work alongside him in Cleveland.

Daddy spent the previous fall and winter commuting back and forth from our home in Zanesville to Cleveland. As a self-employed building contractor, he had to be where his business could best earn money to support his family. Construction activity in Cleveland far outpaced such promise in Zanesville. His days and nights home with us were few and far between.

Daddy's lengthy absences had been difficult for all of us. Mother missed him terribly. We knew because after coming from behind the closed door of her bedroom, her red eyes and puffy face verified the crying we "thought" we heard. And for us, it was tough handling the nasty teasing of neighborhood kids picking on us as we walked to school. "Your dad doesn't live with you because he has a girlfriend in Cleveland," they claimed. We defended him. "You're stupid. He comes home when he can, when he doesn't have a job to finish," we said in some fashion when not simply ignoring their meanness. After all, maybe they knew something we didn't. What if Mother's crying wasn't because she missed Daddy, but because she knew he had someone else?

When the summer weekend came and Daddy took my brothers with him when he returned to Cleveland on Sunday night, I no longer worried. I'm sure he took them because of their antics, but the three of them together, in Cleveland, was proof Mother was the only woman in Daddy's life. He would not have taken them if he had another woman. My parents' marriage was solid. If I could have gone along with them, my life would have been near perfect, I admitted to me.

Getting ready to go, my brothers were excited. Our taunting friends ceased bad talking our family and enviously spread the word that Johnny and Jimmy

Woods were going to see Larry Doby play at the stadium. Boy, did I want to go to that game too. I kept begging trying to make Daddy change his mind. "I can be a helper on your jobs. Please can I go?" Daddy thoughtfully but firmly said I couldn't.

"It's not ladylike, a girl living like us, in one room. Plus, your mother needs your help."

"It's not fair," I persisted. "I'm the same age as Jim."

Later, hearing the stories about their summer, I was relieved to have been spared the experiences.

* * * * * * * * * *

They left our comfortable home that summer for living conditions changed dramatically, and not for the good. My father's Cleveland "home" was in a tenement house in an old rundown part of the city. The substandard housing, part of our daddy's way to keep expenses low, enabled him to send most of his earnings back to Mother. His one room now provided a home for the three of them.

They were not by themselves in their crowded quarters. A couple rats meandered in and out on a regular basis. Daddy continually battled to defend against their visits. His best offensive ploy was to push something heavy against the wall to block the rats' homemade doorways. In time, though, they simply gnawed through another spot.

And those despicable intruders came in the night not just to search for food. In the morning, one of the socks the men had worn that day, taken off, and tucked into the top of a work shoe to wear another day was missing. The whereabouts of the missing sock was not a mystery for long. A rat took it! My brothers and my dad could see the sock, just on the other side of the nasty thieves' little archway. Neither Daddy nor his boys were the least bit reluctant to reclaim what had been lifted by the crafty and unwelcome visitors. Jimmy told me either he or Johnny or Daddy reached into the rat hole, snatched the sock, and wore it.

Maybe the rodents wanted the soft easy-to-drag material for nesting purposes. Whatever their reason, Daddy didn't intend for them to continue their nightly acquisition. One night he tied all six of the socks to the bed railing. His tactic worked. Doing that every night, the socks remained where Daddy anchored them. It was one rat challenge Daddy won. Whatever the long-tailed creatures' reason for coveting the socks, they eventually had to do without.

* * * * * * * * * *

Daddy was a building contractor minus a truck. He was a building contractor who did not own any kind of wheels to ease his travel from home to work, from one job to another job, from a job back home. He carried a heavy metal toolbox that held everything he needed. It was at least four feet long and eight to ten inches wide and deep. Lugging the toolbox, he walked and took the city bus from one place to the other.

Seeing him, if folks thought about it, they may have considered our father was a handyman. Daddy didn't mind. He said a handyman was simply someone who was skilled—able to do a multitude of construction tasks just as he could. He was a contractor who could be found dry walling, plastering, doing masonry work, pouring concrete, laying brick, framing, painting, etc.

When Daddy needed tools or equipment too large or bulky to carry such as ladders or scaffolding, he arranged delivery and pick up by acquaintances in the business with a truck. Daddy never appeared to experience any inconvenience or hardship because he didn't have his own vehicle.

* * * * * * * * * *

Their meals were eaten out, never in their room. For breakfast, it was usually a place on East 61st between Central and Quincy. The waitress accustomed to seeing them, a man and his two young sons obviously without a lot of money, insisted on them ordering a huge hoecake not the three little biscuits offered on the menu. They got more to eat for the same dime charged for the biscuits. Jim said her consideration was not lost to Daddy who, after they had been paid for a job, left an extra tip on the table. He made it a point to tell his sons the importance of letting folk realize, when you are able, their thoughtful attention didn't go unappreciated.

* * * * * * * * * *

There was the time Daddy had a job replacing bay windows in an empty and exceptionally old house. It was a job they needed to finish because Daddy didn't have any money. Even Johnny and Jimmy knew sitting down to a full meal that night depended upon them completing the job in time to get paid.

Throughout the morning and past lunchtime, they worked steady and hard in the raggedy structure being cautious around all the rusty nails as they carefully dislodged the old windows. As they yanked out the big center window, an amazing thing happened. Without any warning, *coins* started raining down on them—all kinds, including half dollars and quarters! The money poured out onto the floor, through ragged breaks in their floor on through the ceiling of the room below, and down to the next floor. Coins tumbled down the exterior of the house into the weeds and shrubbery. They couldn't believe their eyes. Coins were even embedded in the plaster between the wooden lathing. They had a new priority—get that money! Daddy led the way. No one returned to work until every coin, inside and outside of the building was recovered.

Hearing this story, I was sad, puzzled dealing with my father not hesitating to claim ownership of the windfall. Hearing no mention of considering who might be the rightful owner of the coins was inconsistent with how he talked to us about not taking other people's property. I understand though. People had not been in the building for years. Whoever stashed the coins was most likely long gone. He saw the find as a blessing. They had meal money for the entire week.

* * * * * * * * * *

On their way home from work one evening, Daddy took them by a drugstore for a can of soda for dinner. Suddenly, while inside, they heard a woman outside, screaming, piercing screams. The three of them ran out of the store to see what was going on. The woman was jumping up and down, clutching her face, wailing, "My baby, my baby." She would move toward a baby carriage standing a foot or so from her, in the middle of the sidewalk, and then shrink back, screaming, pointing into the carriage. Heavenly days! Oh my goodness! Sitting there on top of the baby's blanket, slowly licking milk off her baby's face, was a big rat.

Telling the story, Jim says, to this day, he can still see the rat's pink tongue on the baby's cheek.

Daddy chased the rat away.

* * * * * * * * * *

At times there were no lights in the room my father and brothers called home. There were no lights anywhere, in the tenement building, on the street. The electricity had gone out. It happened during heavy rain storms, those accompanied with loud cracking thunder and big bold lighting streaks. Following these electrical storms, the utility company took forever to restore service to the neighborhood where they lived.

When the electricity went out after they came home but before going to bed, they had no problem stumbling about in the room, getting into their pajamas and going to bed. However, when the lights went out during the night, while they were asleep, it was a different story. It was pitch black when they woke up. Rising before dawn, maneuvering in the dark, washing up, finding their clothes, and dressing for the workday was not easy.

Jimmy thought he had it perfected and was quick to brag about his ability to get his clothes and dress in the dark. He approached becoming obnoxious, bragging profusely about being able to identify each of their clothes in the solid black, darkest morning. Grudgingly, they admitted he was good. Then one lightless morning, Daddy found an opportunity to tone down Jimmy's self-praise.

It was one of those mornings they woke to pitch-blackness. An electrical storm had knocked out the power. As they washed and began dressing, Jimmy handed Daddy a shirt, fervently assuring him it was his.

"Take it. It's yours, it's yours!" Reaching out, Daddy took the shirt, putting it on without any comment. The father and his sons left their room.

Daddy walked ahead, leading them out into the light of a day just dawning. Then Johnny started laughing. He was looking at Daddy. Jimmy stared at Daddy, who had turned to face them. There he stood a few steps in front of his boys, saying nothing, his face with a quizzical "what's the matter?" look. He was squeezed into a too small shirt, sleeves binding upper arms, fabric stretched from collar to shoulders, buttons straining to meet button holes, obviously not his shirt! Johnny couldn't stop laughing as he aimed his hands in deriding motions at Jimmy. Jimmy looking shocked was speechless, at first, and then he was laughing too.

I know my father, who loved surprising his children with funny *or* scary moments, took great pleasure in his performance that morning.

Chapter 15

Enduring Challenge

Summer 1949, Johnny spent the entire season in Cleveland working alongside Daddy helping provide for our family and learning about life through the words and example of his father. Jimmy wanted to go with them, but Daddy ruled my twin brother should stay in Zanesville. Jimmy had a newspaper route that helped the family. Plus, Mother needed the assistance of her tall eleven-year-old son at home. She would have at least one of "her men" around to give a helping hand.

Johnny's eagerness to apply the skills Daddy patiently taught him allowed Daddy to reduce cost of labor and add more of the money the contract provided to the family's income. The past winter had been a challenge. A new baby came. We needed money.

My little brother Larry Robert was born in November 1948. We were a family of nine, just enough for our own baseball team. Looking at me, Daddy suggested, "How about naming him after your favorite player, Larry Doby?" I was thrilled. His middle name was for Uncle Robert, Daddy's brother. Larry was the little brother Johnny began begging for ever since our twin sisters, Cynthia and Sharon, were born.

Our new baby brother was a new incentive for Mother to encourage her husband to stop working out of town. Daddy didn't make it home many weekends. The strain on Mother was noticeable, especially the increased loss of patience with us if we didn't do what was expected; she didn't laugh with us like she used to, and she stayed in her room more. Her conversations with Aunt Cora let me know her prayer was for her husband to envision the better life they could have if he took steady employment in Zanesville and they had a regular paycheck to manage. But to outsiders, she faithfully struggled to hold things together through another financially tough winter.

Yes, too many times that winter Daddy couldn't be with us or send money home either. Then when a break in bad weather let Daddy do enough on the job for the client to make a payment, the amount was usually short of the dollars Mother needed for the overdue bills and household necessities. If a payment was made against the mortgage, it was likely the electric bill was pushed back. Or there would be minimal to no heat in the house—no money, no coal delivery.

Food was the last necessity we did without, but it happened, once or twice, to an uncomfortable degree.

I can remember Mother on the verge of calling some agency for help so she could feed us and money arriving that day from Daddy in a special delivery letter from the post office. Then she sat in her easy chair and with notepad and pen in her neat precise script wrote a grocery list for Johnny and Jimmy to take to the store. That list included, for each of us, a pint of our favorite ice cream; a reward for how we had endured.

I believe we kept our dire circumstances to ourselves. For me, our situation was difficult only to the extent I surmised both school and neighborhood friends had everything I did not. I didn't feel as if I "belonged." At times, I pretended I wasn't interested in activities I knew would cost money. Once in a while I told Mother about a birthday party someone was having. Interestingly I got to accept the invitation, take a present, and have fun with my friends. (Perhaps I should have asked more often.) Actually, it wasn't difficult banding with my brothers and sister to keep our situation in the family. Guided by our parents' obvious care, love, and respect for each other, we Woods children also had an unspoken bond between us built on the same foundation as Mother and Daddy's relationship. Our family's dire circumstances were only related to money.

Mother's family knew how Iva and her children were faring. Unannounced but much appreciated, Aunt Cora sent food to us—fully prepared, a ham, beef stew, baked beans. And, yes, sporadically, Uncle Arkley brought us a truck load of coal. Without a word, he backed his truck into our side yard (intended to be a driveway when the house was built). Standing with my brothers and sister at the dining room window, we saw our tall uncle—dark hair peeking from the flat cap he always wore, in his usual dark blue, always clean, denim bib overalls—dump the coal outside the side back basement window of the house. With the briefest wave, he climbed into his truck and drove away. Uncle Arkley wasn't a big talker, but those moments left me knowing he truly cared for and loved his sister and her family.

One winter morning we found a cardboard box of groceries on our front porch, pushed against the door, filled with staples and treats. It wasn't from family. I didn't know who the benefactor was, perhaps Reverend Holt, I thought.

When Daddy wasn't home, I knew he was with us. In fact, it saddened me knowing Daddy worried about the sacrifices Mother managed alone. It had to be hard on him being far away, insistent on doing things "his way."

Mother, a trusting, loyal ally of her husband, confident in front of us (even when her concerns became more serious) did her best in every way. She ran the household, parenting her seven children with love, patience, discipline, and creative resourcefulness. Mother did not crochet and knit, but she was a topnotch mender, speedily repairing socks and underwear, ragged knee holes in blue jeans, torn shirt sleeves, and collars hanging by a thread—saving many a garment that seemed destroyed. She was innovative in the kitchen, preparing meals with whatever she had on hand. I smile recalling the afternoon she suggested we could devise a recipe for a no-egg cake, and we went right to it.

And overcoming Daddy's objections, Mother took in ironing. Regular customers brought baskets of rough dried laundry to our back door, weekly. Mother "sprinkled" on Wednesday, dampening the clothes and linens with water shaken from a sprinkling bottle (usually a recycled soda pop bottle with a corked silver colored metal sprinkling cap). She rolled and stored each item layer by layer in a straw laundry basket. Thick toweling draped over the top, tucked tightly into the sides of the basket held the moisture in the rolled pieces until they were ironed. It was critical that nothing dry out or, worse, mildewed. On Thursday, standing at the ironing board giving each piece her quality attention, the ironing went smoothly and quickly. Folks picked up their belongings on Friday. Saturday we could count on Mother's ironing money for emergencies or a welcomed good time; for my brothers, that meant going to a movie.

Spring came. Larry was five months old, and Daddy's work had picked up. Daddy was giving job estimates and getting contracting jobs, one overlapping the other. He still couldn't come home many weekends, but money did. Bills were being paid. The family was comfortable. We had survived our harsh winter.

* * * * * * * * * *

Johnny tells this part of our family story. I was not there, only he and Daddy.

It was early summer 1949. School had closed for the year, and Johnny had been in Cleveland a week or so. One evening after work, Daddy and Johnny were in a restaurant off East 63rd Street where they met Mr. Dank Jacobs. Mr. Jacobs told them he had driven into Cleveland from the country where he raised pigs. He made the trip every few weeks or so to bring cured meat to Mr. Saunders, the owner of the restaurant where they sat eating dinner that evening. Although Daddy knew Mr. Saunders since he frequently had meals in his restaurant, it was the first time he had met Mr. Jacobs. They enjoyed talking to each other.

Dank Jacobs spoke about being the caretaker of a large house and one hundred acres out his way. Daddy spoke about his contracting business he had been building for several years. Mr. Jacobs, interested in what he heard and impressed by the man with the young son, gave Daddy a lead to another job, a big one. He told him the men he worked for were looking for a contractor to build a bridge on the property out there. It would span a small creek from the roadway to their front yard. The place was sixty-four miles from Cleveland in Andover, Ohio. "Come on out and put in a bid," Dank invited.

The next Sunday, my father and brother made their way east on Route 322 to Andover to see about the job. In fact, they were given a ride out to the country by the man whose job they had finished that week.

Daddy met the property owners, assessed what had to be done, and submitted his bid; an estimate of the cost of labor and materials needed to do a good job. He factored in some cost for a laborer, but having no aversion to hard work felt he could do pretty well by himself, especially with his son helping. He had perfected an ability to leverage and balance sizable things, enabling him to move something from one place to another all by himself. He won the bid and took the job. He and Johnny had been able to rent a room in the big house on the property owned by those who hired him. My dad and brother no longer lived in Cleveland.

Summer weather changed to more like fall weather as they worked long hours to finish as much as possible before Johnny had to go home for school and before the onset of bad weather. In the process, a man came by asking Daddy to consider putting in a bid to finish a house he had started to build "down the road." The site was maybe ten miles from Andover on County Line Road. In the midst of the bridge job, Daddy signed a contract to build the house. The owner wasn't in a big rush, which was a good thing. Daddy was pleased to continue having work in the farming community.

Andover was a farm town of small retail and service businesses with dairy farms surrounding on the north, south, and west. On the east was a man-made lake, the Pymatuning,[10] a product of President Roosevelt's New Deal[11] program. At that time, in the late forties recreational facilities were just beginning to be developed around the Pymatuning.

People living in and around Andover, essentially all white folk, were open and friendly with the hard-working black man who had come from Cleveland "to build that bridge west of town." They were used to meeting blacks from Cleveland who returned to Cleveland, or at least did not choose to stay in their bucolic environment.

Daddy was one black man whose viewpoint was different. He had been working away from his family too long. He wanted them near. Yet Zanesville held no promise for his work and a metropolis such as Cleveland was not where he wanted his children raised. In a short time, he had two big building contracts in the area. He recognized opportunity for him and his family to thrive together.

Johnny worked until September when he returned home to begin eighth grade at Grover Cleveland Junior High School.

Before Johnny left, they had been able to demolish the barn on the back of the property. That was a major accomplishment. The contract called for Daddy to use the barn's timbers for a significant portion of the material to build the bridge. Of course assembling the bridge required a multitude of strenuous challenges, as well. Just carrying the heavy timbers to the building site on the front was cumbersome. Johnny helped get most of that done. Johnny says he remembers he was paid well for his work. He had every item of shoes and clothing he wanted for school that year.

Not too many weeks following Johnny's return to Zanesville, inclement weather restricted Daddy's work on the bridge. Fortunately the interior work on the house he contracted to finish kept money flowing to the family. Throughout the fall and into the winter, Daddy working by himself dealt with important thoughts as he pushed his body to make significant headway each day. Unfortunately, he wasn't able to make enough money to cover all that was needed by his family. Still, his mind was engaged, churning, brainstorming a plan to improve circumstances for his wife and children, for whom life yet again had become financially tough.

At home bill paying was a juggling act Mother performed as best she could. Utilities were usually the first casualty of a "no money" phase. Once, word circulated that my sister and I were buying candles because we did not have any electricity. How anyone found out was a mystery to me. I had taken the trouble of walking eight-year-old Kathleen with me to buy our candles a far distance across town where no one knew us. Yet somehow it was not a secret the utility company had disconnected service to the Woods's fine house. I was embarrassed when kids who lived on the next street over asked how it was not to have any electricity. I lied and said we did. Later I learned Mother's friends were aware of the family's plight but were careful not to speak of it when "Iva's children" were nearby. Obviously, around their own children, they were not so careful.

I found several benefits to living without electricity. Some household chores couldn't be done, and for sure, we had more free time in the evening to play. Mother didn't bug us to finish our homework. I guess she assumed we did it at school as we were told. Those were her instructions since darkness came not too long after we got home. My grades didn't suffer. I was an "A" student. No one knew at night when I was supposedly sleeping I had transported myself into another world vivid in one of the books I read in bed by candlelight. Best of all, many evenings, before we went to bed, we played made up games using hearing and touch, including a version of hide n' seek. I only remember being a happy contented child when I snuggled into bed each night.

Another neat memory, a result of not having electricity, is when I would be in the basement, cooking a meal over the hot coals in the bottom of the coal furnace. At the time, I imagined myself in the dark woods, cooking over a campfire. Mostly, I remember the scrambled egg dinners. Upstairs, the eggs were prepared, thoroughly mixed, and poured into our big cast iron skillet, usually by Mother. Jim carried the heavy skillet to the basement and kneeling down on the concrete floor in front of the furnace placed it flat on the hot coals. Cautiously, I scrambled the seasoned eggs, careful not to splash them into the coals and ashes. Those eggs were tasty, better than what we scrambled on the electric range in our modern kitchen.

* * * * * * * * * *

I never knew how much of the following my mother was aware of at the time. You see, Daddy had made a discovery while riding on a different road one day heading out to work in the house on County Line Road. (Daddy still didn't own a car or truck; new friends dropped him off and picked him up.) This one special day down a new road, my father's attention was drawn to property for sale on South Lake Road in the township of Williamsfield, a dairy farming community only eight miles or so from Andover. Daddy explored the premises, verifying what was all too visible from the roadside. The house and farm buildings were in bad shape, run down, and the grounds were terribly neglected. The property for sale included not quite one hundred acres of land, considerable acreage to a city person, not so much to a serious farmer. The eastern border of the property sat on the Ohio/Pennsylvania state line.

Investigating, Daddy learned no one lived there and had not for several years. The last inhabitants had been renters. The owner would rent again. Daddy was seriously interested in the property. He saw the potential for his family. He did not want to rent. He wanted to buy. He had a plan.

In Zanesville, Mother was fending off bill collectors and their starkly worded notices for payment, particularly the mortgage, which was seriously delinquent.

Whenever Daddy came home, Reverend Holt with great empathy for his independent-minded friend engaged him in serious discussion about going to work for someone. "A regular paycheck is what your family needs," he preached. Afterward, I heard Daddy talking to Mother. His intentions remained firm. "The only way a Negro has a chance of getting ahead in America, to accumulate anything for the future is to run his own business," my father stressed.

However, First National Bank intended Mr. Woods meet his obligation to them. The mortgage had to be paid, *sometime*. Mother had explained the bank knew Daddy would catch up and make up the difference owed as soon as the weather broke. Eventually, she told her older children, his income over the good weather months will be enough to carry the family through the lean days of winter. In later years I learned John Woods's mortgage holder had been lenient and respected the construction worker phenomena for several seasons. However, Mr. Woods's income growth, considering his payment record with them, consistently failed their expectations. Many times not even the interest was paid on the mortgage payment.

That winter, soon after the New Year, the bank had had enough. Written notices more adamantly threatened foreclosure, and then Mother received the outright promised immediate foreclosure announcement. They were seizing our property for Daddy's failure to pay.

In a few days, Daddy came home, requested, received, and sat down for a face-to-face appointment with the officers of the bank. They assured him his continuing inability to bring the account current could no longer be allowed. He left the meeting knowing the wheels were still in motion for the bank's foreclosure action against 622 Cliffwood Avenue.

Confident about the promise of the construction business he struggled night and day to build, Daddy proceeded in a direction totally opposed to the resounding advice of family and concerned friends.

With a goal toward saving foreclosure costs and thus being able to realize financial gain, my father introduced an alternative strategy to the bank officers. He wanted to be the one to sell the home designed and built for his family less than ten years prior. The bank listened and ceased their foreclosure initiative, allowing Daddy to put his house on the market and sell it himself. He had successfully negotiated for the future he wanted.

My father continued to work on his plan.

Chapter 16

Moving Along

I don't remember a "House for Sale" sign plunked into our front yard or any "For Sale" sign at all. Friends of the family bought "the house John Woods built." They were a couple who lived in a much smaller home a few blocks behind us. No doubt a sign proved unnecessary.

From the profit Daddy gained selling our house, he made a $200 down payment on the not-quite one hundred acre nonworking farm he discovered one winter day riding to work down a different road. And he bought a pick-up truck.

For me, when I learned we were moving, it was a God-sent moment. I didn't care if we would be country kids. We would be with our father, where he had been living and working—all of us together, every day. The misery and insecurity I secreted inside me melted away. Our family was *not* breaking apart, forever.

The past winter months, gossip had resurfaced about Daddy having another woman in Cleveland. The kids were saying Daddy was in a wheelchair and his woman was taking care of him. The story caused me much sadness. Then as I thought about it, the mind-boggling news my father was disabled, I started feeling better. Those kids had gone too far. Their whole story was a lie. If Daddy could hide another woman from Mother, he couldn't hide being crippled in a wheelchair. Mother would know. The unity my parents exhibited in public and at home gave me that confidence. Knowing such, Mother would not carry on as she did, only unhappy with his not being home but in charge, with purpose, finding ways to keep us content and happy. No, she would be trying to get to him; commotion and attention focused on that. And Mother would be in her room, a lot, crying. Yes, their scenario putting Daddy in a wheelchair was too much. The stories were not true—only kids being mean.

Once we began preparing for the move, life was greatly improved. Surprisingly, our parents let us teach ourselves how to roller skate in the house. The layout of the living room and dining room and the smooth hardwood floors made a perfect arena for skating fast. Over and over, we went from the front doorway through the two rooms to whip around the dining room table. Mother and Daddy agreed the damage our skates did to the floors would be corrected when the new owners had them refinished. Hopefully that was so. For once we learned how to skate, we circled and swirled and chased and followed and raced and skate danced. Other kids were invited to bring their skates and join us. It was the place to be. What fun!

Mr. Floyd Blackmore sold Daddy the acreage, house, barn, and other farm buildings—machine shop, granary, and large chicken coop. Daddy agreed to make regular monthly payments to clear the balance due. Their written agreement provided Mr. Blackmore could reclaim the property if Mr. Woods missed a payment. (I will not leave you in suspense about that. My Dad never lost the property.)

Actually years later, another local businessman confided the fact that Mr. Blackmore had made the sale at a bargain rate because he expected to get the property back within the year. Mr. Blackmore figured our family would immediately clean and fix up the rundown property as we made it livable and attractive. Then when Daddy defaulted as he juggled his sporadic income to provide for our big family, Mr. Blackmore would make a more profitable sale to another buyer impressed with the improved grounds and buildings.

Something else happened. He got to know my father and respected the interesting, well-read, responsible, hard-working family man. Even though Daddy was late with a number of payments, Mr. Blackmore became his supportive good friend and never instituted the default provision.

It was mid-June 1950 when John W. Woods, Jr., relocated his family from the city to the country.

That lovely Saturday morning our family was in Zanesville, and our modern house was emptied of what we wanted to take with us. We loaded the last of it all into two vehicles—Daddy's pick-up truck and a U-Haul truck. Mr. Payne, who we learned worked for Daddy, had come to help us. He drove the big U-Haul. We left the piano behind.

Both vehicles were crammed with family and household as we rode away from the city where my parents met and married and my six brothers and sisters and I were born. In fact, the excitement of it all, what with beginning a more than two hundred mile journey, soon became an uncomfortable adventure. Three adults and seven children, ranging in age from Johnny's practically fourteen years to toddler Larry, eighteen months old, strained the passenger seating both trucks normally accommodated. We managed because Jimmy and Johnny willingly made space for themselves wherever possible in the back of either truck. Before nightfall, we were in Williamsfield, Ohio, exploring an old farmhouse, our new home.

As the men and boys unloaded everything into the house, it was shockingly clear we were embarking on a vastly different lifestyle. The house did not have inside plumbing. We did not have running water. There was no bathroom in the house!

Mother and Daddy's bedroom was on the first floor as was the room Cynthia and Sharon shared. Behind theirs was a smaller room that was Larry's. There were two bedrooms upstairs; one for Johnny and Jimmy and the other for Kathleen and me. They were off a tiny foyer at the top of a beautiful open staircase looking over the living room. From the first, I loved the novelty of being upstairs. I loved not having to worry about being frightened by anyone loitering under my bedroom windows.

Daddy's commitment to self and family produced results he had long envisioned. We were together, and John Woods's contracting business was the foundation of our good fortune. Life had taken a promising turn for the Woods family.

The four oldest—Kathleen, the baby,
surrounded by Jimmy, Johnny,
and me. Photo taken around 1945.

Summer of 1956 and the
second set of twins in our family,
Sharon and Cynthia, pose in
the play yard in Williamsfield.

It's Larry and baby Roy's turn.
Taffy is the family pet staying involved.

Chapter 17

Beginning a New Lifestyle

The next morning, looking out of the large window in our bedroom facing north, I saw a view amazing to my eyes. Out over the porch roof fanned a wide-open field of *country* grass—different heights, different textures, no bushes, and colors mostly various hues of green. It all flowed into thick woods (surely like those described in fairy tales) edging the upper quadrant of the field against the horizon, except where a distant pale blue body of water shared the horizon's line. (I was to forever appreciate having this view of the Pymatuning Lake from my bedroom window.)

The wooded area looked as if it was home to bears' and wolves' dens deep inside. I learned a variety of brambles, bushes, and many short, tall, thin, and wide trees flourished in our woods. Deer ran through. There were raccoons, possums, skunks, snakes, squirrels, rabbits, groundhogs, and turtles. But there were no bears, wolves, or fairy tale elves.

I stood at the window, mesmerized by the different outdoors before my eyes. There were no sidewalks at all and no paved or even asphalted streets (excuse me, roads) in sight. Our nearest neighbor seemed the equivalent of two city blocks or more down and across the road. But there was no time that first morning for me to linger absorbing our new surroundings.

Soon I was downstairs helping Mother who was up and about much earlier. The sun beamed brightly through the double-sized kitchen window facing the east.

Daddy had reloaded his truck with tools and materials to start a new plastering job. He also had a job underway in Bristolville, a town thirty miles or so from us. He was building a concrete block foundation under a restaurant. Daddy juggled these jobs and each day simultaneously worked with his sons to significantly improve conditions around our new place.

The exterior of the old house appeared okay, compared to the interior. Inside, the floors were worn grey splintery wooden planks. In rooms where there were electrical outlets and a light fixture, usually the light glowed with the pull of a string, turning on the naked bulb in the center of the ceiling. The basement floor was concrete, ancient, and crumbly; the walls were cement blocks, dusty, dirty, and accentuated with spider webs, making the area more a dungeon than a basement. I could only imagine how my mother truly felt, seeing her "new" home for the first time. Inside, it appeared we had moved into a ramshackle haunted house.

Thank heavens the kitchen boasted a wall switch for the ceiling light because the room also served as a nighttime hangout for rats. They must have thought we invaded *their* home. I was frightened in spite of Daddy's unfazed promise those creatures were more afraid of me than I them. After a few days I fixed it so mornings when I was the first one in the kitchen, I could flick on the light and drive the rats scurrying away before my feet touched the floor. Before going up to bed the night before, I carefully positioned kitchen chairs—a couple of them in line from the staircase into the kitchen for my feet to proceed on the elevated walkway of their seats as every rat scurried from *our* home.

A first priority was to rid ourselves of the rodents who were more than a horrible visual distraction. They were destructive, chewing holes, getting into packages of food and filthy, leaving droppings everywhere. Still I envisioned one springing flat on my chest, and that was my concern. Maybe that's why I learned to stifle frantic screams when I glimpsed the long oblong body and longer menacing tail of a rat disappearing, though slow to leave. At least he was going, not positioning to attack me. In the weeks before we were able to get rid of them, I so dreaded the rodents I took pots and pans upstairs to bang and clang on my way down the steps in the morning, intent on scaring them out before the light did. Finally Daddy found the right stuff to get rid of our unwanted housemates, and the rat problem was gone forever.

Very soon Daddy replaced the grey weather-beaten outdoor toilet down the narrow path from our back door. No, he didn't have plumbing installed in the house. He and my brothers built a classy four-hole new outside toilet, "so you girls can go together if you want to," Daddy said. They put a framed window pane high in the center of the back wall, a nice mirror on one of the front walls, a newspaper rack on the other, and two toilet paper holders, one on each side wall. The new 'bathroom' was placed between two heavily foliaged plum trees that provided beautiful blooms every spring and cool shade in the summer.

The family scrubbed and cleaned inside the house, tackling what could be done to make living conditions healthy and comfortable. But the poor condition of the house was not our only concern.

Every building, the house and the dilapidated barn and the other once purpose-filled farm structures appeared to be drowning in acres of waist-high weeds, unlike anything our city-bred eyes had known.

The place looked better as Daddy, Johnny, and Jimmy cut the weeds and grass to create the beginning of a fantastic rolling lawn. When they completed their work, our house, to us, seemed to be sitting in the middle of a small park. The lawn flowed from the front porch, which was actually on the side of the house facing the driveway. The lawn extended into a play yard across the driveway. It circled across the back of the house, coming around to meet a deep front yard where eight perfectly spaced tall maple trees bordered a wide roadside drainage ditch. It was a ditch of neatly cut grass serving as a barrier to any vehicle heading onto the yard should it accidentally swerve off the road. Now surrounded by a manicured lawn, the appearance of the once-abandoned house was greatly improved.

The first time Cynthia and Sharon, not yet four years old, played in the front yard all by themselves, the twins ran hysterically onto the front porch, scrambling to open the screen door. "Mother, Mother," they cried, "those cows are looking at us." There were some fifty or so black and white Guernsey cows in the electric-fenced pasture across the road. They belonged to the Cole family, our neighbors. The Coles were full-time dairy farmers. It was interesting watching their herd, every late afternoon, like clockwork, stroll to the barn to be milked.

For many weeks, it was an exciting change. By the time school started some two months and more after we moved in, excitement had turned to merely adjusting. Going outdoors to the hand pump in the backyard some ten feet from the back porch just to have the water we needed became necessary routine. For sure, the initial exciting novelty of pumping our cold, fresh-tasting well water wore off soon. Housekeeping was strenuous—carrying well water into the house, heating it on the electric range to wash dishes, cook, do the washing, take a bath, and then lugging the dirty water out the back door to discard in the "weeds," the tall grass bordering the backyard—hard work! Each night before going to bed, the water bucket in the kitchen sink had to be filled. (Johnny and Jimmy made trouble for themselves by managing to get caught drinking from the water dipper hanging suspended inside.) Water pitchers in the refrigerator had to be filled before we went to bed as well as the ice cube trays in the refrigerator's tiny freezer compartment. Two buckets of water three-quarters filled were left on top of the stove to heat in the morning for everyone to wash-up for the day. Not having hot or cold water running through pipes throughout the house to a toilet and washing machine and to spigots in a bathtub, lavatory, and kitchen sink was a consequence of our move I never considered exciting. It was a necessary change, and I didn't fret.

Time and the new outhouse helped me forget the beautiful amenities of the bathroom *inside* our home in Zanesville.

By the time school started, I seemed to be the only one still scared silly at the sight of snakes, huge ones, middle sized and small, wriggling through our yard or across the driveway or slithering across the road. It didn't seem to frighten anyone but me to look out Mother and Daddy's bedroom window and see the grossly colorful milk snake[12] curled up, warming itself in the morning sun beaming down on the cellar doorframe underneath their window.

Running down the long driveway to the road to get the mail out of the mailbox was no longer a cherished task—just another interrupting chore someone *had* to do.

Hot summer nights were almost unbearable. We were in northern Ohio where a night breeze cooled somewhat, but when no breeze at all wafted through the screened windows, I missed the comfort of the central air-conditioning in the house Daddy built.

* * * * * * * * * *

Everyone marveled at the variety of fresh fruits growing on our land, ours for the picking. Wild strawberry patches produced enough fruit for Mother's yummy shortcake dessert. There were several different apple trees around the property, and Mother readily made pies and cobblers. We found a proliferation of big sweet blackberries growing on blackberry vines scattered in many patches on our land and the neighbors' property, too. Mother canned fruits and made jellies, jams, and preserves.

Blackberry picking was a preplanned all day activity. Mother said she needed to clean, cook, and/or serve the berries within twenty-four hours of being picked, hence the preplanning. For instance, we couldn't go berry picking if Mother planned to iron clothes the next day.

Selecting the picking site was a serious decision because each of us had our favorite and we had to stay together as a group. No one was to get lost! Mother had to know our destination. If we told her, "We're going to Pennsylvania today." That meant we were heading to where our property line and the Ohio/Pennsylvania state line were one and the same. There was a heavily laden, but small patch of briars on our land near the fence. It wasn't a favored spot because it was small and farther away. When we did go, we climbed over the wooden rail fence to sit and eat the lunch Mother and I had packed for each of us. Sitting under the shade trees in our neighboring state was relaxing because crops were planted that gave the appearance of acres of beautiful lawn under a wonderful blue sky. It was also neat anticipating Mother pretending shock when we announced, "We went to Pennsylvania for lunch today."

Each of us had our own berry-picking bucket and tried to come home with the most berries. If, altogether, we picked at least a full galvanized bucket of berries, the one contributing the most to that bucket was rewarded with their very own blackberry pie. Because of the prize, we were careful not to eat or spill the fruit, which meant no horseplay and wrestling by the boys.

We wore berry picking clothes. Daddy insisted long-sleeved shirts, heavy jeans, and tall sturdy rubber boots gave important protection. The prickly berry vines rose from thick underbrush at the edge of a field under a stand of small trees or in wooded areas. The vines were in places where there was no people traffic. We dressed to offset the risk of a snakebite or stepping on a field mouse or other critter or suffering a sting or painful bite from any insect, especially a spider. Before we moved to the country, Daddy never let his girls wear pants. The move from the city changed that. Almost everything we did in our new environment could not be done well or with propriety in dresses or skirts.

* * * * * * * * * *

We didn't plant a garden that first summer; we did the next. Daddy borrowed a tractor and tilled the soil across the driveway for the grandest garden we would ever have, perhaps a half-acre plot. We planted, weeded, cultivated, and harvested pole beans, green beans, lettuce, tomatoes, corn, potatoes, and carrots. It was such a large bountiful vegetable garden, the following year we did not have one at all. Mother said Daddy had not recovered from the last summer's major effort. She was busy too, canning vegetables from early morning to late afternoon. When we did plant again, our garden was reduced to tomatoes and green beans, maybe sweet corn. Still it was difficult finding time to maintain—weed, cultivate, and then harvest. I was thrilled when we stopped gardening altogether. We city folk had learned all the fresh vegetables we wanted for eating or canning could be bought for a great price from the many roadside stands the real farmers had throughout harvest season. We were their customers.

Daddy and Mother kept us occupied with time-consuming chores. Daddy had his boys busy repairing things around the house, cutting grass, or going to work on the job with him. Kathleen and I helped Mother cook, do the laundry, clean house, and watch after Cynthia, Sharon, and Larry. Being strangers in essentially a strange land, home and family were very much our only community that first summer in Williamsfield as we worked together.

* * * * * * * * * *

Summertime recreation included some of the outdoor games we had enjoyed in Zanesville such as tag, hide n' seek, and catching lightning bugs. We also enjoyed playing baseball games on a miniature diamond laid out in the front yard or on the larger one made over in the play yard. Once in a while, Mother joined in for an inning or two. Daddy played too, more often than Mother, or he umpired.

Long summer evenings, Daddy took us on drives, exploring our new neighborhood, now the countryside. I heard minimal and short-lived complaints about the unbelievable change to how we lived. The family was all under one roof every night.

Chapter 18

The Birds, the Bees, My Parents, and Me

Almost every day Johnny and Jimmy went to work with Daddy. What a surprise the evening Daddy invited me to go with him in the morning, not the boys, just me. It was a plastering job—the living room of the house he built. He said he was finishing the "brown coat." "It won't take long. You can be my helper." I felt special. In the morning, just as *we* did for "the men," Mother packed my lunch for me to take to work with Daddy.

It was a Saturday I'll never forget. You see, it was the day my father told me about the changes I would experience as my body developed from a child's body into the body of a woman.

Working, standing balanced above me on his scaffold, my father talked. His left hand gripped the handle of a tray piled with first-coat brown plaster mix. His right hand gathered and then firmly and precisely applied a trowel of the compound to the strips of bare wood lathing covering the wall. Through the oversized window beside him, the sun was streaming into the room empty of everything, except us and what he needed to do his work.

Daddy talked about the choices we have in life, about the importance of thinking, about self-responsibility, consequences, stuff he always taught us. As I continued kind of reading the book I had brought with me, I listened and was his helper, too, handing him whatever he needed. I was wondering what I had done wrong in recent days to earn me this lecture, his private lecture. I could not think of a thing. Then his subject matter was no longer general life topics. He had lingered on me, specifically—my age (I was twelve years old), what grade I was going into when school started in a few weeks (I would be in the eighth grade).

Before I knew it, my father had segued into talking about changes affecting my body that could start soon and happen each month and continue for almost the remainder of my life. He told me what he was saying was personal business, not to be discussed with anyone other than Mother—certainly not with my brothers and my little sisters. He talked about how the change would cause my emotions to fluctuate, but "knowing it is going to happen, you can make the decision to be in charge of your personality that time of the month," he said.

He even spoke of the need to carefully take care of personal hygiene during those days. "Those days each month could easily be your secret," my father told me that day.

I learned the change about to happen meant my body would be able to make a baby. He talked about eggs and sperm, male body parts, female body parts, everything!

I was so glad he was high on that scaffold and I was far below him, practically on the floor. I was sitting on a bucket I had turned upside down, my eyes focused on the book on my knees. Thank heavens I couldn't see my father's face and he couldn't see mine.

Daddy told me, for the best chance of having a good life, I should make the choice not to get pregnant until I was a grown woman, had my education, had married well, and could take care of myself and a baby. "You must be a good example for your little sisters," he said. "I don't want to look up and see you coming down the road with your belongings in brown paper bags bringing home a baby you cannot take care of."

My father's tone was somber, just informative as he covered it all.

It was good he did talk so much because there was a lot I had wondered about. Not many years prior, I found myself analyzing the possibility of a cabbage patch or a stork actually having something to do with babies appearing. That was before the Christmas Eve birth of Cynthia and Sharon at home on 622 Cliffwood Avenue in Mother and Daddy's bedroom. The entire night I lay wide awake in my bedroom, listening. The doctor came to the house, but for sure no stork or cabbage had been involved.

After the birth of my twin sisters, when I thought about how a girl could keep from having a baby (and I worried about it a lot because of the dire head shaking accompanying rumors someone's daughter had gone away to have a baby), I decided perhaps the poor girl had let a boy look into her eyes with extra-special sincerity. I would make sure not to let that happen.

Actually, after moving to the country, my thoughts on the genesis of babies had been elevated to a different and absolutely yucky level to my mind. Living in Zanesville, I was not outdoors in a way that enabled me to witness nature as I did in the country where the unbridled habits of four-legged animals were there for all to see, including me. Still, I couldn't fully accept the possibility men and women did anything like I saw happening between those dogs, cats, cows, and pigs.

At the end of our day together, Daddy had cleared up everything, having conveyed all the facts having to do with having a baby. One thing remained a puzzle, but I didn't ask the question. I could not understand why a girl who knew how pregnancy happened and certainly didn't want to be pregnant would let herself get pregnant. Several years later, I understood the challenging complexity of managing self-control when strong, wonderful, overpowering emotions are involved.

When I came home from my day of learning with Daddy, Mother asked if I was okay and if I had any questions. She told me where she had stored any toiletries, personal items I might need. But she stressed I should tell her when my body changed. I did, several weeks later, and never had further discussion on the matter. It was all my private business. I felt grown-up.

Chapter 19

The New School

It was Tuesday morning after Labor Day, and Johnny, Jimmy, Kathleen, and I watched a big yellow school bus approach from the south coming down the road to pick us up for our first day of school. (Taking a bus to school was a new concept for us. In Zanesville, we walked and talked with friends along the many blocks to school.) Now, a bus stopped at the end of our driveway and we climbed on, our first summer as country kids officially ended. We trudged down the aisle, selected seats—my brothers sitting together, me sitting with my sister. Settling back we watched others get on at driveways along the way to our destination, Williamsfield School on Route 322 just past Route 7.

The residents in our new community some sixty miles from Cleveland, forty miles from Youngstown, and one hundred miles from Pittsburgh, Pennsylvania, had witnessed, throughout the years, several black families come and then leave. That September we were the only blacks enrolled in Williamsfield School. From Mother and Daddy's conversations, I learned the local folk hadn't been the least bit reticent about questioning, in a friendly way, our plans for staying in the community. The Woods family had no plans to leave.

Our new school differed significantly from those we attended in Zanesville. Williamsfield, a much smaller community, housed all twelve grades in one school building. And grades one through eight were dual classrooms, i.e., two grades in one room. Kathleen's fourth grade teacher welcomed her to a classroom of third and fourth graders. Jimmy and I were in the eighth grade, in a class room divided to teach seventh and eighth grade students. Johnny, a ninth grader, started high school where classrooms held one grade only. You see, students from the neighboring township of Wayne came over to Williamsfield for their high school education, so the ninth, tenth, eleventh, and twelfth grade class sizes were larger than the elementary grades.

Anyway, absent any curiosity, fanfare, or hysteria, the Woods children brought integration to Williamsfield. As far as I could tell, there was nothing special about us because we were black children in a student body that had previously been only white children.

Some years before, at Wilson Elementary School in Zanesville my color was a concern I had to handle. It was in the fifth grade. I had been named a member of the School Girl Safety Patrol. The School Girl and School Boy Safety Patrols helped students cross streets going to and from the school building. Being selected to be a patrol girl was an honor and a privilege. I proudly rushed home to tell my parents the news. I dearly hoped they would sign the slip giving their permission. They did! I was assigned to the kindergarten class. I was one of the patrol girls who walked alongside lines of the smallest children marching two by two from the schoolyard. We looked after them as they walked the sidewalks toward the street corners in their neighborhoods. We stood guard near the corner until they safely crossed to parents or other grownups waiting for them.

One afternoon, walking, patrolling the curbside line of the four- and five-year-old boys and girls, alongside a little girl with curly strawberry blond hair, I felt a lingering, timid touch to the back of my hand. Looking down, the child's finger still touching me, her little face looked up into mine.

"If you wash real hard, won't it come off?" she quietly asked.

Her question truly surprised me, but I was quick to calmly and lightly, and with pride, say, "No, it won't wash off. I'll be this color all my life."

I've often wondered what, if any, conversation she had with her family concerning her curiosity about skin color different from hers.

In the new school, Mr. Fobes, our teacher in the seventh and eighth grade classroom scared me somewhat, at first. He never smiled. He was a no-nonsense instructor and disciplinarian whom I exasperated by whispering during class time. And I only whispered once in a while, I thought. Not having heard what my teacher said. I might ask the person at the next desk, "What chapter? What page?" No teacher before him had ever been out of sorts with me. I had a teeny glimmer of thought that maybe his consternation was predicated on my being black. Then one day when tears spilled from my eyes after he verbally chastised me for the entire room to hear, he sent me to the cloakroom. Following me, inside he lectured about whispering, "Raise your hand and ask me if you don't know." Then, turning, motioning I should exit the doorway ahead of him, he blurted words that immediately brightened my spirits.

"I've never seen such spoiled children from a big family," he said.

You see, my twin, Jimmy, was, of course, in the class with me, and at times he found ways to disrupt quiet moments with fun stuff. He could easily make one or two in the class laugh without doing anything disrespectful to anyone or out of line in a bad way. In fact, it was usually when Mr. Fobes's back was turned. But our teacher knew it was Jimmy causing the commotion. Mother used to say being the class clown was obviously Jimmy's major goal in school.

I took Mr. Fobes labeling the two of us as spoiled as a tribute to Mother and Daddy and our family. His muttering acknowledged us to be the self-assured individuals our parents raised us to be. I no longer hurt. My unhappy teacher's critique placed me on a pedestal I liked. For whatever reason, he and I had no more problems with each other. I found it special to be thought of as a "spoiled child," coddled and respected by my parents.

My love for school continued in Williamsfield where I wouldn't think of missing a single day, even if I was sick. Homework was a welcome challenge. I tried to present the neatest, most complete assignment. I enjoyed everything about taking tests, the pressure of timed exams, the necessity for no appearance of cheating, making sure I had the required #2 pencils, sharp and ready to go. I anticipated doing well on any test whether it was a pop quiz or a widely promoted exam. Diligently working hard for and then getting the best grade possible was my objective every day.

Unhappily, I've never forgotten the C I got in biscuits in seventh grade home economics at Zanesville's Grover Cleveland Junior High School. I was totally distraught.

It was mandatory for home economics students to work in pairs. When the teacher came to me and my partner's work station to grade our biscuits, I was prepared for her to quiz us individually about our part in making the biscuits. But she didn't ask one single question of either one of us. She picked up a biscuit, gave it a good visual examination, gingerly pulled it apart, examined it for texture, etc., popped a morsel in her mouth to taste, and then wrote her grade next to our names on the evaluation sheet taped to the counter top. Seeing the C, I flipped! It was my partner's fault. I knew how to make biscuits. At home, from the age of seven, I had been making tall, light, fluffy, delicious biscuits without any help whatsoever. I didn't deserve a C.

I ran from the room crying. Our teacher caught up to me far down the hall, sobbing against the shiny yellow block wall.

"'C' is not a bad grade," she said.

I wailed, "It is bad. It is next to a D and that is next to an E and that is FAILING."

My teacher said the biscuits, done in partnership with my classmate, merited a C, which was fair. And it wasn't "bad" for the experience gave me a learning I referenced many times—do not act independently when you work as partners; do all you can to work together for the good of the team.

Of course she was absolutely correct; I applied the lesson learned that day many times in my life.

Satisfaction with school life only increased as I participated in extracurricular activities. I sang in the school chorus, was active in drama productions, worked on the school newspaper, and was involved in intramural sports, particularly basketball and volleyball.

In no time, even the daily travel to and from school included great times with new friends who became best friends riding the school bus. The new school was wonderful.

Chapter 20

Christmas Growing Up

The build up to Christmas Eve when I was a youngster is remembered as a magnificent time of yummy anticipation. Maybe Santa Claus would come. Maybe, somehow, presents would appear. For sure there was an abundance of homemade goodies to eat and family fun time. I also became absorbed with reacquainting myself with the story of Jesus's birth. Without a doubt, though, that interest was trumped by the secular amenities embodied in Santa Claus, presents, fun, and goodies.

Yes, Christmastime, on weekends and perhaps a couple evenings during the week, our house was fragrant with aromas from making fudge, baking cookies, cakes, cupcakes, and luscious nut-filled brownies. We made several different kinds of cake frostings, cooked and uncooked. Pies and cobblers were also very popular with us.

Mother and I did most of the cooking and baking. As Kathleen got older, she had specialty items she made, primarily layer cake. Jimmy and Johnny played an important role since we didn't have a rotary beater or an electric mixer. When our arms were too tired to continue, my brothers were enlisted to beat cake batter. Holding the large mixing bowl and whipping the mixing spoon round and round in the thick batter "two hundred times" and more was no problem to them. Daddy's delicious contribution was the snow ice cream he made, when there was snow.

Everyone, except Daddy, decorated our freshly made Christmas cookies. Popping popcorn was a treat all winter, and making popcorn balls and stringing popcorn was a favorite activity, especially for the youngest of us during the holidays.

One year Mother developed a top of the stove fruit cobbler that became a favorite (both blackberry and apple). It was the Christmas a heating coil in the oven broke. Daddy wasn't able to have it fixed right away. With Daddy's encouragement, we persevered. "Do you have to have an oven for everything?" he asked. "Can't you figure out a recipe that doesn't need the oven?" Sweetened fruit and thinly rolled narrow strips of pastry dough interspersed with butter, generously dusted with spices and more sugar were layered in a huge kettle and boiled in just the right amount of water. The new recipe became a forever-after requested dessert even when the oven was working.

We made fudge as if we had a contract for supplying a candy store. Ours was the most delicious vanilla, peanut butter, and dark and light chocolate fudge, with and without pecans, walnuts, or almonds.

No one pressured us during Christmas season about eating too much. All the specialty baking and cooking, a huge part of celebrating the season, did come to a halt after New Year's Eve. Until then, it wasn't unusual for Mother to oversee portioning an evening's batch of cookies or fudge evenly between her children. Each had his or her very own crisp brown lunch bag of homemade treats under his or her absolute control.

We were ready for humorous drama when Jimmy or Johnny, who had wolfed down their bag of sweets, embarked on a diabolical, yet cute, campaign to get Kathleen to share her candy or cookies with them. Kathleen was known to hold her brown bagged supply for days, until her big brothers discovered it existed. Then their goal was to get it for themselves. Johnny's ploy was to beg, or be sad and needy, and then graciously charming. It worked. Kathleen's stash became his.

Jimmy was more entertaining and just as successful. He pretended to be a kitten or puppy, wriggling on all fours, mewing or yipping and yapping around her feet and ankles until his little sister, giggling profusely, fed him all he wanted of her carefully hoarded treasure.

When we were older, Daddy called for family talent shows on a weekend night. We recited poems we had memorized and sang Christmas songs and carols. Everyone singing Christmas carols was my favorite time. We had a variety of Christmas songbooks that were put away after the holidays to be brought out the next year. We also had what was known as "popular song" books. Songbooks, magazine format, were popular in the 40s and 50s, and Daddy brought them home periodically. Every verse of the song was printed but not the music. They resembled magazines of poetry and were wonderful for singing along with the radio or the recording, if you had a record player. During the holidays or not, Daddy enjoyed sitting back in his favorite chair in our living room with his pipe to be entertained by his children singing or reciting poetry.

Christmas season found both parents with time to join in playing board games, particularly, Chinese and regular checkers. When we reached high school age, Daddy taught us how to play cards—gin rummy and bid whist, which became a favorite pastime. We had some serious bid whist tournaments—just family.

The Christmas spirit existed without the widely recognized material enhancements or trappings of the season.

We had no decorations unless we hung those we made at school. And the one Christmas tree I recall during my childhood was an especially luxurious, floor to ceiling, live evergreen in the living room on Cliffwood Avenue. Every year I pined for one. (A pleasant memory after I married was my husband calling our annual Christmas tree, "Marva's Tree.")

Receiving gaily wrapped presents was not a guaranteed occurrence for the children. Nevertheless in my younger days, as I listened to the radio disc jockey on Christmas Eve give updates on which cities Santa Claus's sleigh was approaching, I squeezed my eyes tight in silent prayer he found his way to us or that somehow there would be presents in our house on Christmas morning. And it did happen a few times.

There was the time I got a new doll carriage and a wonderful doll. She was a colored doll—looked to be a toddler and so beautiful. That day as Mother fixed Christmas dinner she and I named my doll. It was quite a serious undertaking. We alternately suggested and considered different names until we agreed "Dixie" was perfect.

Another year when we were able to get some of what we asked for, I got a brown dress. I had asked for a brown dress because I wanted to be a Brownie in the Girl Scouts. My parents said I couldn't. The only brown dress I had ever seen for a little girl was the Brownie uniform. Surely when Mother and Daddy realized that was the only brown dress in the stores, they would change their mind and let me be a Brownie. Mother and Daddy beamed with pleasure as I unwrapped and unopened the box to find exactly what I had asked for, a brown dress. It was deep chocolate brown sprinkled all over with teeny yellow and pink flowers. I was quite a little actress that morning because I looked surprised and happy when I was only surprised, actually shocked and sad! My parents so happily shared the difficulty they had finding a brown dress for a little girl.

The most memorable Christmas Eve was when the twins, Cynthia and Sharon, were born. They were born at home early that morning. In fact, the day started when Daddy came into our bedroom to tell Kathleen and me we had just received an early, very special Christmas present, two new baby sisters. That year, Christmas Eve and Christmas Day were truly unique.

As I got older, I looked forward to making Mother and Daddy a gift in art class at school. Once I learned how to sew and do needle work, I embroidered handkerchiefs and doilies. I liked hiding from Mother's eyesight in my bedroom where I sketched the flowers or other designs I embroidered. I finished the rolled hem with neat hand stitching. Mother always seemed surprised, which pleased me.

The enthusiasm generated and maintained by the goodies produced in our kitchen and the fun and games we shared with each other in our living room sent a house full of children to bed on Christmas Eve with happy thoughts dancing through their heads. And even though they were never apparent on

Christmas Eve, the next morning we had a plentiful assortment of fruits and nuts, including sweet tangerines and the biggest oranges.

Traditionally on Christmas Day our family enjoyed a special breakfast, including pancakes, ham, biscuits, and eggs. Early in the afternoon we had a turkey dinner with all the trimmings.

Christmas is a memory of reading about Mary and Joseph and the enemy King Herod; marveling at the star in the heavens that guided the shepherds and the Three Wise Men; looking at the brand new sweet face of the baby Jesus, the gift to the world lying in the stable with the animals around, and understanding once again the promise of it all. It is a memory of a family finding joy in what they had, never misery for what they didn't have; all of it working together to make for a joyous season. Christmas was a beautiful time in our home when I was growing up.

Remembered

Daddy
1902–1960

Mother
1911–1987

Kathleen
1941–1991

Sharon
1946–2003

Chapter 21

New Friends—New Lessons

This I believe—the color of one's skin needn't hinder the formation of a great friendship, and good friends are of immeasurable value for one's personal well-being. I credit Williamsfield Township School for strengthening those relationship learnings, which have significantly enriched each phase of my life. Our first year in Williamsfield my brothers, sister, and I found all others in the school system were white—students, teachers, staff. In fact, my five years there, September through May, day after day at the tall red brick asbestos siding wrapped school, except for my sisters, I was the only black girl in the student body. (During those years, a black guy or two enrolled; one came my junior year. He was tall and handsome. Here I admit, I fantasized that he and I might become boyfriend and girlfriend—it never happened.) Still, my unique heritage and color was never a defining issue in the classroom, hallways, lunchroom, or anyplace at Williamsfield School. Classmates, friends, and I studied, laughed, shared, and faced challenges meeting goals together. To me, our different skin tone and features didn't matter one iota. I felt appreciated and worthy to accomplish anything I prepared for and wanted in life.

For John and Iva Woods, once school started, it was quickly apparent, our relocation to Williamsfield moved race relations up to a level of parental concern we had not known. Mother and Daddy seemed to have no worry about us fitting in with the other children or our level of happiness in the new school. My father and mother were concerned for our safety as black children and fixated on providing guidance to better insure our personal security.

It was 1950, just a few years since the country helped other free world nations victoriously end World War II. When it was all over, brave and accomplished black and white Americans had fought and died together for that victory. Yet the racial discrimination and legal segregation those soldiers left behind when they went to fight in foreign lands continued to exist when they returned home to America. In the Southern states, "Whites Only" signs, "No Colored Allowed," and other postings directing the separation of blacks and whites prevailed as they had before. Patience throughout the country for maintaining such a revolting human rights status quo had waned to a point where proponents of both sides of the issue passionately fueled the public with information, rhetoric, and action. In many large cities in the North and throughout the South, meetings were held; emotional dialogue transpired. Radio commentators, newspapers, and magazine articles reported on the pros and cons expressed. Race relations in our country evolved into a serious, life-threatening issue for many. Folks not wanting blacks and whites to be treated equally and incensed about the strong possibility of segregation being outlawed took strident steps to thwart any movement toward laws enforcing equality. Crosses were burned on the lawns of blacks and whites well known for working for voting rights and integration of the races. On quiet dark nights, bricks were hurled through windows to forever ruin the peace and comfort of the home of someone working for equal rights. Children taunted other children with racial slurs. In the face of all of this, people favoring the end of racism in America became more adamant and bravely proceeded to successfully enlist greater numbers of blacks and whites in their effort. That good only spotlighted the evil carried out by segregationists, usually under cover of night. For the most part, blacks had no proof who the perpetrators were, the identity of those who may have civilly passed by them during the day and then did harm to them after dark. Who could be trusted? Most overt aggressiveness against blacks took place in the South. But in the North, as well, there were incidences of racial violence. However, there were no violent or even unpleasant racially based incidents anywhere near where my family lived. Still my parents were on the alert and monitored our activity in the new community so unlike the one we came from. Zanesville compared to Williamsfield was a relatively cosmopolitan city where by sight the Woods children were not special. Our family lived in a predominately black but mixed race neighborhood. We attended predominantly white but mixed race schools. In Williamsfield, although Mother and Daddy and all of us had nothing but good experiences with everyone, my parents invoked a strategy for keeping their uniquely black children safe. Nothing was left to trust.

My father reacted to a truth; the just and equal treatment we experienced in our school didn't represent real world for blacks in America. He was cautious for us. He felt our visiting in a friend's home or in the popular hangout having a hamburger and pop or with friends in any public place could bring trouble. We might be faced with handling mean insensitive words, attitudes, or actions from folks who didn't know us. Daddy instituted an isolating strategy that grew from an intention to protect his children from prejudices, subtle and overt. Tightening our socializing circle was his strategy to avoid such experiences.

Daddy, with Mother's full support, didn't allow me to participate in after-school activities. I couldn't socialize in my friends' homes or anyplace other than in school or on the school bus. Thus, the camaraderie I enjoyed with schoolmates ended when I arrived home. My friends and I didn't see or hear from each other until the bus picked me up the next school morning.

My brothers were about as socially restricted as I was. Perhaps the impact wasn't as drastic for Johnny and Jimmy because they were allowed to attend after school sporting events when they had time, which wasn't a lot. Most weekends and some evenings my brothers helped Daddy finish a job. Their friends also had work responsibility, just different work, farming. They didn't have much time to play either. And there was the homework factor that plagued my brothers. They very seldom willingly picked up their school books, so Mother's "have you done your homework?" invariably received a no answer and gave her legitimate reason to keep them from a pick-up baseball game or finding adventure in the thick woods all around everyone's acres of cleared land. If my brothers were home and had done everything expected of them, they were allowed to be with friends.

The social restrictions imposed by my parents served to impress on me the fact that being a black person was a really big deal. Daddy taught us we were no different than other human beings, but that most white people thought we were, and we should not, could not, ignore that. My father viewed the self-segregation he imposed on his children as harmful to no one and important to our well-being, our safety, and our futures.

Of course I wanted to share good times with my friends, and on occasion, especially when they begged me to "just ask if you can go," I asked first Mother, and then Daddy. And as if he had not preached his message many times before, Daddy patiently reminded me why I couldn't have fun with them. "Your blackness might invite an unnecessary problem, even danger," he warned. This precipitated him into bringing home, for weeks after, black newspapers such as the *Pittsburgh Courier* and the *New York Amsterdam News*. "Read the editorials and every article. Know what people are thinking, what's going on. Your mother and I want to do our best to help you handle yourself, to keep you safe." Once, he shared this parable illustrating his cautious reasoning.

"Picture yourself sled riding on a bright sunny day, having fun skimming over the deep pile of fresh white snow, zooming down the hill and all at once appearing out of the blinding bright sunlight, there is a tree in your path. What would you do?"

Before I could answer, he was saying, "You would do everything in your power to avoid smashing into that tree, wouldn't you?"

"Y-e-e-e-s," I said, almost disrespectfully.

"Well," he continued, "remember to be wary of obstacles suddenly appearing in your path as you make your way in the world. Know that something unexpected could come between you and what you've anticipated, worked hard to have. The most formidable hindrance you will face is *discrimination*. People will place roadblocks in your path to keep you from going forward, because you are black. How you choose to handle it will determine the quality of life you will have for yourself and those you care about.

"Be on the lookout for discrimination to raise its ugly head when you are sailing along being good, doing and expecting good. Just as surely as that tree in the middle of the snowy hillside appearing through the sunlight will cause severe damage if your sled smashes into it, so can discrimination cause great damage, turning you from your objective when you had thoroughly assessed the situation and didn't envision 'losing' a possibility.

With open eyes and a firm grip as you steer and using all in your power, your muscles, your arms, your hands, each finger, even your finger tips, guiding your sled, you need not be afraid to enjoy the promise of the ride down the snow packed hillside. So it can be in living your life if you are alert at all times, not stunned by unanticipated, unwanted possibilities!

Your Mother and I are doing what we can to equip you for handling discrimination and to maintain pride in yourself. We want you to have the confidence to pursue any of the good options you'll have for a quality life. Some discrimination you will need to sidestep. Other discriminating experiences you'll find you must deal with, someway. It's up to you to think and have the tools and resources so you can make the decision that is best for you and your family.

I'm not going to let good times now fool you black children into assuming you and your friends have a lifetime of equal choices in front of you. You'll have different and difficult challenges. Concentrate now on learning all you can. There will be plenty of time to socialize in college."

The self-segregation our parents imposed kept my attention on the continuing plight of our people and those trying at the time to change things for the better. If Daddy had permitted me to gaily mix and mingle with my friends, would I have been interested in the radio and printed accounts of prejudices and discriminating actions against people of color? Would I have been receptive to going off to a black college as he planned? His strategy infused me with black awareness I could easily have lost.

Those teenaged days when I felt sorry for myself because I couldn't go to a sock hop or a wiener roast and hayride; for sure the prom; just thinking about moving on to college buried my unhappiness so deep it vanished. You see, I had my father's promise to look forward to. "You'll go to a black college, live on the campus, and decide for yourself which invitations you will accept." My focus was the future, and the isolation imposed by my parents gave me plenty of time for self-development.

Daddy's parenting philosophy encouraged both work and study as important preparation for opportunities affording us the best future possible. We were to learn all we could as well as develop skill and talent for making a living doing what we enjoyed. We should be able to "work for ourselves" and never have to rely on wages from others.

He taught his boys every contracting skill he had. After Daddy confirmed there wasn't a test or other activity at school they shouldn't miss, he took Johnny and Jimmy to help him on a job and miss a school day. It wasn't unusual for other boys in their classes to miss school because they helped on their family farm. The day the principal sent Daddy a letter telling him he couldn't keep his boys out of school is memorable to my brothers. I heard Jimmy say he was glad Daddy got the letter. "School is more fun than working," he mumbled. Daddy read the letter, put it down, "well, I'll take care of this," he promised to no one in particular.

We heard about Jim being surprised the next morning to see Daddy in the school hallway, walking toward the principal's office. Jimmy says Daddy glanced at him, didn't say a word, and went directly into Mr. Kirker's office. That night at supper the family heard a replay of their conversation.

Daddy reiterated how he told Mr. Kirker he knew other families—all he named being farming families—took their sons out of school, without a problem, if they were needed to hay and plow, etc. "Well, I'm not a farmer. I'm a plasterer, and if I need my boys once in a while to help me, they will. I'll see they study their lessons and do their homework." There was no more problem after that. In an emergency, my brothers were absent from school, on the job with Daddy whose words stressed school was priority. He saw to it they kept up with schoolwork.

* * * * * * * * * *

Teen years are remembered as busy and pleasant. I had a nice airy bedroom I could escape to when my jobs were done. I constantly read—newspapers, every day; library books, whatever book I could get my hands on, even Daddy's bulky hardcover concrete grey one entitled *Construction* and the even larger, dirty brown hardcover tome, an intellectual informative reference book about the Bible. Magazines were entertaining distractions to me, whether serious, socially informative, or foolish. I had plenty of time to amuse myself with what was at hand.

I could thank Cousin Ellen, Aunt Cora's daughter, for the foolish magazines I found to read. She mailed her thoroughly read *Romance*, *True Confession*, and *True Love*, or some such titled magazines to Mother, her Aunt Iva. Mother hid them. I know because I inadvertently discovered their hiding place. Once found, what a wonderful time I had slipping away and wrapping my emotions in the words and innuendo of tantalizing, forbidden subject matter, relationships, love, love making! I couldn't have a boyfriend, but I had sufficient material to imagine a personal romance.

Daddy ordered me to seriously read the "good stuff." He regularly brought in *U.S. News & World Report* (no pictures, only fact detailed columns) and *Time* and *Newsweek* magazines. For sure, once a week, he assigned an article for me to read. In the evening after supper, my father settled back with his pipe or cigar to hear my extemporaneous report on the material.

Then Mr. John Johnson began publishing *Ebony Magazine*. That was fabulous because Daddy never failed to bring us the latest issue of the entertaining monthly magazine. Similar in size and glossy presentation to *Life Magazine*, it was filled with articles and color pictures dealing with black life and popular and not so popular black personalities. You can imagine the excitement in our home when Daddy brought in the issue with an article featuring Mother's brother, Uncle Cleo and his radio/television repair shop in Ravenna, Ohio. His youngest daughter, Cousin Helen, was the newsworthy subject. Uncle Cleo had so trained Helen, that at twelve years old she was a repair technician in his shop.

Radio programs enlivened our days until bedtime, bringing the world into our home. Mother listened to Arthur Godfrey every morning. I liked him too. There was nothing pompous about Mr. Godfrey. He seemed so ordinary, genuine. Hearing Arthur Godfrey's relaxed commentary about Manhattan and casual chitchat about his chauffeured ride to work, especially down Riverside Drive, invited thoughts of other options for my own life. In fact, my mind first conjured up the possibility that as an adult, I could experience New York City—drive down Riverside Drive and see across the Hudson River to New Jersey.

Daytime serials or soap operas as they were called filled the air weekday afternoons. There was a reason they were known as soap operas. It wasn't because they were "operas" in the sense of the actors singing arias to tell a story. The shows were bankrolled predominantly by soap product manufacturing companies such as Colgate Palmolive, Procter and Gamble, and Lever Brothers. We used the products too, Oxydol, Rinso, and Lux Soap. Each day the ongoing drama took the listener through emotion grabbing experiences in the fabricated lives of men, women, and families. Story lines centered on continuing characters dealing with life's challenges and finding, holding, losing love, and romance, through deception, trickery, and tragedy. Mother wouldn't miss an episode of *Ma Perkins*, *Stella Dallas*, and *The Guiding Light*. As I listened, involved in the intrigue while at the ironing board ironing clothes, afternoon very soon approached evening, and the ironing board had to be put away before the men came home for dinner.

I liked Ralph Edwards's *Queen for a Day*, a show that did exactly as the title implied—showered attention and gifts on a woman named to be "Queen for a Day." She was selected from letters written by listeners supporting someone in their life that should receive the honor and all the gifts. A woman who struggled unselfishly for others and needed something she couldn't afford and dreamed of having would be picked. As I lay belly flat on the floor, chin resting on folded arms, listening intently, my fantasy was to write a letter suggesting Mother be selected. They would pick her and give her a much deserved brand new, top of the line, washing machine. I knew I could only daydream about the possibility since the letter would never be sent. That I couldn't do to my mother. She would be embarrassed with the invasion into her privacy and mortified with the notoriety no matter how glorious I thought it could be for our family. Listening to *Queen for a Day*, I was impressed with how special Hartmann Luggage must be since the announcer profusely exclaimed over the gift to each winner of "a set of Hartman luggage!" In fact when I began my career, wanting to have more than brown paper bags to hold my belongings when I came home for a visit, one of my first purchases was a Hartmann Luggage Garment Bag.

Daddy consistently listened to news broadcasters. Two of his favorite commentators were Gabriel Heater[13] and Lowell Thomas.[14] Daddy also enjoyed the comedy show *Amos n' Andy*,[15] not universally appreciated by blacks. The title characters were seen to be portrayed as "yassuh," subservient black folk. But Daddy made us sit and listen with him. We were to notice how the writers lifted up the characters' intelligence, had them actually outsmart their foes with strategy, by thinking, using their brains.

Baseball continued to be a family favorite. We all gathered around listening to the Cleveland Indians games, day or night. Most games Larry Doby, due to his amazing power hitting, kept me a nervous wreck. He was a fantastic long ball hitter. Unfortunately he was also a leader in the strikeout column of the stats. Always my favorite player, he gave me grief when he wasn't "superman" and great joy as he saved games with his bat and glove. He was an outstanding centerfielder, chasing down fly balls the play-by-play announcer had projected would drop out of reach to be a double or a triple. What a thrill when he stretched the entire length of his body forward and snagged a ball in his glove just before it fell to the outfield grass, or flinging himself up and against the fence he caught the ball intent on sailing into the stands for a home run. We didn't see the action, but the play-by-play broadcast coming from the face of the radio gave my mind a perfectly clear picture.

I liked listening to all kinds of music, especially popular songs, country western, classical music, and religious. We always tuned in to hear the outstanding black singers of the time. Nat King Cole was a favorite of mine. Mother liked Arthur Prysock and Tennessee Ernie Ford too. Marian Anderson and Lena Horne were vocal talents who overcame discriminatory practices to become popular performers appreciated by not only blacks but whites as well. No one matched Marian Anderson, a classical singer who traveled the world and sang in many languages. She was regarded as the world's greatest contralto. Lena Horne, a beautiful woman, mesmerized audiences with her sultry singing style. She starred in clubs, concerts, on records, in Broadway musicals, and in the movies. There was also Dorothy Dandridge and Josephine Baker. My parents debated over who was the better artist, Dorothy Dandridge or Lena Horne. However, there was no comparing Miss Josephine Baker to anyone! Born in St. Louis, she had gone to Paris in the '20s and was highly publicized as sultry and continental, singing to packed rooms in cabarets in Europe and America. The deep-throated spiritual music of Mahalia Jackson was well known in our home. Mother and Daddy talked of not being able to get good gospel music to come in stronger than the static. Country and western music, particularly the Grand Ole Opry from Nashville, Tennessee, made it through the airwaves late at night.

Grandpa, Mother's dad, had given me his Victrola and his entire set of old records from when my mother was young. All you could play was one record at a time. Also you had to manually crank the record player as tight as possible to keep the turntable going throughout the song. Still I spent hours in my bedroom playing those ancient records. "It's a Long, Long Way to Tipperary," "When You and I Were Young, Maggie," "Baby Your Mother," "You Tell Her, I Stutter," and Jo Stafford's "You Belong to Me" were records I sang along with till they were memorized. With little hesitation, I could give you a few lines of each today!

Sewing was an activity of mine that made time fly. I sewed by hand and also used Mother's electric Singer sewing machine. I made all my skirts, blouses, dresses. The summer after sophomore year of high school, Daddy enrolled me in a correspondence school pattern drafting course. The school's package was delivered each week to the post office, and Daddy brought it home to me. Right away, I completed the assignments and mailed them back to be evaluated. The evening Daddy brought home the package with instructor comments and grades was great. The comments were supportive and the grades good. I was proud of my work but wondered if they ever gave a bad grade. After I finished the course, I proudly made my patterns instead of buying *Simplicity* or *McCall's* or others sold in daily newspapers. No, doubt, I had learned the lessons well.

I enjoyed mornings in the kitchen, baking, especially cakes and pies and cookies. One summer I spent perfecting a recipe to enter the annual Pillsbury Bake-Off Contest, generating hopeful energy and interest involving everyone in the house. Daddy brought home ingredients I needed. He never lost interest or patience no matter what was going on with his business (and in the summertime, his general contracting always went well). He and Mother faithfully made thoughtful suggestions, which I welcomed. I kept detailed notes, recording ingredients, temperatures, weights, measures, utensils used, pan size, shape, every detail. My parents and brothers and sisters cooperated fully in judging (eating) the production of the day. In fact, if I did not have something for the men to test when they came home from work, they didn't hide their disappointment. Finally we all agreed on a version of a recipe I developed and perfected that we named Banana Nut Cake. I carefully filled out the entry forms, which Daddy took to the post office and personally mailed. Surely my Banana Nut Cake would be selected. Our confidence didn't dim until we read the listing of winners, including honorable mentions, in *Good Housekeeping* or whatever magazine carried contest results. Not receiving any recognition, we believed my entry was lost in the mail or more likely misplaced.

One summer Daddy introduced me to the activity of writing for publication. He wrote several articles for *Look Magazine*. I was his editor and typist. One piece dealt with changes he proposed in marketing and managing Major League Baseball so the sport remained popular, the country's national pastime. Daddy was a strong proponent of Bill Veeck[16] and Mr. Veeck's then unusual approach toward entertaining people who came to his stadium for an afternoon or night of baseball. Bill Veeck introduced "giveaways" to patrons. He once hired a little person to play on his team. Daddy was in favor of such innovative promotion. His article supported the merits of Mr. Veeck's thinking and his unusual approach to doing business. My father's writing detailed why it was important for other baseball executives and the leagues to adopt Bill Veeck's approach to revitalize the game. I had a clear vision of how my father's article printed in the magazine was going to look. *Look Magazine* sent us a rejection letter.

At Daddy's suggestion, I wrote a children's book. Jimmy, still a talented artist, drew the illustrations for our book about a baby rabbit lonely in a new neighborhood. In the bunny rabbit's quest to find new friends, he learned about other little animals, a turtle, a baby bird, a duck, their habits, favorite foods, where they lived, etc. We got a rejection slip. I was unbelievably disappointed with that rejection. Someone must have taken my idea as their own. For a year or more I thoroughly scanned articles and advertisements promoting children's books and sections in catalogs selling books for children certain I would see another author had a similar book on the market. I may have been discouraged with the rejections, but the process and anticipation of success kept the household connected, involved, not bored, or dissatisfied with our lives.

At school I freely shared with my friends the activities I enjoyed at home. My friends gossiped with me about their interactions, fun, what took place when I wasn't with them. Sharing our experiences made me feel included, just on a different page. I even shared my father's teachings with one of my very best friends, Kay, who I felt was genuinely interested in my dad's perspective on black and white interactions and understood the truth in my father's teachings just as I did. Kay and I were scholastic competitors; she won out was the class valedictorian. Kay also helped me circumvent my father's "no lipstick" rule. It was her idea to share hers with me at school in the restroom before we went to homeroom. The act warmed my heart as I went about the school day looking like a teenage girl should. As far as I knew, Daddy never found out.

I graduated from Williamsfield High School the class salutatorian, ranked second in academic achievement,[17] member of the National Honor Society, senior class president, and editor of the school newspaper, and elected by the class as the girl most likely to succeed.

The summer after high school graduation, before traveling south to yet another entirely different environment to attend college, I designed patterns, bought fabric and materials, and made my college wardrobe.

That summer of 1955, Emmett Till,[18] a fourteen-year-old visiting in Mississippi, on vacation from Chicago, Illinois, was murdered by white men. News accounts reported Emmett Till's horrible murder happened because those men decided the black child had stepped out of "his" place as a black person.

Chapter 22

Parenting Practices

My siblings and I had no doubt our father was on his parenting job 24/7 whether he was in town or out of town. He laid down his rules, and we were to follow them. "Do your chores, your homework, and mind your Mother!" were his standing orders. Mother, a "stay at home mom," had consistent parenting habits also. Her manner was far from Daddy's stern approach, but she expected obedience and when we fell short, verbally chastised us. Daddy, hearing about any transgression (as Mother always warned), might dispense additional disciplinary attention, depending on the level of our bad act.

Johnny's Geography Test

There was the time in the fourth grade when Johnny brought home an E, a shout-out of "failure" like today's F. He had flunked his geography test. Johnny knew he had to bring the paper home and didn't have the option of tossing that test in a wastebasket to pretend he never got it back. (Jim and I knew he had used that tactic before and gotten away with it.) He couldn't this time because Daddy had been asking, faithfully, "How did you do on your geography test?"

"Teacher didn't give 'em back," Johnny answered. Daddy said no more and just asked the same question the next night.

The fateful day the test was returned, as soon as we got home, Johnny handed his, with the loud red E in the upper right corner, to Mother. What a dismal afternoon as we waited for Daddy to come home from work. We knew there was big trouble for Johnny, once he heard the news, which Mother wouldn't tell in our presence. It was their usual habit for her to join him after he had washed up and gone to their bedroom to change. It had to be the time she let him know about her day, our day, from her perspective, the good and the bad experiences. To Jim and me, Johnny's test result overshadowed any good she had to report that day.

After supper, Daddy settled in his chair with the newspaper, unconcerned, it seemed, about confronting Johnny until my brazen brother pitched him the golden opportunity.

Johnny announced he was going outside to play. "I've done all my homework."

Oops! He opened the door to disaster, for sure.

Daddy quietly responded, not taking his eyes from the paper. "How could you fail a geography test?"

Jimmy and I hunched over the dining room table, sitting elbows anchoring upper bodies bent over school books and writing tablets as if we were seriously studying. I was only listening, waiting to hear how Johnny would extricate himself from what was surely going to be a pretty uncomfortable scene. Our big brother did not fail me. He was a kid, stupidly elevating himself to a "reckless" kid. He took a chance, and with a shrug of his shoulders, he gave the smoothest answer. "No one in the class passed," he answered.

Daddy turned, peered at him over the wide open newspaper, repeating Johnny's words in question form, emphasis on the first two words, "No one in the class passed?"

Without hesitation, Johnny embellished his lie, with a stronger, more certain tone, "Yep, the whole class got an E."

Our father said nothing and went back to reading. Johnny took that as permission for him to exit, and he did. After all, he didn't have any homework to do. He went outside to play, and no one stopped him. There were no fireworks—that night.

In a couple days, Johnny says he'll never forget it; there was a knock on his classroom door. Mrs. Bloomhall opened it to see Mr. Woods standing in the doorway. The class heard him apologize for interrupting, but not the rest that was said.

At home, we learned what transpired after Mrs. Bloomhall excused herself and pulled the door shut behind her as she stepped out to talk to the concerned parent.

"I was hoping to observe your geography class," he told her, adding, "I can't imagine why everyone failed the test."

Daddy confirmed what he suspected. Johnny was one of only a very few who didn't pass. The teacher took the opportunity to convey more.

"Mr. Woods, your son is very bright, a smart little boy. But he obviously did not study for the test. Johnny does not apply himself in class. Yes, he turns in his homework, but it's done carelessly. He can do so much better." That night, Johnny got a lengthy, detailed lecture and quite a spanking. Daddy did not believe in sparing the rod.

Mother was the "good cop" parent, but not a softie. She too had rules and behavior expectations, though you did not feel the doom you felt when you provoked Daddy's ire. Mother spanked, only sometimes. You knew there was a chance you could "get away with it" if you broke one of her rules and somehow convinced her you learned your lesson from the experience and her lecture.

If Mother wanted you to talk, she questioned for a while, but for sure, she gave up if you could hang tough, not give in and spill the beans. Daddy? No way. He stopped what he was doing, if he saw that was necessary, took you aside, and settled in with eye to eye conversation. He didn't inflict corporal punishment to find out what he wanted, only to impress on you that your deed was intolerable and couldn't happen again.

Teenage Boy–Little Girl Encounter

My first memorable personal example of the solid parenting partnership of my mother and father had to do with me doing my best to keep secret something troubling me and not share my dilemma with anyone. It was the summer I was five years old. An extremely personal problem was ruining my days and nights. I wanted it resolved without anyone knowing the embarrassing situation I had gotten myself into.

Aunt Cora and Uncle Herb lived in our neighborhood, a nice residential area of all single-family homes. Their home was behind ours on Matthews Street. All we did was walk through our backyard, and then cross the alleyway to be in their backyard.

I usually asked to go along when Mother visited her sister. Mother resisted, reminding me, "You'll get bored and want to go home before I'm ready. Why don't you stay here?" If I insisted on going, thinking of the good time ahead if my cousin Ellen was home and let me hang around with her, Mother let me tag along.

Ellen, Aunt Cora and Uncle Herb's only child, was a neat cousin. She was a beautiful teenager, thirteen- or fourteen years old, and so lucky to have a lot of long wavy light brown hair that she wore "out." My own long very curly hair was braided neat and tidy into two pigtails, we called them, down to my back with a colorful ribbon bow on the end of each. It was oh so b-o-o-r-r-ring. My cousin sometimes let me brush her hair, which I could never do with mine and which was also much more fun than even brushing my doll's hair. It was great when Ellen was there to play with me.

On one particular summer day, I went along with Mother, and Ellen wasn't home. She had gone off with her friend. Eventually I asked permission to go outside to play. Mother and Aunt Cora were happy I wanted to since they resorted to whispers as they gossiped and laughed about things they didn't intend for me to know.

"Stay in the yard," Mother said.

My aunt's backyard had very little play space. One side was widely bordered with her flower garden, and the other was almost all vegetable garden. Still I had fun. When I remembered to bring my jump rope, I practiced in the grassy lawn patch between the path and one of the gardens, that is, if the weekly washing was not hanging out to dry.

I also liked to skip from the backyard on around the west side of the house and across the front yard onto the narrow, heavily shaded, beaten dirt path, between the east side of Aunt Cora's house and the neighbor's tall, thick hedges. Returning on the shrubbery-shadowed path into the backyard, skipping and singing, the only light being the pale blue sky above, it was an adventure, a journey through a mysterious tunnel.

This particular summer day (when I was only five years old) I was happily hopping and skipping along the almost dark path toward the sunny backyard, singing softly to myself when there sitting on the incline that held the hedgerow was a neighborhood teenage boy I knew, asking me to "stop a minute." I had not seen him until he spoke. I was startled. He motioned me to come over close to him. I did. I knew him. Right away, he asked me to pull my pants down. I was wearing a dress.

"No," I said, as it flashed into my mind that my underwear and what was underneath was my private, personal business not to be shared with anyone, I added, " I can't do that."

"Come on," he begged, reaching out to the skirt. "I won't hurt you and no one will know."

With an adamant no I backed away, and then mumbled I had to go in and hurried away.

I was embarrassed. I did not tell anyone a thing.

It happened again, the next time I went with my mother. He asked the same thing, "Pull your pants down." I got away. Still I kept *his* bad action to myself. I did decide never again to play on the pathway around Aunt Cora's house. I would avoid him.

The next time I went to Aunt Cora's with Mother, I stayed inside, making myself scarce by playing in a corner of the kitchen or on the staircase behind the kitchen. When they realized I was not asking to go out and play, they invited me to. I said, "No, I'll stay in here." They wanted to know why. I didn't have a reason, only a soft shrug of my shoulders and a closed mouth "I don't know." Jokingly they suggested perhaps I discovered it was more fun listening to them than playing outside. That was not to be. Shooing me out the door, Mother dispensed her routine order "stay in the yard!"

He was there, hiding in the hedges.

One more time I managed to escape as I kept saying no. I was scared. I did not know what to do to make it stop. He had not tried to hurt me, but this time, he offered money, pennies and nickels.

"How is this going to end?" I worried. It so frightened me that I started dreaming about him. Still, I did not tell anyone. I simply decided not to go to

Aunt Cora's house with Mother again. When she announced she was going to visit her sister, I showed no interest in what had been my opportunity to be with her, away from my brothers and sister.

Mother was puzzled, which surprised me. I thought she would be glad I didn't beg to tag along. But her concern was, "why?" I had no reason, shrugged my shoulders, and claimed, "I just don't want to go." Mother decided my behavior was strange and told my dad, which I did not know until he questioned me.

My father was mostly patient in handling his children, but he also had a demanding, "I will control this" approach he used if he felt it was necessary. Talking to me alone at the dining room table, him sitting in his armchair at the head of the table, he did not bully, but he was empathetically persistent. He made it clear to me that he knew there was a reason I did not want to go with Mother, and he had to know what it was. I tried to resist telling, but his manner and my fear that things would get worse if I did not tell someone was the catalyst that worked.

Hearing the story, from the beginning, Daddy was quiet, somber. At the end, looking past me, at nothing, in a second or so, his eyes turned to me. "Don't worry," he said. "I will take care of everything. You will not be bothered again."

I recall hearing snippets of him speaking with Mother about watching after me and not letting any of us out of her eyesight for long periods of time. Mother, stunned, was in complete agreement. It wasn't Mother's fault. I was not out of her sight that long, and I was in my aunt's yard.

Daddy spoke to the teen's father telling him it was up to him to see that his son never again approached any of his children. "But if you can't keep your boy in check, I'll check him." The kid was a problem, used to terrorize my brothers, loved taking their baseballs from them. Daddy did insist on talking to the boy, in the presence of his parents. Daddy emphasized his continued inappropriate actions would not be tolerated, promising penitentiary was the next punishment he could expect because Daddy would see to it. We had no more problems with the neighborhood bad boy. No one did.

The Trust Factor

One day Johnny had Daddy's permission for him and Jimmy to go out to the fairgrounds to play baseball and watch a baseball game. That is what they said they were going to do, and that was fine with Daddy. However, the boys were going to the fairgrounds to watch motorcycle races, which they knew was a no-no. Daddy slipped up on them sitting on the grassy border against the inside of the fence around the track grounds engrossed in the motorcycles zooming around. They didn't know Daddy was there until from behind their backs they heard, "So this is a baseball game?" His voice, they say, scared them to death. They got lectured (we termed it "a bawling out")—a strong explanation on the pitfalls in life one would have by lying, and not being trustworthy. He warned about the life-threatening danger being where those motorcycles could leave the track and careen into them. I don't remember, but they say, "They got it good"—a spanking that is.

Boys Must Be Boys

Jimmy, maybe four or five years old at the time, was playing with one of my dolls—posing it in chairs, eating at the doll furniture table, having it walk, having it talk through his voice, simply having fun pretending the doll was a little person. Daddy, in disgust, challenged him. "So you want to be a girl, play with dolls."

Daddy had Mother sew Jimmy a doll of his own. She made it out of heavy striped mattress cover fabric. My twin remembers it was a stuffed, somewhat flat doll with beady eyes.

Daddy wasn't through. He ordered Jimmy to change into one of my dresses. "If you want to be a girl, dress like one, too," he said. There he was in my dress walking around holding his own doll. He was mortified, so upset he fled down to the basement and sat on the bottom step, crying. Finally, in a fit of defiant, though violent bravery, he sat there in the dark, slamming that doll around, beating it to shreds. He says he never again played with a doll.

How different our lives may have been if Daddy had taken a far different and still creative approach to his small son's interest in imagining life through playing with a doll. He and Mother could have initiated the booming business dolls for boy children became many years later. The Woods family would have a more prosperous reflection to conclude this recall of what is only a story of embarrassing torment remembered by my brother.

Girls Must Be Girls

Daddy had firm convictions as to how to raise a daughter to become a proper woman, a lady. A girl child must adhere to certain protocols—at least, his girls would. We could not wear trousers, except if safety was involved. His daughters need not wear trousers while playing because being proper young ladies, we would never find ourselves falling down rolling about on the ground be it grass that made a lovely thick carpeted lawn, or gravel, cinders, rocks, or dirt. And, our legs must never be elevated higher than our knees; be demurely positioned at all times when sitting in a chair, in a wagon, on a swing, wherever, so there would be no worry of our personal privacy being compromised.

"Girls shouldn't walk around whistling," Daddy told me when I was four or five or about. It was Sunday morning, and we were walking to Sunday school—

Johnny, Jimmy, Daddy, and I. Daddy started the whistling. My brothers joined in, as did I, a marching song. We had just made it down a steep hill and had picked up speed, swinging our arms in rhythm with the tune. I was feeling proud of myself having successfully followed Daddy's instructions on how to walk down a steep hill. "Bend your knees, turn your toes in." It worked. My feet didn't slide down; I didn't fear I would topple forward on my face as the steep decline forced my body forward. Walking, knees bent, toes in, I was in control of my descent. It was fun, the four of us marching along whistling "Marching to Tipperary," until I was reigned in by my dad's words.

"It is not ladylike for a girl to whistle in public." He didn't say why. I remember mulling it over in my mind, over and over. It was just "whistling." Was it unladylike because it made my face look ugly? I didn't know. I asked Mother. She said it was unladylike because it drew the public's attention to me. "A lady wouldn't draw attention to herself by showing off, preening, sauntering around a crowded room all by herself for no reason and certainly would not whistle in public." To me, it was only more evidence that boys got to do the most fun things.

Think Before Reacting

Jim asked if I remember when I tried to murder him. "You don't remember throwing a butcher knife at me?" he said disbelief in a high-pitched voice. Well, as soon as the words "butcher knife" reached my hearing, I remembered. It was an incident I chose to forget. It was so scary—my stupid and dangerous reaction to a terrorizing brother.

We were thirteen, going on fourteen. The day was over, or at least it was evening after supper. Mother and Daddy sat in the living room, Daddy reading; Mother listening to the radio and sewing, mending something from her mending box. With seven children, Mother always had some piece of clothing that needed the skillful attention of her needle and thread.

I was in the kitchen washing dishes. It was my turn. All the other kids were playing, doing whatever they wanted. Jimmy wanted to antagonize me. He noiselessly darted in and out from Cynthia and Sharon's room just off the kitchen. He kept pestering and teasing me because he knew how angry I was. Kathleen and I were the only ones in the rotation to clean up after meals. He knew how I resented him and Johnny never having to wash dishes or do housework because Daddy said those tasks were "women's work." If Daddy did not have a truck to unload or load with tools and materials, Jimmy and Johnny usually had nothing to do in the house except take care of the furnace, putting in coal or wood to keep the fire going. I resented doing dishes that evening.

Jimmy kept teasing and wouldn't leave me alone. It was his inane chanting, "yeh, yeh, yeh," doing a silly little jig and saying, "Is that clean? That fork's not clean?" He was menacing quietly keeping Daddy from hearing him. I didn't want my brother to get in trouble, so I tried to make him stop by threatening, in a slow and low voice, "You better get out and stay out. I'm gonna tell Daddy." It wasn't working.

When I picked the butcher knife from the dishwater to wash it, an idea to do some terrorizing myself came to mind. I motioned, threatened throwing the knife at him. He wasn't afraid. Laughing, he darted about and dared me, a couple of times. Squinting, giving my final warning, I threw it.

I remember how mortally miserable I felt when the wide-bladed, black-handled knife left my hand, floating, it seemed, across the kitchen toward my brother. If only I could grab it back. I was immediately sorry I had thrown it.

Jimmy sidestepped the oncoming tragedy. The big knife plunged upright in the linoleum covered floor where he had been standing. I shuddered then. I shudder now at what could have happened. I was scared. I was so ashamed of what I had done; my stomach hurt. I started crying.

My shocked brother ran to tell Daddy. I knew I was going to "get it," and I deserved the beating it would be. Thank God the knife didn't hit him. I could handle Daddy's punishment.

Daddy's reaction was totally unanticipated. I heard him calmly tell his son he had no business being in the kitchen anyway. Then putting the paper aside, he rose from his chair, walked past Jimmy looking at him, and dismissed him, saying, "You know the kitchen is for women, off limits for you boys. The only time you should be in the kitchen is when you are walking through or if you're called to eat."

Slowly walking into the kitchen, Daddy reached down, pulled the knife out of the linoleum, and brought it to me. Surely I appeared as traumatized and remorseful as I felt—washing dishes though my tears, sobbing, and shoulder shaking so I couldn't stop. But my father had not come to comfort me.

"Violence is never the solution to a problem," he said. "The most significant difference between human beings and other animals is our ability to make decisions." Staring into my eyes, his never wavering, mine neither; Daddy said he hoped I would never again lose control and do something as dangerous as I had just because I was angry. "Don't let your emotions decide the action you take. Think! Think about what will happen once you have acted."

Surprisingly, for this most horrible bad act, I was not a recipient of Daddy's corporal punishment. For sure, though, the pain I felt then and for a long time was worse than any spanking I ever got.

On Being a Good Loser

There was the summer Sunday when I was very young. The family went to Union Baptist's church picnic in Zanesville's Putnam Hill Park. It promised to be so much fun. Our picnic basket was filled with good food, sandwiches, deviled eggs, cupcakes, fried chicken, baked beans, snacks, fruit, and vegetables to munch. The church provided so much ice cream stored in "hot ice" it never ran out, and there would be plenty of pop to drink also, plus the yummy food in other people's picnic baskets. Everyone shared.

And we would play games. Prizes would be awarded to winners. I set my mind on winning a first prize. I almost won the potato sack race—came in second. It looked like a tie, but I got second place. I cried and couldn't stop. Daddy took me aside, walked us across the evenly cut, thick green grass to the edge of the park grounds. All the while he was talking to me about being a good loser. I kept blubbering, saying there was no reason to call Jeanne Guy the winner. Daddy warned I seemed to have a little envy and jealousy in me, two personal characteristics not at all good. "You're a poor loser and envious of others." He cautioned I must work to overcome those traits or I would be an unhappy person—one people wouldn't want around.

Many times throughout my life I have pulled his words up to help me in a personally trying moment be a gracious person.

Decades later, when Oprah Winfrey went national, I was secretly resentful because it wasn't me. Ms. Winfrey was a caring, personable, articulate, energetic, intelligent black woman—like me. She was a media success like I thought I could have been, if only. For years I thought, "If only I wasn't overweight and black." Then on scene came Ms. Winfrey. Body image and skin color did not stop her. I was *jealous* and also an adult, educated woman with children of my own. I found myself recalling my father's advice at the church picnic. I overcame my jealousy of Oprah Winfrey.

Truth and Honesty

Kathleen was a favorite of Aunt Cora, who easily found reason to give my little sister a toy or a special barrette for her hair, even new clothing. She may not give the rest of us something at the same time, but it didn't bother us. Maybe because Kathleen shared Aunt Cora's middle name, Marie, we understood and accepted her receiving our aunt's special generosity.

Our first Easter away from Zanesville, Aunt Cora sent Kathleen a beautiful dress—pale oranges, pinks, yellows—pleated A-line from a square framed neckline. My sister was absolutely beautiful, herself, in her new Easter dress. Kathleen hated it. I couldn't believe she hated it. Mother gushed over her. Daddy had her pirouette and pose, admiring her. I was envious of how wonderful she looked. Kathleen cried between poses. There was something about the dress she despised.

"What's wrong? What is wrong?" Mother asked, puzzled and consoling.

Kathleen wouldn't say, just sobbed.

Mother, after pulling her close and holding her, gave Kathleen permission to take off the new dress. "Go hang it in your closet. When you have a special occasion, I'm sure you will be happy to have this dress. It is very pretty," she said as she undid the buttons Kathleen couldn't reach. "Take it upstairs."

Since moving to the country, we had not been to church, and there were no other special occasions—until several weeks later. Kathleen was in a concert at school. Mother casually talked about Kathleen having the new dress from Aunt Cora to wear. When Mother had Kathleen bring it to her, Kathleen returned and reported she could not find it.

"I told you to hang it in your closet. Where did you put it? It isn't in your closet?" she worried.

Mother directed an accusing question at me, wanting an answer. "What did you do?"

"Marva, where is her dress?"

I've surmised Mother recalled the green glint of jealousy she had noticed in my eyes because the "beautiful dress" was not mine. Honestly though, I knew absolutely nothing about the missing dress.

Daddy held an inquisition like none other. He berated my sister with stern questioning, verging on hints of a spanking, then moved on to reasoning tones, and then resignation—with laughter or hints of humor, "Okay, your mother and your sister have looked everywhere," chuckle, chuckle, "tell them where you hid the dress."

Kathleen shook her head slowly—opened her beautiful dark eyes as wide as possible, looked at Daddy, and said, "I don't know where it is." That's all she said.

Many days passed and the dress was apparently forgotten. It wasn't a topic of conversation.

I was puzzled. What a mystery! I believed my sister. She had no idea what happened to her dress. There might be a ghost in our old farmhouse!

The dress dilemma faded away until nature brought it back into our lives. Living in the Snow Belt, under the Great Lakes, we had heavy snowfall long after Easter, which was in late March. Sometime after the last big snowfall had melted to only dirty mounds on the ground in darkly shaded spots, Jimmy and Johnny made an amazing discovery.

Consistent warm weather had melted even the pile of dirty snow banked in the southeast corner of the house, under the pantry window. The beautiful spring colors of the missing dress were exposed, stuck in a frozen mass of sooty snow for my brothers to find when they were outside playing.

The family was astounded. Kathleen only looked scared. She knew she had it coming, a beating that is. She never got it. She did get Daddy's constant and varied lectures about lying, about the unacceptable trait of being deceitful, and about the importance of being trustworthy.

Opportunity to Learn Is Everywhere

Larry tells how he liked riding to work with Daddy when he was three, four years old. "That's when I learned how to drive," Larry shared with me over the telephone one recent day.

"He taught you how to drive when you were that young?" I practically yelled.

"No-o-o-o—I liked standing in the front seat of the truck beside him. Daddy would tell me to sit down."

"Then I won't be able to see," Larry said he whined.

"Sit down and look at what you *can* see," Daddy ordered.

Larry did. What he saw was Daddy's foot on the brake, the gas, the clutch, and his hands on the steering wheel. He watched the moves Daddy made driving—starting, stopping, turning curves, backing up, parking, and experiencing the feel of the car with each action. It was later in his life Larry learned he had indeed learned how to drive, looking at what he could see.

Many years after Daddy died, Larry completed his high school driver's education course and needed a car to take the driving part of his test to get his license. A friend's adult brother willingly lent his. Larry, an hour or so before the test, was shocked to find the car was a stick shift. He had learned on an automatic; had never driven a stick shift. The car's owner patiently let him try to drive the car. Larry was able to resurrect what he had learned those many times abiding by Daddy's suggestion that he pay attention to what he could see. Larry drove the stick shift automobile for his driver's test, passed, and got his driver's license.

On Preparing for a Future

"Focus on your homework." When my brothers, sisters, and I listened to the radio and did our homework at the same time, Daddy made us turn the radio off.

"Prepare for your future. They've got theirs—get yours! After putting in time and effort, getting prepared, they are using their skill and ability making a living entertaining. What can you do to make a living for yourself and your family? This is your time to prepare for a career doing what you'll enjoy, just as they enjoy their work."

Never before had I thought about *enjoying* work. I began mentally questioning myself. What did I enjoy doing that could be the way for me to make a living? My father's insightful response to our study habits guided my thinking toward becoming a professional singer. I enjoyed singing. Yes, singing would be a fun way to make a living. But I was *fat*! Not to worry, so was Kate Smith, and she was a popular singer. "Yes, I just might become a singer"—my first career possibility of serious consideration. Thereafter, my interests and learnings in each grade, broadened through classroom studies and extracurricular activities, were pivotal as I considered all options for my future. I valued and enjoyed participating in class plays (always a "prompter," there were no parts for a black girl). I played on, even captained intramural sports teams, sang in the school chorus, and worked on the school newspaper and served as editor. Notably, learning how to type in high school gave me earning power I gratefully made good use of years before I chose a career path.

Chapter 23

College Years—Mostly About Money

If it wasn't for my father's passion for AM&N, I would have campaigned to be sent to Howard University or Spellman or Tennessee State or even stay in Ohio and go to Wilberforce. Those black schools were frequently mentioned in newspapers and magazines. It would be easier to talk to my friends about any one of them. What I knew of Arkansas State AM&N in Pine Bluff, Arkansas, I learned from my father. He constantly told me about the historically black college's growth since he was on the campus many years before. AM&N was a school where he said teachers cared about students. His northern born and raised children would travel south to AM&N, the successor of Branch Normal College, where he had gone. I wasn't emotionally bonded to any college. I simply wanted to be a freshman on someone's campus when it was my time (preferably a black school).

Because money stayed on top of our family's critical needs list, in my mind, going away to college wasn't a sure thing especially since my parents had another baby. Roy was born just weeks following Johnny's high school graduation. My doubts changed that August when Daddy drove Johnny to Warren, Ohio, for the train beginning his long trip to Arkansas. Johnny didn't even like school, and I excelled. Surely my Dad would see that I had the opportunity when it was my turn, and so it happened.

The next year when Johnny returned to AM&N for his sophomore year, Jimmy and I joined him as freshmen.

I was a satisfied seventeen-year-old sharing a room in the freshman girl's dormitory. Having a roommate was comforting since I had shared a bedroom with a little sister since I was four years old.

At home Kathleen must have savored the newness of her world. She had sole proprietor rights to our room in the small farmhouse. Now "the big sister" in the house, she replaced me as Mother's number one helper. She and baby Roy (full name, Roy Roger, after the Brooklyn Dodgers' star catcher, Roy Campanella, and Uncle Roger, one of Daddy's younger brothers) would forge an endearing bond that lasted a lifetime. When we left for college, Kathleen was fourteen years old and in high school—no older brothers and sister influencing her actions, if we ever did. There were only younger siblings far behind her in grade school and toddler Roy at home. Perhaps any middle kid syndrome was gone. Yes, it was easy imagining how she must have treasured the change in her life.

At night my thoughts flew home to them as I hugged my pillow lying in the strange bunk-like bed gazing at the three-tiered red brick bell tower majestic in the middle of the quadrangle. My dormitory was one of two architecturally similar dorms facing each other across the quad. Jimmy had a room in the freshman boys' dorm directly across from mine. Johnny's room was in the sophomore boys' dormitory next door to Jim's building. The sophomore girls' dorm was across the quad from Johnny's dorm and next door to where I lived. Those four dormitories surrounding the quadrangle were filled with young people—all of them black like us, living away from home and family, blessed to be in college. I felt undeserving, being thrilled to be there. Looking at the moon high over the campus, I pictured Mother and Daddy and Kathleen, Cynthia, Sharon, Larry, and Roy in Ohio seeing that moon the same as me. I missed them so much. My sadness lingered as I considered the sacrifices of my family that caused the happiness I felt. The gloom passed because I knew I was exactly where my parents wanted me to be and I had to do well. I vowed not to let them down. For sure, Daddy must have been proud of the accomplishment—his three oldest children in college as he planned. Many nights those first days on campus, I went to bed knowing it was astounding that I was actually *there*. I succumbed to melancholy until I fell asleep.

Daddy's contracting business was good, contributing to a predicament not experienced in several years. He had to hire helpers, increasing his labor costs. His "best men" were in college. Larry, barely seven years old, went on the job some weekends and earned Daddy's praise as a quick learner and a big help. Larry was pleased. All my brothers seemed to enjoy working with our father.

My going away instructions were to study and do well, not worry about anything. Actually throughout the better part of my first year, I didn't know about our financial situation with the business office. Daddy had made an agreement that expenses due when the semester began, but not covered in full, would be paid by year end. I didn't know the extent of Daddy's challenge to pay the bills in order for the three of us to stay on campus and take classes.

Money from home for incidental expenses was extremely rare, but not a problem to me. I believed I had everything I needed and should not want for anything. After all, I was assured of a place to live and meals once the business office cleared me to register for classes and authorized me to move into my assigned room. I was doing just fine.

A quote by Henry David Thoreau strengthened my contentment for what I had and dispelled any dissatisfaction over what was missing. "A man is rich in direct proportion to the number of things he can afford to let alone."

There were many things I knew I could afford to let alone, therefore I was rich. I didn't need any more clothes, accessories, or shoes than I brought with me. I didn't need to buy magazines or go to movies or other entertainment. I would have to replace school supplies, pens, pencils, and paper when they ran out and to have toiletries and buy soap powder to keep up with my laundry.

My meal ticket gave me three meals each day except for Saturday and Sunday when on Saturday there was only breakfast and lunch and on Sunday only breakfast. Through the week, I saved the apple or orange and crackers picked up at other meals to snack on tiding me over when the dining hall was not open. A few times I was a little concerned about eating on weekends.

Neither Daddy nor Mother suggested I get a part-time job. After a couple weeks into the routine of attending classes, all of them, on time and with assignments done, I realized sixteen credit hours of course work did not make for a tight, strenuous schedule. I had more than enough free time for study, socializing, extracurricular activities, and taking care of myself. *I had time to work, to get a job.* I need not fret over lack of spending change. I decided to find a job.

Without saying so to anyone, I looked for part-time work on or off campus. I was lucky. A posting on the bulletin board in the administration building by a lawyer in town described a job I knew I could do.

Attorney Flowers advertised for a student to work as a secretary two to three afternoons a week, to type and file, "able to work without supervision." I took a bus into town for the interview, conscious I must sit at the back of the bus. All at once, that was a crucial fact of my new life.

It was September 1955, and in Pine Bluff, I was a Negro living in one of the forty-eight states in America where laws said, because I was a Negro, I had to be alert for situations where it was against the law for me to mingle with white people as they mingled with each other. In Arkansas, I was a legally segregated person. Aware being a Negro was a serious negative to eyes peering from white faces was intimidating. I had been in Arkansas for several weeks but hadn't been scared about the segregation rules. We were told on campus there was nothing to fear. Now I was off campus, in the public, and had better sit in the back of the bus or risk harm.

Surprisingly, entering the bus, heading to the rear wasn't a problem to me; it was an embarrassment when I realized the back corner seat was where I *wanted* to be. I could see more. The back of the bus was my preference because of the pure novelty of riding through a new environment on a city bus. My experience on busses was primarily limited to the school bus ride everyday on rural roads through the countryside to a school on a country highway, more fields and farmland than anything. Now, here I was a curious teenager who wanted to see the neighborhoods, the sights in this new world of mine in Pine

Bluff, Arkansas. Even if any seat, in the front, the middle, wherever had been available to me, my personal choice would have been to hurry to grab one in the back. I could stare at approaching sights and continue examining whatever caught my attention as the bus steadily rolled past and even turn around and keep looking if I wanted to. I could visually analyze the strange Southern folk. I could watch the white ones standing and walking about their business on the streets outside the bus windows. I could surreptitiously peer at those who got on the bus, who moved in a "superior than thou" manner in the midst of "coloreds," people such as me with perhaps "tint of skin" being our only, for sure, difference. Many of those Caucasians had hair curlier than my mother's and lips as shapely as mine, noses not so different—but they were white folk, accustomed by law to act as if I was less a human being than they were.

My curiosity was not for the whites alone. I studied the black people, too, trying to imagine their real feelings—those already seated and those boarding. All were subjected to my veiled scrutiny. They were dignified, proud, in conversation with a traveling companion, or alone, relaxed, and composed. It was business as usual for each of them.

The scene, the reality of it, was clearly denigrating toward me and my black brothers and sisters. Due to my experiences in the fully integrated environment I came from—had succeeded in—and so recently knew, I wanted to think some of those white people were troubled with such despicable laws that separated one group of folk from another so precisely. I struggled to appear as if it was all normal to me also.

Once on the bus, with serious countenance, ashamed over my inward pleasure at doing so, I walked to the seat I preferred, in the back corner.

Safely arriving at the law office, I confidently waited for the interview. All those years, listening to my father, I had prepared myself to earn money doing office work while studying for a career. I had taken every office practices course offered—shorthand, typing, and bookkeeping. I had been typing since the ninth grade, and working on the school paper was a favorite extracurricular activity. I could file and use an adding machine and mimeograph machine. I had never been a secretary but didn't let the fact daunt me. The interview went well. Attorney Flowers hired me to start immediately.

The attorney, a highly regarded black lawyer in the state, primarily needed my typing assistance. Each afternoon I could expect instructions for a basket of work set aside for me. Of course, the first several days, the woman in the office for the full day stayed with me. Then I was all by myself to do what I had to do. Thus, it was important I could "work well without supervision." Being alone turned out a blessing. No one was there to watch me overcome my nervousness, make mistakes, recover from making mistakes, and learn how to do a good job and manage the assignments in the few hours allotted. At the beginning, it was difficult producing error-free letters, lengthy documents, and memos.

I knew I wasn't expected to be 100 percent perfect; still, I didn't want them to find a wastebasket filled with my incompetence. Word processing didn't exist. The convenient copy machine routinely enjoyed today didn't exist. Carbon paper between sheets of paper provided the lawyer's required several copies of everything. Typing errors had to be erased. I soon realized making a typo took too many anxious minutes correcting to produce smudge-free work. If I made the mistake early in the document, my best next step was to start all over. Some work I corrected, throwing the errors in the wastebasket; some I tore, crumpled, and stuffed in my pockets to trash in the dorm. The yet-to-come after-hours cleaning crew would have been nice.

Another pressure was finishing my work in time to get back on campus before the dining hall closed. I was obsessed with not using the money I earned to buy food when there was a nutritious, well-rounded paid-for meal on campus. Those first weeks my bus ride, then hurried walk through campus to the Student Union dining hall, each pocket crammed with crumpled paper, must have been a mysterious concert of crispy, crackling sound for those nearby on the journey. If the dinner line closed before I got there, it was early to breakfast the next morning. Hunger lingers after studying late at night on an empty stomach. I knew.

Working in the law office was a privilege with excellent exposure to something new, but it was lonesome leaving the friendly campus to work alone most of the time. I shook off my dissatisfaction until I learned the executive director of the Alumni Association was looking for a part-time secretary. I was interested. The Alumni Office was on the second floor of the Student Union Building in the middle of the campus. The announcement said you could set your own hours. I applied for the position. Vanessa B. McHenry, the executive director, selected me, and I gave notice to Atty. Flowers and began a three-year stint in the Alumni Office.

I also typed term papers for students, charging fifteen to twenty cents per page. Once I missed seeing and hearing Dr. Martin Luther King, Jr., in Caldwell Hall because I chose to finish typing a student's term paper. All my life, I've regretted that decision.

Christmas vacation break, my senior year I worked in a hotel in Little Rock owned by one of the professors in the Business Department. He offered fulltime jobs in his hotel's housekeeping department to a number of out-of-state students. We had a section of the hotel to live in at no cost, and we could put in an eight-hour day as many days as we wanted, but at least five days a week. It was a good hourly rate of pay. We had to have permission from our parents, which I got.

A good thing occurred for me on our first day. The hotel staffing office was in a tizzy because the pastry cook hadn't reported for work. Pies were popular on the dining room menu. Hearing their critical need as I stood listening waiting with my college mates for our housekeeping assignments, I volunteered I could bake pies.

"What? What kind?"

"All kinds—apple, blackberry, peach, cherry, lemon, pumpkin, sweet potato, chocolate, all kinds," I repeated.

The others were given room-cleaning and bed-making duties. Not me. I was taken to the kitchen and told to make an apple pie and a sweet potato pie.

They never assigned me to housekeeping duties. I was the hotel's pie chef throughout the entire period. It was amazingly unbelievable to earn money (higher than housekeeping paid) doing what was recreation for me growing up. In those two weeks or so, my take home pay was sufficient to cover graduation fees, buy a beautiful white eyelet and lace dress, and shoes for graduation.

Using the training and skills I had gained at home and in high school, I didn't worry about having spending money.

The same was not true about money for tuition, other fees, and room and board charges remaining due at year end. The Woods students from Ohio always owed the business office. We couldn't take exams until after Daddy paid our bills over the summer. When we returned to campus in the fall, we took the previous semester's final exams.

The end of senior year was different, much better because the previous spring, Junior Year, I entered the campus-wide election for Student Government Association Officers. The four students elected president, vice president, treasurer, and secretary were awarded a year's scholarship, tuition, fees, and room and board paid in full. I mounted a vigorous election campaign for treasurer running against an extremely popular and gregarious, totally competent, guy. I distributed flyers and position papers and spoke to small groups and larger groups. My favorite effort was the sizable campaign poster I designed and displayed on an easel in the Student Government Building. The colorful poster had a headshot photo of me smiling yet businesslike, with an oval 5 x 7 mirror securely centered at eye level on the poster. The message—"Look in the mirror and who do you see? Someone voting for Marva Lee. Vote for Marva Lee Woods for Treasurer of Student Government." Those filing past in the dinner line couldn't avoid the strategically placed interactive advertisement. They looked and they laughed. Enough of them also voted for me, because I won. Thanks to the full scholarship for senior year, I had no outstanding bills in the business office as the year and my undergraduate college days ended.

Daddy received nary another bill for my college education after he sent the business office money due the school following my junior year of classes.

Chapter 24

College Years—Romance and Recreation

If AM&N had been a person greeting me with a welcoming handshake, she would have deemed me a proud confident young woman beginning freshman year on campus. My grip would have been firm, my approach certain, not in any sense reluctant—and why not? High school had been a well-met challenge with notable achievement and happy times. Good memories of school days and home life floated around in my head. Yet I was far from being self-assured. There were a number of developmental experiences missing from my life that had to be routine for my classmates. I was socially insecure, scared about fitting in, and taking part in new activities with new friends. I worked hard to hide my fears and confidently participate just as my father promised would be my opportunity once I was in college.

It wasn't an easy segue becoming the-me-I-wanted-to-be. I envisioned myself a relaxed person receptive to invitations to join others for a good time. But the last party I attended, not held in school, I was nine years old. And I had never invited friends to my home for a party or simply to hang out, never been to a sleepover, and not once attended a school dance. Here I was a college freshman who never had a boyfriend or even a hint of a boyfriend, you know, like exchanging mutual glances of interest or hanging around with one who wanted to be near me. All of the above I took as legitimate reason for my difficulty in overcoming inner shyness.

Still, I was confident my hidden insecurities would be mastered because there was nothing lacking in my self-esteem. And as an avid reader, I wasn't oblivious to the details involved in the socially related aspects absent from my life experiences. My mind could sketch the moment-to-moment scenes—with sound—of parties, dances, and such and fully imagine how to successfully conduct myself. An important prerequisite was to make friends and nurture good friendships. That was no problem. Knowing how to listen, laugh (with folk, not at them), and be considerate was all good. (Being a good scholar helped as long as you had the right attitude.) Now, away from parent-imposed boundaries, I knew it was up to me to become the socially adept adult I chose to be.

One issue I excessively thought about, I did not to mention to anyone. I never had a boyfriend, and it didn't bother me. I mean, I didn't agonize over wanting a boy or wanting to be hugged and kissed. When *South Pacific* was a hit on Broadway and the song "Some Enchanted Evening" became popular, I learned every word and imagined a handsome guy seeing me "across a crowded room" and the rest becoming romantic history. But all through high school, I had never been kissed, never fantasized about being kissed, or yearned to be kissed. That kind of scared me. Was there anything wrong or different or special about me to keep me from one day loving a guy and having a family? Perhaps my destiny was to be a nun, or maybe I was "frigid."

Gathering stuff and packing to go away to school, I made up my mind to work toward getting kissed as soon as I got to college. I had to find out if I was "frigid," cold with no interest in sex. That was the big topic in the *True Confession* magazines I used to sneak out of Mother's bedroom to read. From what I read, I might be a first class candidate, because I didn't ache to be adored by a guy. Then again, maybe God picked me to be a nun. I dared to hope not and supposed since I was not Catholic, it may not even be possible for me to be a nun. Being "frigid" was possible, I decided (from reading those "love magazines") and could be a problem, since I wanted to get married one day and have a Dick and Jane[19] family. I had to know if I liked being held and kissed.

I may have been anxious for a boyfriend, but I knew I wouldn't do anything risqué. After all, my father had made it clear I was the oldest girl and had a responsibility to the younger ones to be a "good girl." From the time I was twelve Daddy warned me if I got pregnant, I need not come home to be a bad example for my little sisters.

Still, churning in my mind was how to somehow get myself a boyfriend and a kiss once I got to AM&N. But I was afraid. What if I couldn't handle the emotions of a kiss? The fear quelled any eagerness to make it happen. I couldn't open my physical senses to emotional turmoil resulting in me losing control and getting pregnant. So I kept myself consumed with all there was to do managing myself away from home for the first time ever. I had no problem keeping opportunities for kissing far away from me.

If a guy I had no romantic interest in made his intentions clear, i.e., openly pursued me obviously seeking a boyfriend/girlfriend relationship, I kindly but consistently discouraged him, and he moved on. If a young man was simply nice, easy going, just friendly, it was great. He was a friend, not a boyfriend, not someone to kiss. I relaxed and enjoyed our friendship. Then I discovered I didn't know if a boy I liked was interested in me as his girlfriend.

Throughout all these years, I've never forgotten one special guy I let get away early in my first semester at AM&N. I actually was interested in Rudolph, who was in several of my classes. I liked his quiet, serious personality and clean-cut appearance. I liked him. It was so easy talking with him. At times, when we left class, he hurried to catch up with me on the sidewalk, and side by side we made our way together. We had good conversation, about our assignments or instructors, nothing personal, I thought. He was tall and thin, with pecan brown skin and a soft crooked smile and thoughtful dark brown eyes. Then one day he suggested we go to the library that night and study together. I thought it was a great idea and brightly answered "okay." He added he would come by the dorm for me. Hearing that, I did wonder if it was a date, but shrugged off the thought. We were only studying together. He was so cute. I was nervous but happy because I liked him. We did the library thing a second time. That evening a friend who lived on my end of the hall walked down to the lounge with me and sauntered along, the three of us headed from the dormitory. She and Rudy laughed and joked together. I was quiet, only smiling. It was the last time Rudy and I went to the library together. She and Rudy became a couple. My underdeveloped social skills and study-focused attitude couldn't produce conversation and inviting tactics quickly enough to move him from the "on deck circle" into the batter's box of my life.

The two of them and I were good friends all four years at AM&N. After graduation they married. Much later, he became principal of Little Rock's Central High School, the site of Arkansas Governor Orval Fabus's unsuccessful effort in 1957 to keep out the Little Rock Nine.

My first semester on the campus came to an end, and I had not been kissed and didn't have a friend I could call a potential smooching partner.

I enjoyed new friends. I stayed on top of my studies, was involved in several activities, including the Drama Club, Dormitory Organization, and Sunday school. All of that along with my part-time work gave me ample opportunity to socialize in the limited way I was accustomed to—doing tasks I had committed to and finding a reason to say no to impromptu get-togethers like sitting around in the Lion's Den gabbing over hamburgers, hot dogs, soft drinks.

I have good memories of hanging out in the dorm after hours with fabulous dorm mates. The guys visiting in the first-floor lounge had to leave at ten, so we usually gravitated to one of the usual gathering rooms upstairs to gossip about the day. A group of "Little Rock" girls hung out in a room on the first floor. Once one of them got a "goodie box" in the mail, not from home, I assure you, because nestled in the well-wrapped and tied box was a fully cooked hot dog in a bun slathered with mustard and relish and who knows what other condiments. I assure you it hadn't been sent express mail. Considering how gross it was, the sight, the smell, so yucky—one might have thought it came by pony express! For sure, the surprise receipt of that stinky package generated the hilarious attention of everyone in the dorm that night.

If I wasn't studying somewhere or down the hall doing my laundry or visiting in a friend's room on our hall, most likely you'd find me hanging out with the gang in Gaitha and Arletha's room. I would be one of five, six, or more friends sitting around on the desks, the beds, the floor talking, laughing, and teasing. I got teased a lot because of my accent, my Ohio accent—and about having only white classmate pictures in my wallet. They found it incredible that I had gone to what they termed "a white school."

"It was not! It was the school for my town. Everyone went to the same school." I tried to explain.

Weekends we might have a card game going, usually bid whist, maybe gin rummy. Or Arletha might be doing someone's hair—perhaps mine!

I was relaxed and happy with college life, except I had not been kissed, which no one knew except Magalene. Magalene, a great friend, was not a regular participant in the talking, card playing, gossiping sessions. (No surprise she had her PhD not many years after we graduated.) She was a trustworthy very best friend to keep my secret.

Second semester, well into the winter months and I still had not been kissed. Could it be that deep down in my heart I didn't want kissed? I truly hoped that wasn't the case because one day having a husband and children was definitely part of my life plan.

The very top of my "to do list," before going home to Ohio for the summer, was to know what it was like for my lips to be involved with the lips of a neat guy. Would I like it? Would he? That was a disturbing question that led me to realize kissing a campus guy introduced a problem. What if I was a stupid, silly kisser? He might tell. I didn't want to risk it. I needed to kiss a stranger, someone I didn't know but trusted. Magalene and I worked out a plan. When the next visiting basketball team came on campus, I was to choose one of their players and get the job done.

The travel bus from a college in our conference usually pulled up to the front of the Student Union Building the afternoon before the next night's scheduled game. The guys, in for the two days or so, flirted with the campus girls. And the girls flirted with them. Certainly, after dinner hour new couples strolled the walks, visited in the Student Union, or talked on the front steps of a girls' dorm. When the next team came to AM&N, I would be one of the girls walking around the campus with a guy just off the bus.

I was to choose a player that first afternoon and only his last night on campus, let him kiss me. Mag was encouraging; "sure you can get one interested in you." I believed her because guys had flirted with me before, light stuff, a nod of the head, a lifting of an eyebrow and grin. I pleasantly shrugged off the attention. "Not interested," my actions clearly said. This time, I was going to be interested in a boy I selected, not one who targeted me.

As they hopped off the bus, Mag and I looked over the candidates. They were basketball players—tall, which we had not considered. I didn't want someone extremely tall. I saw the one I liked, pointed him out to Mag, and we kept our eyes on him. He was neat, seemed sensible, not rowdy, had a friend or two, didn't talk all the time, and wasn't that tall. We agreed he was it.

Mag and I got in line for dinner just as the team came along so I could make the initial conquest. Mag was quietly aggressive with the teammate nearest "my guy," which placed my guy and me in a position to strike up a conversation. It wasn't difficult. I had his attention simply opening with, "Hi, bet you guys are hungry."

Small talk came easy. He was from Texas. I was from Ohio. He shared their schedule, their agenda, how they had to be in team meetings, practice, etc. He walked me back to my dorm, talked about us meeting later that night. I couldn't. He asked if I would be in the Student Union for breakfast. I would. We talked about the time. "I'll see you then," his voice almost questioned as he dropped my hand. He turned to leave after watching me go up the steps and into the door.

We met at breakfast, but of course there was no time for us to be alone, just conversation and another great stroll back to my dorm. He'd be occupied all day. The basketball game was that night. The plan was working.

After the game, the team's last night on campus, we went walking. When we returned to my dorm, I had been kissed. From what I could tell, he had no idea his was my first kiss.

Still, after taking the longest way back to the dormitory, I was glad there was no time to talk. As we approached the dorm, the bright light in the center of the porch ceiling was given a quick "on and off" as happened when it was time for the fellows to leave. I actually had to rush inside interrupting his arranging for us to meet for breakfast the next morning to say good-bye. It was his plan, not mine. I was too shy and insecure about our kisses and hugs in the dark corners of the bell tower that night to show my face in the morning.

That visiting team bus left our campus after breakfast taking away a nice guy who has a special place in my memory. His name slipped away years ago, but the short time we spent together and my first kiss, I've remembered as wonderful. I never again worried whether it was my destiny to become a nun or if I was "frigid."

Romance never became important in my college years. I was a busy person and was not ready to be in love, and I didn't need the worry about getting pregnant. After all, I had little sisters for whom I must set a good example. It wasn't difficult for me to continue consciously discouraging serious attention from the first class guys I went to school with. Not ready to start a family, I kept the stress of a love relationship out of my life.

* * * * * * * * * *

Early in my college experience I knew Alpha Kappa Alpha Sorority was the sorority I wanted to join and hoped those women would pledge me. I was very happy when I learned they were interested in me as well.

Cora, the Dean of Pledges for Alpha Kappa Alpha, as required at the time, wrote my parents for their written permission before involving me in the process to become an AKA sister. She told me the response from my father was like none they had ever received. His lengthy letter articulated why he would not approve his daughter wasting precious college time in a *sorority*. He discussed the challenges black people faced in our country and how we must use our time and abilities to be prepared. "She is on that campus to study, learn all she can, not join sororities!" I seriously begged him to let me become a member of the Alpha Kappa Alpha Sorority. "You will not have to pay anything. I'll take care of everything. The AKAs do worthwhile work. As an AKA, I can help others." I told him I could join after I graduated, but I wanted to be part of their activities, be a "sister" on campus. It was to no avail; he wouldn't budge.

* * * * * * * * * *

I joined a newly organized Campus Gospel Choir. Our traveling group of students and adult sponsor took a program of classic gospel songs on the road to college campuses throughout the state. Unfortunately, the choir disbanded due to lack of funds. But not before the evening I sang a solo and had the distinct honor of being asked for my autograph. I was amazed at the request and never forgot how I hoped I hid my shock as I acknowledged the fan and took the pen and paper she offered. As she shyly, yet sincerely waited for me to finish writing my signature, I puzzled. "What did she see in my performance, hear in my voice? Should I take voice lessons? Could it be I might have a future in show business?" I rhetorically wondered. It was a fun moment.

Acting, playing a character on stage, before an audience, that was my thing. As soon as I could, I joined the campus drama organization, the Spotlighters. I was an all around active participant in the club. When I didn't have a speaking part in productions, I helped behind the scenes. And I can forever claim to be an award-winning actress, having won a Spotlighters acting trophy. I was inducted into Alpha Psi Omega Dramatic Honor Fraternity. I didn't need my parents' permission to be a recognized actress.

Chapter 25

College Years—The Academic Experience

"What does Wally Post have in common with Will Rodgers and the Cincinnati Reds?"

Calculus class, first period in the science building, Dr. Kyle was at it again. With assurance, I pushed my hand politely into the air, the only arm raised in response to our professor's question.

Mathematics was far from my favorite field of study, and calculus challenged my cerebral matter like no other course had.

"Research has shown the average human successfully functions an entire lifetime using only 10 percent of his/her brain," my father told me early in my high school days. Emboldened with that information, I vowed the course wouldn't defeat me. I kept pursuing to tap innate ability, and be the victor. Thus, calculus was simply agony. While Dr. Kyle's class was my toughest course, I could easily answer his mathematically unrelated question.

"Wally Post is the name of the catcher for the Cincinnati Reds baseball team," I answered, adding, "Another Wally Post copiloted the airplane he and Will Rodgers flew when they were lost."

Dr. G. D. Kyle, head of mathematics and physics, praised my quick and correct answer. Several times previous he had effusively heaped his verbal credit on an embarrassed me for my "all around knowledge." In a number of instances, his "off the wall" or random inquiries were related to vocabulary. Those questions were a piece of cake to me most likely due to having studied Latin in high school. "Veni, vidi, vici," he once boomed near the end of class time. "Did you?" he added. I didn't answer because I hadn't. I do remember knowing the translation was "I came, I saw, I conquered." Other questions I answered perhaps due to a lifetime of reading for recreation.

I recall Dr. Kyle telling the class, "Marva may not be the best calculus student, but each of you should cultivate a broad knowledge base such as hers."

He lectured us to "be inquisitive well beyond your narrow world. Being able to contribute to a conversation with anyone you meet could lead to your most treasured successes." I was the example our astute calculus professor used to challenge the class to be worldly, curious, well-rounded people. Dr. Kyle, not one iota reluctant to do so in my presence, told our class, no way would I fail the class. The grade I earned would reflect the value he gave my mastery of general knowledge.

"Thank you," I subconsciously whispered, checking mingled emotions of gratitude and unworthiness. I knew I was flunking calculus, but prayed hard work and a miracle would help me squeeze out a C. I poured over the textbook and paid attention in class; still daily homework results were horrible. The day I knew Dr. Kyle would pass me, I vowed calculus would never be part of my future career plans.

Intuitively I applauded Daddy's insistence I keep up with the daily news and read the work of well-informed writers. Gratitude for my father's perceptive guidance constantly resided securely in the folds of my brain.

My father's guidance influenced my choice of study, the basic college courses I would take. "Major in business administration, accounting, or mathematics," he suggested, dramatically volunteering rationale I could envision. "If you marry, decide you want to work, and have a family too, or you marry a knucklehead and have to make a living for your family, you can hang out a shingle, run a good business from your home. You can be a businesswoman, an accountant, anywhere."

Other advanced insight fueled his thinking. Daddy was certain employment discrimination would soon be illegal in America. "When companies, in order to stay in business, have to hire people they've rejected because of race and are looking to hire a qualified Negro, you'll be the one they want. There'll be smart, ambitious Negroes who have studied to be teachers and social workers. You study business management, accounting, even math, and you'll be the one in demand.

I listened and accepted my father's strong premise. However, I was not at all enthralled with the prospect of being an accountant, at any level. And mathematics, regardless of the more than respectable grades I earned in high school, intimidated me. So with resolve to actuate the words of my father, by process of elimination, I majored in business administration and minored in accounting and math.

* * * * * * * * * *

Those many years ago, when a female student on AM&N's campus stated her major was business, the business education assumption prevailed. Girls were more likely to prepare for teaching business, not running one. I was so proud business administration was my choice it was difficult holding onto humility as those two words confidently left my lips in response to "What's your major?" My plan, if I didn't go into show business, was to become a titan of industry. Two other women in our class earned a Bachelor of Science degree in Business Administration.

It was kind of neat that my chosen field didn't entice girls. Boys outnumbered girls ten to one in many classes. I liked that. After all, from puberty, my exposure to the opposite sex, curtailed by parental curbing of social activities, could only be platonic. Attending class every day with smart, funny, ambitious, and eligible black college men held the possibility I could have new experiences beyond book learning.

* * * * * * * * * *

The instructors I knew at AM&N were exemplary role models in aptitude, appearance, manner, and attitude. Each, like Dr. Kyle, was outstanding in the knowledge of his or her field and obviously personally invested in preparing students to be future leaders. Not one instructor seemed bored, and all, male and female, were *black*.

Dr. H. B. Young headed AM&N's Business Department. He earned his PhD from Harvard and had returned to the South to work in academia at the level his preparedness warranted. In Pine Bluff, seen on campus, in his office, in the classroom he exemplified what I expected of a Harvard man. Dr. Young was an imposing, tall, broad-chested figure who moved about with a quick stride. A brown skinned man, his wide face, pleasant smile, and sparkling eyes provided a warm touch to a no-nonsense instruction style that conveyed a stately businesslike demeanor. He appeared to be more like a CEO of industry than a college professor. I marveled that my small black college in the South provided the good fortune for me to benefit from the expertise of one who had earned a Harvard PhD.

I was attending a black college in the South and finding the kind of education my father said we could never have in a northern college. I learned from black professors who had the opportunity to learn and grow and know respect because of the leadership roles of their parents and neighbors in self-sustaining though segregated communities. Many had attended predominantly black colleges; others journeyed to integrated schools in the north then returned to the South to hold their positions of influence. And, I saw Negroes in business for themselves and Negroes in responsible roles in their communities, their schools. I went to school with young men and women raised in families who had such positive experiences. All were part of the thriving Negro culture my father's observations had promised.

As we grew older, Daddy seemed to love asking us, "How many Negro teachers have you had, even seen, in any classroom?" He knew full well every one of our teachers had been white. "In your black college in the South, you will have to study like you've never studied to be as smart as your classmates who will have had a lifetime of learning from Negro teachers."

I believe my father dropped out of Branch Normal before getting the two-year certificate given by his school, the predecessor to AM&N. I believe he dropped out because I never saw the certificate. I never knew why he didn't finish the program. Perhaps lack of money was the reason. Daddy had vowed to send us to college and to help until we graduated. I intended to earn my degree in four years.

Each fall my father sent me to Pine Bluff; I studied diligently, never skipped classes, and participated in extracurricular activities. From elementary school on, I had been counted among the "smart" students and looked to maintain the image in college. More importantly, I needed good grades to qualify for scholarship money. I faithfully took notes; made sure, no matter how limited my funds were, I had textbooks and other materials needed for class and projects; plus, I studied, researched the unfamiliar, completed assignments, and prepared for every test.

Practically every student I drew near to, who became a good friend, had a study ethic that mirrored mine. As my parents had warned me, college was not like high school; it was tougher, everyone serious. Everyone was there to prepare themselves for a future just as I was. They were outstanding students; many ranked first or second in their high school class, classes larger than mine had been. Their classroom performance proved an ambition to excel equal to mine. I enjoyed all my new friends and a wonderful college experience. I graduated with my class at the end of our fourth year on campus as I planned. There were about 250 of us.

Unfortunately, I could not claim any notable academic rank in our class. Friends were cum laude, magna cum laude, and summa cum laude. Friends of mine were elected to Sigma Gamma Rho, the academic fraternity. I felt blessed with the better than average grade point I did earn. I gave myself an excuse for falling short. From freshman through junior year, the business office couldn't clear me to take final exams at the end of the school year. I took final exams following the three month summer break, a day or two before classes started for the fall term. My grade point average suffered.

Senior year was the only year I took finals with my class. The other years I was called to the business office, and Mrs. Early or another very nice person would tell me my grade would be *I*, for *Incomplete*, until the balance due on my account had been paid and I had taken the final exam. "Your father said he will take care of it this summer." At home, after a couple weeks of total relaxation, I cracked the books—studying, trying to stay on top of the coursework everyone else had put behind them.

September found me sitting in an otherwise empty classroom taking tests for class work completed the previous May. I never got an A on any of those exams. I didn't get Ds or Fs either. I did okay, but I did not excel. Senior year, thanks to my all expense scholarship I took all exams and completed my last year at AM&N with my classmates. My grade point average may not have been something to write to anyone about but being named to Who's Who in American Colleges and Universities certainly implied I had a brain.

I left campus feeling fully prepared to start a career in business. It was a known fact that over the years key members of management in large companies received notoriety for stellar careers recognized after having "started in the mailroom." I wouldn't start in a mailroom, but I was prepared to work hard and smart, help grow the "bottom line," enhance the profit picture of an organization, and thus, succeed with that company. And I had my bachelor's degree!

Still, as a Negro and a woman, I knew I needed more. My intentions were in a few years, after working I would enter graduate school for my MBA, a master of business administration degree.

A Sunday afternoon at AM&N—
Around my chair:
Arletha, Shirley, and Blanche.

Mother enjoying her front yard
September 1958 as I begin my
last year in college.

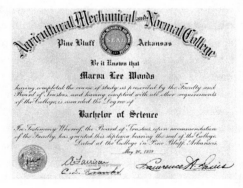

Chapter 26

On My Own

Late spring 1959 on AM&N's campus and graduation was near. My future was in my face with nary an excuse to delay deciding where my tomorrows would begin. The secure haven of college days had been reduced to only one page remaining on the monthly calendar in my dorm room.

Daddy sent train fare home—his decision, not mine. I knew returning to dairy farming country in Ohio wasn't a feasible option. Country versus city life had little to do with my decision. My father's dominating influence did. Choosing home base as a starting point for the real life I wanted meant including Daddy in my decision making. He would insist on adjusting his schedule to chauffer me into Cleveland, Akron, Youngstown, or Pittsburgh or wherever my job search garnered a prospect acceptable to daughter *and* father. Mother planted seeds of that truth my first summer vacation home from college, nurturing the premise in conversations on subsequent visits. Mother's observations were effective reminders of the impossibility of my father "letting go," giving me freedom to make my own decisions. To avoid the emotional unrest his passionate involvement promised me and the family, home couldn't be my destination after graduation.

Summers home from school while Daddy and his sons worked every day Mother and I had great talks. From a little girl, I saw myself as Mother's #1 helper, and with great pride I worked to maintain my position when home for vacation. As I stood at the ironing board set up in the living room and sprinkled rough dried clothes or ironed what had been dampened the day before, serious and humorous thoughts and opinions easily passed between us. Or we were in the kitchen preparing vegetables or fruits for canning or maybe fixing supper. Perhaps we were in the living room—I relaxed listening to the radio while Mother, needle and thread in hand, repaired something from her mending basket. Sometimes we were outdoors, sitting side by side in the apple green, solid but light-weight aluminum lawn chairs that had been moved onto the front porch. We were close, my mother and me. As I dealt with parenting decisions obviously driven by Daddy, the more passionate disciplinarian of the two, Mother worked her "good cop" to Daddy's "bad cop." Without compromising loyalty to her husband, Mother's comforting words drew my mind away from destructive frustration and focused me on the future ahead as a well-prepared adult, on my own. Mother's casual introduction of the concept that once I finished college I should anticipate a life away from there was an important bit of parenting. In my heart, the dutiful child I considered myself to be assumed I should come home to share the rewards of the education everyone sacrificed for me to have. Daddy never suggested absolutes about after college for me. He did speak about the grand life marrying a foreign diplomat could afford. And from teen years on, his theory for me majoring in business was so I could hang out my shingle advertising an at home business. "You can marry, have a family, and earn good money for your family," he had said. Perhaps a "good marriage" was his primary post-college hope for me. Without a doubt, those conversations with Mother freed me to feel secure about building a life of my own wherever I chose.

By graduation, several female classmates were engaged to be married or in serious relationships waiting to hear the big question before summer ended. Others had secured teaching positions. Some were in the process of applying to graduate school or had been accepted and were transitioning to another campus town. Neither graduate school nor marriage was on my "to do immediately" list. There was no man at all in my life.

With my bachelor's degree in hand, I wouldn't initially pursue a master's degree. I was confident the decision wouldn't disappoint Daddy, who hadn't included the importance of an advanced degree in his "get a college education" lectures. Perhaps that was because he believed studying for the BS would motivate my desire for the next degree. I did want the added credential and secretly pined to immediately begin work toward a master's in business administration. Being named to Who's Who inspired me to initiate effort toward going to Ohio State University's Graduate School of Business in Columbus, Ohio. I didn't follow through when it was apparent a good paying summer job and scholarship assistance were out of my reach. While building a career, I could go to school for my MBA.

I wanted a break from money problems. I would make a career connection with an employer whose benefit program included a tuition reimbursement plan. My objective was finding and choosing a prosperous company, getting on their payroll, and being financially secure.

Even though private industry was my goal, for insurance, I took the civil service examination offered on campus senior year. What harm was there in being qualified for a good government job? I passed with scores placing me high on the Federal Register of professional entry-level opportunities. Weeks before graduation, several announcements arrived in my campus mailbox inviting me to interview with the Social Security Administration in Chicago, Illinois. I knew no one, had no connections in Chicago, and was not at all excited with the prospect of day after day earning a living thinking, planning, working in the field of social security. I declined their interviews.

In dormitory gabfests late into the night, everyone helped me explore options as I freely discussed my need to land in a safe, career-promising environment after college. Staying in Arkansas or the south was fine except opportunities in business were not promising. Going back to a northern climate of cold and snowy winters wasn't appealing. Joanne suggested her hometown, St. Louis, Missouri, which was more southern than northern.

My research found St. Louis, known as the Gateway to the West and the largest city on the Mississippi River, had the potential of a variety of employment options for a business-trained recent college graduate. St. Louis was home to corporate headquarters operations for Anheuser Busch, Ralston Purina, Mallinckrodt Chemical, McDonnell Douglas, and others. There were also many civilian Federal Government Installations in St. Louis. And when I was ready, the exceptionally regarded Washington University would be a great school for me to earn my MBA.

I also knew of relatives in St. Louis. Through the years, when Daddy spoke of his sisters and their grown sons with homes in St. Louis, he did it with pride. His big sister, Aunt Modes, came to visit when we lived in Zanesville. She was the only St. Louis relative I had met. Considering the potential for starting a career in St. Louis and family to meet, my answer was a grateful yes when Joanne invited me to come home with her when we left campus, visit a few weeks, and start my job search there.

My postgraduate deliberations had not been shared with anyone at home. Daddy's letters to me were filled with pride about my graduation. Even though I was the first from both sides of the family to earn a college degree, no one could come to graduation. I never let them know how disappointing that was. Neither did I give any indication that I wouldn't be coming home. When Daddy's money order with train fare back to Warren arrived in the mail, without delay, I wrote them about the opportunity to go to St. Louis and search for a personnel or accounting position. My father's money order gave me cash to spare after getting my Greyhound Bus ticket. My father understood as we all agreed I would be home for a visit as soon as I could after I was settled.

I started looking for work the first day with Joanne after barely unpacking. I wanted to be on my own with little delay. Want ads in the *St. Louis Post-Dispatch*, the *Globe-Democrat*, and the *St. Louis Argus* provided my first source of leads. The telephone book was helpful also, especially for reaching out to family.

I connected with relatives sounding quite proud to meet and get to know John Woods's daughter, now a college graduate. But the greatest help proved to be Joanne introducing me to her cousin Helen, who lived near North St. Louis.

She had small children and her own beauty shop. She was a true blessing. Soon I was going on job interviews, looking good! Helen kept my hair in beautiful shape and gave me transportation money. In return, I babysat for her. Finding a place to live before I found work could have been difficult, but blessings continued as Helen and I worked out a perfect deal. I moved in with Helen and her family and between job interviews earned my keep being a much-needed mother's helper. I was succeeding as an independent adult.

Travel from one interview to another was exhausting. I walked and took city buses, getting lost many times, which meant trudging in attractively heeled dress shoes more blocks than I wanted and enduring foot pain I thought would never go away. Most stressful was being almost late for an interview on a hot muggy St. Louis summer day. Before even seeing the receptionist, I had to find a ladies room or somewhere to attend to my hair and repair the little makeup I wore. Through it all, my persistence delivered sought-for results. All at once, I had three job offers to consider.

Should I take the secretarial position in the black-owned and operated construction company? It would be quite a statement if I stepped up and supported the black-owned business sector by beginning my career with one.

Should I accept the full-charge bookkeeper's position in the small cabinetmaker's firm? The work was exactly what I had been trained to handle.

Should I become the medical secretary for a group of doctors in the huge hospital complex? It promised to be the most attractive, pleasant, even fun place to come to every day. Hundreds of people worked in the hospital. Waiting for interviews, I saw men and women, black and white, in and around my age happily doing whatever they were hired to do. I could make a lot of friends. Perhaps I would meet a single doctor, interested in me.

Considering my training in accounting and an ultimate goal to be a personnel manager, my decision was easy. I wouldn't consider the secretarial jobs.

I accepted the position with the cabinetmaker. It was a growing, family-owned and operated company. When it had grown even more, I could become the personnel manager. The owner and his brother sold custom-made cabinets to new home builders. The brothers also worked in the plant with the men designing, building, and finishing the custom-ordered cabinets. I was hired to join their mother in the office and be the office assistant. The mother would be promoted to office manager, dealing with paperwork related to sales, contracts, and promotion of the business and be a secretary for her sons. She was a gentle woman and seemed more a mother than a businesswoman, and she was my supervisor. I didn't see any other black employees, which didn't matter. I was given total responsibility for the books, through the profit and loss statement and including payroll. I envisioned wonderful potential with the company.

How proud I was to write home with the news. My first job after college paid $1.25 per hour for a forty hour week, Monday through Friday. I was a full-charge bookkeeper.

With my first paycheck of forty-eight dollars and some change, I bought things I needed and had spending money to take good care of me until next week's payday. However, the second check was a problem. I didn't know what to do with the money. I had no financial urgencies. I knew I had to start building a wardrobe for going to the office every day but never having *extra* money to spend on me, I didn't know where/how to start the process. I walked around Famous Barr Department Store, looking and thinking until I knew what I should do. I bought clothes for family, for my sisters and brothers at home. What joy it was packing and then mailing the huge box to Mr. and Mrs. John W. Woods, Jr., and family, General Delivery, Andover, Ohio.

* * * * * * * * * *

I could have told you before now about a special person I met just a week or so after coming to the city.

The first time I saw him, he was across the room, a stranger holding my attention with an expression of joy emanating from every feature of his smooth brown face—for sure from his twinkling eyes and smiling mouth. I was mesmerized by the delight I read in his grin, so much more committed than a mere smile. If his intent was to impress me with his "handsome self," standing there just inside my cousin's backdoor, he succeeded. He was gregariously good looking; so much so, I didn't imagine him being truly interested in me. Considering his persona from the kitchen of the sprawling brick ranch home I was visiting, I was fascinated. John Lee Stith, Jr., was a big guy, tall, ample, cute, and funny and handsome, too. A smile wouldn't leave my own face no matter how I tried to soberly control an obviously interested reaction to his flirtatious attention.

"Who do we have here?" he teased.

I remained motionless, practically speechless I recall, back pressed against the kitchen sink, facing him, me grinning too.

That evening I was there as a guest of the Stewarts, cousins from Daddy's side. Their son, Eddie Lee, Jr., a bit younger than me, had invited his friend Lake Stith in for conversation. Lake had just returned to the city from his freshman year at the University of Missouri down in Jefferson City. My newly found family had arranged to introduce two aspiring young black people who might enjoy sharing college experiences with each other.

The evening had ended. It was a good one even though, throughout, Lake had a lot to say and I was mostly trying to hide feeling shy and insecure. I excused myself from Lake and Eddie Lee's conversation to carry our empty glasses that once held lemonade, or whatever soft drink, to the kitchen when John Stith appeared inside their back door. He was "Lake's ride"—his cousin dropping by to give him a ride home once our visit was over. Of course, I didn't know my future started that Friday night from the back doorway of Cousin Eddie's kitchen.

Chapter 27

I Got Married

The night I met him, the big handsome guy never even left the doorway to project enthusiasm in style and words sufficient to upset my world. He was different, like a dab of bright red on a palette of drab grey and tan hues, and he had my full attention. From across the room I looked and listened, motionless like a statue, captivated by his obvious interest in holding my attention.

That night in the several minutes between meeting one another and bidding each other good-bye, I learned John Stith, Jr., only a few days prior had returned from Columbia, Missouri, and his first year at the University of Missouri. His campus experience was fun; practically all fun as he told it. Amazingly, he seemed not to have been one bit influenced by the opportunity and responsibility to study, learn, and cultivate foundations for a constructive well-lived future.

I sensed potential in the apparently fun-loving man and the possibility of a dimension of joy he could introduce, if only briefly, into my life. If he meant to start something fun with me, the pretty, baby-faced young woman, with body frame more curves than angles and brand new in town, I was feeling it. However, I felt he would soon become bored and tired of me once he learned behind the warm smile and inquisitive bright eyes I was different—a focused country girl with no inclination for foolishness. Still, I hoped to experience more of his relaxed self-assured, self-satisfied persona. It was clear I would. Before leaving my cousin's house that night, he arranged to pick me up the next Thursday for a date.

As John Stith exuberantly told it, his greatest accomplishment at "Mizzou" was cupid moves resulting in the marriage of classmates Arnold and Shirley. Arnold, his best friend, and Shirley, John's biology lab partner, "the most beautiful freshman girl on campus," he said, were now Mr. and Mrs. Their romance continued to blossom in St. Louis, on Union Avenue in a lovely modern apartment only recently available for blacks to rent. Within the week, we were visiting them, John holding me close to his side as we played cards, munched on hors d'oeuvres, and sipped drinks sharing the glow of the newly-wed bliss filling Shirley and Arnold's love nest. The smile never left my face as John proclaimed, me blushing, "This is the woman I'm going to marry."

"Not until you finish college," my mind silently cautioned.

The car he drove the night we met and every time after that was his father's brand new blue and white 1959 Chevrolet Impala. Our first date was a driving tour, showing me the sights and places he loved in St. Louis, the city of his birth. The father's beautiful car seemed to be the son's to drive anytime. But for my determination to hold back, and not be so available, we spent all our free moments together. We went to movies, on picnics, even cozily lounged in dark neighborhood taverns, or shared in the fun parties hosted at Shirley and Arnold's apartment or had quiet dinners with them, and then on the way home, we necked in the moonlight under the cover of majestic leafy trees in Fairground Park. Before the end of a summer, never imagined by me, I was no longer a virgin. Happy but not thrilled, I wanted my guy to want to finish college. Dating, being together exclusively was sufficient for me, but not for him. He wanted to be married.

I wrote home about John Stith but omitted any mention of marriage. My parents knew he was in college; his dad was retired from the Pennsylvania Railroad and worked in real estate, and his mother was a registered nurse in the prenatal unit at Homer G. Phillips Hospital. All of the above was short of the mark acceptable to my father. The man I married should be a college graduate, established in or at least on the threshold of a professional career, or my father's most favorite image, my husband would be in the foreign service if not a foreign diplomat. My father would not have welcomed details painting the picture of a serious relationship with a young man who was simply a good guy from a good family.

I, too, wanted to marry well. As the oldest daughter, I valued being a good example for my little sisters. Thus my resolve to stall the possibility of marriage until John Stith's college graduation was in sight.

John's marriage focus escalated to the point he told his parents he was through with college, for the time being—he wasn't ready. Unhappy is insufficient to describe the disappointment his dad, John, Sr., and his mom—especially his mom Jeannette Stith—expressed when they realized their son had immediate marriage in mind for us. Mrs. Stith insisted he return to the university for his sophomore year.

Compounding the hysteria, his mother did not trust me.

"You don't even know *who* she is," Mrs. Stith screeched one day, unaware of me being on the front porch hearing the family's angst through the screened front door.

"This girl comes to town, says she has graduated from college, *doesn't* have a diploma, and you believe her!" (Our diplomas were not back from the printer when we marched and had to be mailed to us.)

John's father knew me better than John's mom since many times he was with us as we dropped him where he needed to be so we could have the car.

It was clear he was proud to introduce me as his son's girl. And poor business that summer found him having difficulty raising his son's tuition and room and board fees. The combination of his son's unabashed talk about fun times on campus, his poor grades, and now being in love and not wanting to return, easily convinced a cash-challenged dad to see merit in John beginning his independence. For me, it was far from perfect that Mr. Stith liked me and accepted his son's plan for our future.

My best tactic was to hang tough, not agree to marriage even though all our conversations evolved to exactly that. In his heart and soul, he said, the two of us were already "one." He reminded me I had a job as he diligently looked for work. He placed employment applications with the post office, the transit authority, and utility companies. He considered selling insurance as Arnold did. He was certain a job would be found soon. Confidently he stressed we would support each other emotionally and materially.

I got scared. Things were moving too fast. It was a confusing time. I wanted to forever be with John Stith without reservation, yet I couldn't give myself guilt-free permission. Not so with him. His comfortable, caring, and determined self held me close and vowed we would marry.

"It may as well be now as later," he said. "We can work together to build our lives." Loving him, his words were beginning to make good sense to me.

Yet it appeared I was going to be swept into marriage and a life of unnecessary struggle. I needed help. I had to talk to my family, especially Daddy, knowing he would advise against marriage with such a fragile support base as my guy presented. I knew I would listen. His words would give me the strength to convince John Stith our future would be better if we waited until he finished his education. Discouraging all talk of him going with me, I told John I should go home and let them know our plans.

I wrote Mother and Daddy with the good news I was coming for Labor Day weekend. "I'll be at the Greyhound Bus Station in downtown Cleveland 1:30 Saturday afternoon. Daddy, if you can't meet me please write immediately to let me know." They didn't have a telephone, but I knew they would use a neighbor's if something interfered with them coming the almost sixty-five miles to pick me up. Hearing nothing, I proceeded with my plan for a long weekend with them.

As John and I said good-bye at the bus station in downtown St. Louis, truthfully, I doubted ever seeing him again. My dad would strengthen my reasons against marrying. His rational insight would enable me to overcome my emotional bond with the man I saw some merit in marrying. So I would stay in Ohio and find work closer to home, not come back to St. Louis and the adorable man I was having so much fun loving. So, my good-bye embrace was to the tune of words, all lies assuring him I would return. I was sad because I felt totally taken care of with him, or thinking about him. He may not have his degree; he had potential. I could be with him the rest of my life. I did imagine me deciding to stay in Ohio and John Stith coming there for me. Daddy would be impressed with us together and give his blessing. That was the only way I'd return to St. Louis, Missouri.

The trip to northeastern Ohio was a long one in a bus full of families traveling the last summer holiday weekend. Babies were crying. Toddlers and older children were roaming the aisle every chance they could. I was contentedly lost in romantic thought, and then mournful with my doubts. We were delayed in a couple small towns by local Labor Day Parades and festivities. It seemed like forever before the bus made its way into the Cleveland terminal.

I looked forward to seeing my family. I didn't know who Daddy would bring with him. Or he might make the drive by himself so we could talk freely on the way back to the house. I realized I didn't want that; the ride home had to be enjoyable, not the emotional pressure of discussing the marriage proposal before me. Surely Kathleen, Cynthia, Sharon, Larry, or Roy, perhaps Mother would come with him. "He mustn't come by himself," I thought.

"He'll bring Roy," I decided. I had not seen my family since leaving Ohio for senior year of college a year prior. Roy, just four years old, the baby of the family, was Daddy's favorite, a family favorite. I looked forward to seeing how more amazing the smart, cute, now five-year-old had become. "Yes, Daddy most likely had Roy with him." As I walked through the crowded terminal, all at once the anticipation of seeing family was so gloriously powerful it was all I could do to keep a wide grin off my face. And had my luggage been lighter, I would have been running. Where would we first see each other? Anticipating what lay ahead, I forgot all about John Stith.

My family was not in the waiting area. I sat down, perhaps appearing relaxed. I strained to see them when they came within view. It wasn't happening! Concern and then worry crept into my thoughts since my father was a punctual person. Maybe there had been an accident. At the Information Desk, I checked for messages. There were none. The guy said traffic was bad. "It's a holiday weekend!" Of course that was it, I thought, recalling the parades that held up our bus driver several times coming from St. Louis. The same could have happened on Daddy's drive from Ashtabula County. For a few minutes, I knew I must be patient. Then a critical piece of information visited my brain. "They didn't even get the letter and had no idea I was making the trip to Cleveland." Over and over my mind chastised me for not confirming someone would be there.

Once I realized I wasn't going home to family, I couldn't get to a telephone booth quickly enough to call St. Louis and talk to the man I loved. But John's mother answered. Gratefully she abruptly passed the phone to her son. Her rudeness this time was a relief to me. I didn't want to give her the satisfaction of hearing my tearful voice. I have no memory of the words I chose to convey I was stranded. True, I had convinced myself, they didn't get my letter. I didn't believe it though. They did receive the letter. Daddy read between the lines. He knew I wasn't a virgin anymore. He didn't want me around my sisters now that I was living a loose life. He disowned me. It was painful thinking my family didn't want me. The hurt pushed me to cherish my relationship with John Stith, speaking on the other end of the telephone. His calm voice reminded me of all the hours I spent on the bus trying to be home for the weekend and, "after all, it *is* a holiday weekend!" John encouraged me to give myself more time, "they're just late."

He had no idea of the misery I had conjured up; how I had let my "daddy's little girl" thoughts get tangled up with my grown woman needs and experiences. In the face of my emotional turmoil, John L. Stith, Jr.'s mature objectivity impressed me. All at once I didn't want to lose him. I couldn't wait to return to the smart, considerate man who said he loved me. I just said I was coming home and later we would visit my family in Ohio as husband and wife.

Sixteen days after my failed Labor Day weekend trip, John Stith and I married at the justice of the peace in St. Louis. At that time, Missouri state law required parental consent for a person under the age of twenty-one to obtain a marriage license. His father signed for him. Fortunately, only one signature was needed. We were married on September 25, 1959. Not one family member, from his or mine, was present.

Chapter 28

Daddy

My father had not disowned me. He arrived at the terminal just after the bus departed taking me back to St. Louis. Labor Day parades along the way into Cleveland as well as traffic congestion in the city caused the extensive delay that kept my father and me apart that weekend.

My family had eagerly anticipated and prepared for my visit; they bought my favorite foods, plus all the ingredients for what I would help prepare in our large country kitchen. They had planned a special Labor Day weekend. It wasn't difficult to imagine the joy in the little farmhouse because, "Marva's coming!" But I didn't and they wouldn't know until Daddy returned that evening without me.

Telling this story brings uncontrollable tears as I vividly see everyone happy, restrained, not rushing to the car as it came up the driveway. Daddy always stressed emotional restraint, not the exuberance of uncontrolled excitement. My brothers and sisters would have been calm, subdued, but I would have felt their joy. Mother would have stayed on the porch, watching, smiling in anticipation, until—unbelievably, I didn't get out of the car. Today, sadness prevails as I know I so regret not calling a neighbor to confirm our arrangements.

By letter I let my family know what happened. They regretted not having a telephone and not contacting me to let me know they received my "I'm coming for the weekend" letter and assuring me they would pick me up. Still I was never certain they believed I arrived that Saturday.

Shortly after our marriage, John and I learned we were expecting our first child. We postponed any talk of us traveling until after the baby's birth. In the meantime, my husband and my father had a fine long distance relationship. Actually, Daddy's letters told of road maps he had collected and studied and his strategy for driving the entire family to come visit us in St. Louis.

However, during my pregnancy, Daddy had been intermittently, and I would learn too late, seriously ill. How could I have been so unaware of the gravity of his condition? He died November 15, 1960, having been rushed to the hospital after collapsing with a heart attack while working.

Daddy never met my husband or our baby daughter, Farah Diba, his first grandchild. Farah was three months old when her grandfather Stith sent us home via train, a berth in a Pullman car, to be with my family for her grandfather Woods's funeral.

Chapter 29

About My Career

I got married, and my passion for a business career vanished. I quit the full-charge bookkeeper position. I forgot all about having decided it was a great career opportunity for me, a black woman, in 1959 doing such important work in the growing manufacturing firm. I would say I resigned from the job due to low pay and the work location of the company. That was not the whole truth.

Unashamedly, I remember allowing the fun time I enjoyed as a new bride become more important than my job. Too many times I started my day at the office explaining why I was late, always a created excuse. I couldn't admit my husband and I hated me leaving our cozy apartment. I hated being late to work. It was stressful. After he was hired by the post office, we learned we were pregnant, and the two of us easily decided I should quit my job.

Staying home became a bore, so when morning sickness subsided, I took another job. Plus common sense invaded our reverie and told us additional income would be helpful since there was a baby on the way. I was glad to work and liked all I learned in the office although I was only a clerk typist. And amazing to my husband and me, as a clerk-typist I was paid more than I made as a bookkeeper. The temporary position ended when I started maternity leave.

* * * * * * * * *

My resume encompassing the next four years consisted of temporary or entry-level positions. The most personally promising assignment was as a television production assistant at the public education station on Washington University's campus. I envisioned parlaying the experience and exposure into a television career. I also considered starting work on my graduate degree at Washington U. Neither was to happen. We had our second baby, bought a house, and adopted a puppy. We also dealt with learning our children had sickle-cell anemia, and because of that, the best "next steps" for all of us. We cherished, even more, good times with family and friends. Our focus was family life. The quality of my career wasn't on the radar screen.

* * * * * * * * *

By the mid-sixties Dr. Martin Luther King, Jr. and the civil rights movement had led the country to realize our constitutional law was imperfect. The nation went to work to right past wrongs. Laws passed by Congress and signed by President Johnson opened doors of opportunity to people who had been excluded in several ways, including getting jobs with greater responsibility and better pay. Employers advertised to find and hire qualified minorities in job categories not usually considered for them.

I updated my resume, giving greater emphasis to college courses and work done using that training. I aimed for a position at higher than clerical level. The doors had opened and as a black woman with credentials, i.e., a bachelor's degree in business administration, I had success in my job search. Soon I was involved in the interview-selection process for a position requiring work experience related to the job duties, or a college degree.

The State of Missouri hired me as an employment service placement technician. The basic objective of the work was to fill a company's job order after interviewing candidates for employment and matching them to the open position. The position proved to be a tremendous opportunity to learn about the structure and staffing requirements of many different kinds of businesses.

My starting salary was higher than I ever earned. Yet I needn't worry about having to work overtime. Our agency, they said, never approved overtime work. Very seldom could state employees expect the financial bonus of overtime, which didn't displease my family. We wanted me home. We could expect a regular pay raise as long as my performance was satisfactory.

Summarily, it wasn't pressure-filled work interrupting the family life so vital to us. Important to me, I was employed doing professional work on a career path that could lead to one day becoming a personnel manager.

Chapter 30

A Dick and Jane Life

"Dick and Jane," sunshine yellow hair, polite, the little boy and girl at play indoors or outdoors in perfect surroundings with perfect toys impressed me when I met them in Wilson Elementary School in Zanesville. They were the core characters in a fictional family living in the pages of my first grade reader. My first serious personal goal took form as I learned to read studying the pictures and words about their happy, lovingly secure days. One day, I would have a family like theirs.

The problem-free existence of Dick and Jane's household pleased me. Their being white people had nothing to do with the role model status I afforded them. Yet if Bill Cosby's Huxtables had been on the scene, I may have chosen to aspire to their lifestyle not because they were a black family but because Dr. Huxtable involved himself in parenting his kids as my father did us. The fact is, though I never spoke about it, I promised myself when I grew up mine would be a family that lived a Dick and Jane life.

My home would consist of "Father," a wonderful man who found and married me, and "Mother", me, comfortable and happily living with our children and dog and kitten in a neat house surrounded by a green lawn and white picket fence.

It almost happened.

Seventeen months after welcoming our first child, my loving husband and I brought our new son home from the hospital. Joining his big sister, he made us a family of four in the spacious upstairs portion of the two-family house we rented on Lexington Avenue in St. Louis. The birth of John Darin Stith in December 1961 blessed us with two bright, adorable children.

John was the true breadwinner in the family. He worked for the postal service while studying for his real estate license. He also kept additional part-time jobs. But unlike the mother in the fabled "Dick and Jane" story who was home all day providing the amenities of relaxed cozy family experiences, I went to work every day also. We prospered, and with our love and hard work came close to having the lifestyle I dreamed of.

Then on a hot St. Louis summer day, we learned about sickle-cell anemia, a genetic health condition for which there was no cure. Darin was eight months old. His little hand was swollen, and nothing we did gave him relief. He seemed to be in pain and kept crying. It could have been an insect bite or perhaps somehow he had sprained his hand. Finally we took him to see a pediatrician in Children's Hospital.

"Do you have other children?" the doctor asked me. "Where is the father?"

Puzzled with the intensity of his questioning, I looked him directly in the eye and told him my son had a sister and, "their father will be in. He's parking the car."

Darin's blood test results showed he had sickle-cell anemia disease, an inherited condition. In no way did I look anemic, so my thought was they were thinking the father must be anemic. When John Stith walked into the department, mouths fell open as they regarded a guy more than six feet tall who clearly weighed more than two hundred pounds and didn't appear at all anemic. Our blood tests showed we each had sickle-cell trait, the precursor for our offspring to have sickle-cell disease. And my thinking had been wrong. A person with the disease or the trait may never *appear* anemic.

Only when our children were diagnosed did we learn men and women with sickle-cell trait should be cautioned about having children with each other. The risk factor is that 50 percent of their offspring will have the disease. Was Darin our only child with the disease? We were instructed to bring Farah in for testing. I balked. After all, she had recently passed her second birthday and had not shown one symptom. I was absolutely skeptical when they told us tests confirmed she was afflicted. Not until some two months later when she had a painful sickle-cell crisis did I accept the diagnosis.

From the beginning, bravely and intelligently their father and I coped with the news of an illness no one in the family or our circle of friends had known about. Candidly, I had difficulty keeping my ears from hearing some type of syphilis when the doctor was saying sickle cell. "Perhaps they had only jumped to our baby having 'syphilis' because we were black!" But I was wrong. "Sickle cell" was the diagnosis.

"There is no cure," the doctors at Barnes Hospital told us and, as I remember, followed up with the information that "Research finds the disease is more prevalent in blacks and East Mediterranean people." "Well, no wonder there is no cure," I scornfully contemplated, "it's a disease indigenous to people of color."

The doctors told us Farah and Darin, throughout their lifetime, would suffer, without warning, extreme pain and organ impairment due to their imperfect red blood cells. They would be in a sickle-cell crisis. Those sickle-cell attacks would lead to their hospitalization for oxygen and intravenous pain medication and blood transfusions to replace lost hemoglobin, such loss the cause of tissue and organ damage.

When they weren't in crisis, they might be tired and listless. Yet there would be good times when they had a long stretch of time, weeks, even months when they would feel and be so fit, we would think they didn't have the condition. Unfortunately, this debilitating disease also promised the dire possibility of a life expectancy of only forty years.

Still their father and I dredged up optimism. Researching, we discovered scientists were working for a cure. Until one was found, we knew our children must have everything they needed. We convinced ourselves we could help our babies avoid sickle-cell crisis by providing excellent living conditions—quality nutrition, a comfortable clean environment, stress-free rest, and relaxed happy times. John left the post office for a better position in private industry that could eventually enable me to stay home and take care of our children.

Our extended family responded wonderfully to help us. His mom and dad, and sister, still in school, were attentive and supportive. My mother and brothers and sisters almost a thousand miles away in Ohio were a fine source of moral support more than anything, but would eventually provide much more.

It was essential we have in-home childcare. First there was a lovely older lady who took good care of them and did ironing and housecleaning as well. My father-in-law brought her to us every morning and delivered her back to her door at day's end.

It became *the* priority to buy our own home. John sold our new car, a Plymouth Valiant, to lower our debt level and assure qualifying for the best mortgage. We looked at property in the county where neighborhoods invited outdoor activities for children. The realtor found the perfect home in Richmond Heights, Missouri. It was a sunny, well-kept modern house with evergreen shrubbery and a grassy front lawn. We installed a white picket fence around the tree-shaded backyard. We took our children to the Humane Society and picked out a puppy. Angel, though a mix-breed, had the appearance of a miniature Lassie. She turned out to be a movie-perfect dog—playful, obedient, intelligent, and a protective, watchful pet.

Then Kathleen relocated from Williamsfield, Ohio, to be live-in help for us.

Throughout my college years, Kathleen and I didn't keep in contact. Mother's letters reported the news about all my sisters and brothers. Kathleen was in the process of getting her adult life on track when Daddy died. At that time, her high school graduation had long passed. Never interested in going to college, she convinced Mother and Daddy she wanted to be a nurse. She set her sights on finding a nurse aid job in a hospital and then enrolling in nursing school. Daddy took her to apply at hospitals and other places until his health began to deteriorate.

Following our father's untimely death, Kathleen was a big help to Mother, who had four other children ages six through fourteen to care for. We all worried about their future out there in the country. Mother loved her home and didn't want to live anyplace else. But how would they get along? Thanks to family, neighbors, and friends, especially the Fullers and the Watsons, she was able to make it work and didn't have to give up the home Daddy had worked so hard for his family to have. After a year and half or so, she had made it through her deepest grief over the loss of her husband—her friend, lover, and leader. She became openly concerned about Kathleen's future. Throughout it all, Kathleen hoped to find work in the area but had not been able to do so.

Mother and Kathleen found it a perfect proposal when we suggested Kathleen come live with us in Richmond Heights. We needed her. She needed us to help her start her career and prepare for her own independence. She could look for work in between caring for our toddler daughter and son while their father and I worked.

Kathleen was back into the rhythm of my life, part of our family, a blessing to all. My husband and I had no worries leaving our babies in bed sleeping as we hurried off to work. Their doting aunt was in charge.

We had no trouble coordinating our schedules as Kathleen chased down job openings advertised in newspapers and listed with the State Employment Service. She found the work she diligently sought. Her first nursing job was in a nursing home. Soon she was called for an interview and was hired by Barnes Hospital, a premier medical facility in St. Louis. She was hired for the night shift she wanted. Our children had around-the-clock attention, and Kathleen had stepped across the threshold to a nursing career.

* * * * * * * * * *

It was several years later when I was not able to avoid another peril not mentioned in Dick and Jane's world. Trouble surfaced in our marriage, and the family fell apart.

For this writing, the details of the break-up are not necessary. I will record some documentation to evidence I did not let the outcome happen easily.

From the beginning of troubling incidents, I made excuses to our children about their previously devoted father's absence from the home. My tears were held back until I was in bed, alone. During daytime hours I stayed as busy as possible. All the while I silently prayed for his return to our routine while simultaneously praying the dark of night came quickly so I could get back in my bed and cry and figure out the real reason for my husband's absence.

Constructively, I thought, heeding the advice of girlfriends, the other half of still happily married couples in our circle of friends, I attempted to bring my man back under our roof. I was a more focused housekeeper. (He had asthma and couldn't tolerate the minutest particle of dust.) I would be sexier. (Candles, provocative lingerie, silk sheets were nice but the best was the day he opened the front door to find me "dressed" only in Saran wrap, vacuuming the living room.) I could change my public businesslike image. (Trading in my just paid for, four door, dusty green Ford Fairlane sedan and bringing home my brand new, bronze with cream colored soft-top, Chevrolet Impala convertible was exhilarating.) I forced myself to exhibit independent self-sufficiency, becoming heavily involved with our children's extracurricular activities. Even as I earned and accepted more responsible and visible assignments with my employer, I took on the den mother's position with Darin's Cub Scout pack. I edited and typed the newsletter for Farah's class at West Richmond Elementary School. I took lead roles with the PTA, even serving as president.

For a very long time, I wouldn't give up and accept my marriage was ending. We were simply experiencing an example of "worse" in the "for better or for worse" phrase embedded in our wedding vows. We would get through it. I was so certain we were two people meant to grow old together; I wouldn't let myself think divorce. I thanked God each day I could say I was married to my husband.

Then I began to consider possible consequences, all troubling. He and I were joint owners of our family's home. He was out of the home—doing what? What if he had an automobile accident causing a lien to be placed against our property? I realized I had to look after the well-being of our children. Practicality overcame emotion. I found a good lawyer.

Too soon our family unit was broken, unable to be fixed. He was gone. I was emotionally shattered. Four months before my thirteenth wedding anniversary, I was divorced. I had our white picket-fenced house, our two children, the family dog—all mine, alone. We were left alone in my wannabe "Dick and Jane" world.

Acknowledging the divorce could seriously derail the quality life I planned, I recalled my father's guiding words from my teenage years. I vowed I would continue to forge my vision of a good family life in spite of the father's absence. I would hold myself and my children to standards and goals, insuring as enriched a lifestyle as possible.

I had been content with a career maintained while succeeding as wife, mother, and homemaker. Now I needed a position in private industry where there was greater opportunity to make more money. Then I would regain my self-respect.

After all, those many years before, Daddy had encouraged me to "finish college, be prepared to have a career so you will be able to care for your family if you marry a knucklehead who shirks his responsibilities."

Our dog Angel in front of
the house that would have a
white picket fence.

Kathleen Marie,
Farah and Darin's
beloved Aunt Kathy

John Stith, Jr.— Dad and his children—
Darin's birthday, December 1965.
Farah says she remembers wanting
to hurry and cut the cake.

Chapter 31

Title VII

Title VII of the Civil Rights Act of 1964 prohibits discrimination in employment based on race, color, religion, sex, or national origin. The Equal Employment Opportunity Commission was created to enforce this legislation. Title VII catapulted affected classes of people, which included me, being black, onto the playing field entitled to full consideration and participation in all categories of work for a right sized entity engaged in doing business with the U.S. government.

Prior to Title VII making fair employment a federal law, fair employment laws existed in many states and local communities. Thanks to the civil rights movement, those employers in all states and local municipalities, in the North, the South, the East, and the West, were required to engage in fair employment practices.

Race, color, religion, gender, and heritage were no longer factors most employers (without possibility of redress) could find negated my ability to satisfactorily perform their job. I believed as long as I appeared clean, neat, polite, and presented the good aptitude and understanding an employer expected of any applicant, that employer would honestly consider me for the job opening.

Once hired I anticipated receiving fair pay, training, benefits, and additional compensation as available under company policy and granted to others similarly classified. I also expected, as warranted, promotion consideration based on competitive work-related factors such as training, experience, performance, and accomplishment. Under Title VII, it was illegal for an employer to exclude me for reason or reasons based upon the non-job-related factors of race, color, religion, gender, or heritage.

Chapter 32

AAP

Equal Employment Opportunity legislation at the federal level gave birth to the Affirmative Action Plan (AAP).

A business organization's completed AAP paints a statistical portrayal of demographics describing the employer's workforce. Along with other information, the data reported provides an analytical concept of the reception and treatment of affected classes, i.e., those certain groups of employees that included blacks and females, who are in the organization and have been considered (or not) to be part of the organization.

Employers with contracts to do business with the federal government must implement an affirmative action plan and undergo regular or scheduled compliance reviews conducted by the Department of Labor. When the company's AAP shows the right numbers in the right boxes, the Department of Labor could conclude minorities or "affected classes" were treated equitably. When the company's statistics are not in acceptable range, the AAP shows the company's good intent by acknowledging those shortcomings in hiring, etc., and, provides narrative establishing the company's action goals toward correcting unsatisfactory situations.

An AAP includes the company's commitment to be involved with sources proven able to assist the company's effort to bring members of affected classes to their doors. The AAP lists those community-based organizations involved in employment and training that they contact for assistance in achieving the company's fair employment goals. In the 1960s and 1970s, such outside organizations, among them the National Association for the Advancement of Colored People (NAACP), the Urban League, and Congress of Racial Equality (CORE) were well known in our black communities for their good relationship with employers. It was highly likely one or all three were listed on every major employer's affirmative action plan as a source for finding qualified job applicants representing members of the affected classes.

An acceptable AAP provides a valuable safeguard to the employer. It is instrumental in protecting an organization from the litigation of discouraged, frustrated, feeling damaged, affected classes who might scream "foul" in their interactions or lack of with the company. In spite of an applicant's detailed play by play of an unsuccessful attempt to be hired or an employee's detailed report of what he or she considers constant mistreatment and disregard in that company's dissemination of responsibility and compensation, if the AAP statistics and narratives are within guidelines, the applicant's or employee's complaint is likely to be deemed frivolous. The judgment made as to whether a company justly played the game in its quest to fairly hire, promote, and retain employees, to me, hinged greatly on how that company fared in its periodic Affirmative Action Plan Compliance Review.

Chapter 33

Affirmative Action Opens Doors

In 1972 a major consumer products manufacturing company, part of a worldwide corporation, hired me to be a personnel assistant. The entry-level management category job was in their St. Louis plant within easy commute of my home. I was the first black person and the first woman to hold the position in that plant. I considered corporate America the "big leagues" for business management opportunity. That June day in 1972, I felt I had been admitted to play in the big game.

The Urban League, after crucial networking on my part, was the conduit to my groundbreaking opportunity.

It all began in my seventh year of what had become a career with the Missouri State Employment Service.

A few years earlier I was promoted from a placement technician to an employer services representative (ESR) and thus was an "outside-sales" person for MSES. Via on-site visits to all types of companies in St. Louis city and county, I encouraged company officers or employment staff to list their job openings with the State Employment Service (SES). I was in a unique assignment for a black woman. Hopefully I helped open doors for others.

One of the criteria for the job was to pass a test for placement on a selection register with military veterans receiving the extra points giving them veteran's preference in the selection process—perhaps a reason most employment service representatives were men. My peers were men who had been ESRs for a number of years. Most were also veterans of the armed forces who had been high on the state's selection register for our coveted positions.

My co-workers were fine gentlemen, good businessmen, and indeed "salesmen." From the beginning when I partnered in the office and then "in the street" with any one of the seasoned ESRs, each co-worker was generous in sharing written and unwritten rules, nuances for every aspect of the position that was invaluable for succeeding.

As wife, mom, and homemaker, going to work everyday as an ESR was wonderful. I had the freedom to schedule and hold productive appointments and on lunch time or en route to a meeting take care of some family care matter. I had a job perk not possible if I was locked into a stationary work site. "Major in business," my father had said. "Then, if necessary, you can work from home."

As an ESR, I never worked from home; however, I thought of my father's advice when I darted into the dry cleaners or rushed to a meeting at the school that I had scheduled for my convenience. It was convenient not being tethered to an office or a classroom.

Confidently I left the office each day armed with our agency's pamphlets, brochures, and data to give company personnel I visited. I was also well equipped with researched information about *their* operation and particularly staffing requirements. When I walked into the Ultimate Chocolate Place, or Arnie's Tool and Die, or Worldwide Shipping and Storage or Monsanto or Mallinckrodt Chemical, I discussed solid facts about the skills needed and the materials, tools, and processes used by the company to bring their product to the market. And it was a satisfying accomplishment convincing them the government entity I represented, which their tax dollars helped fund, could improve their business. The employment service's placement unit would send good workers at no additional expense to their overhead. It was an excellent day when I returned to our office with a signed job order authorizing the State Employment Service to refer applicants for consideration as a new hire for their business.

The personal satisfaction of being an ESR was also couched in my success at bringing job orders to the placement unit earmarked for minority candidates. Good jobs, usually meaning paying union wages or higher than minimum wage, hadn't been so available to the minority community. My work helped open the doors to better paying jobs for the unskilled.

Having a college degree was the important prerequisite for me surviving the selection process to gain the promotion. It was clear that once on the ESR team, exposure I gained in researching the business structure of a variety of organizations served to prepare me for better career opportunities for myself.

Discussing business management issues with company officers at the highest level and with respected managers in large and small organizations were day-to-day opportunities and challenges that pleased me greatly. But opening doors for others to opportunities my father had said would be out there for black men and women one day gave me tremendous joy.

* * * * * * * * * *

My career with the Employment Service was more than satisfactory until my husband and I separated and it became clear a divorce was inevitable. Then I faced reconciling the importance of money earned versus quality time with my family. It was not difficult reaching a conclusion. If I could better provide for my two children to go to bed each night feeling secure, confident, and happy with their lives, I must. Also, whatever was on the horizon for our family structure, I had to insure as best I could there be sufficient income and quality time for my family in a single-parent household. Getting a second job was not the answer.

It came to me that I was away from my children X number of hours a day to perform a job that paid Y amount. Because X was necessary, I had to maximize Y. I could use my qualifications and do better in private industry. I would search for a position paying more money, with no less than my current benefit packages, and projecting opportunity for advancement to higher levels of responsibility and compensation.

Networking, I shared with family, friends, and neighbors my intent to leave the Employment Service. "Please tell anyone you think can help that I am in the market for a career opportunity in personnel." I was reservedly candid about the personal aspects guiding my decision to abandon the employer I found personally and professionally energizing through so many years. My networking reached out to everyone except co-workers at any level and contacts made carrying out my duties with the Employment Service.

One memorable Sunday morning I lifted the telephone off my kitchen wall to hear words on the other end leading to a new chapter in my life. The voice was that of a good friend's husband, a man for whom doors to a better job had opened due to the positive change for blacks and others due to equal opportunity laws. The man now held a plum executive position in a worldwide company headquartered in St. Louis. He said he heard about a job opening that sounded perfect for me.

Over drinks the night before, an Urban League placement representative had shared his misery over failure to find the right candidate for a job opening the Urban League had been trying to fill for some time. It was in the personnel office of a well-known manufacturing plant. My neighbor told the man about me and my job search. He wanted to hear from me.

Early Monday morning I made the telephone call and connected with the rep who, in a rather bored tone, told me about the specifications spelled out on the job order. A company in the area was looking for a qualified black woman for an opening in their personnel department. They wanted to hire a personnel assistant and had been demanding, in fact stubborn, about the necessary qualifications. The Urban League had referred several excellent people, all with college degrees but not in business. Neither did the candidates have business-related work experience. The Urban League had been hopeful each referral might have been accepted in view of outstanding background and solid work experience. But without business training or business experience, the company didn't want any to come back for further consideration. They had given up and wouldn't see another candidate. It was a waste of time. They might promote and train a person already with them in a clerical position.

As the representative rambled on, I remember tuning him out, thinking the man must have hoped his openness would make it easier for me to accept the unwelcome news he would finally convey. *"The job order's been closed. They will not accept another referral. You're not going to be considered."*

Then through the fuzzy matter regrouping in my head to craft and express gracious words of thanks and understanding over my bad fortune not to get the interview, I heard him exclaim, "They want to see you! I was able to talk about your qualifications, your business administration degree and your work experience. How soon can you go to their office for an interview?"

What a thrilling moment. My father's words had become actual fact in my life. Big business earnestly sought a black person with business training, and they wanted me. Here was my opportunity for the career I wanted in private industry. I was ready.

When could I go for the interview? My mind was churning. I had arranged a day off that Friday—a vacation day, I had said. (There was no reason for anyone to know Friday morning I was scheduled to be in court for the judge to grant my divorce.) Marge and Shirley, my two character witnesses, and I had reservations for lunch afterward in a fine restaurant in Clayton. Now it was clear, after our lunch, I could go for the interview, not home to cry as I probably would have done. It was perfect. I would be divorced, not separated. I hated having to tell a potential employer I was "separated"—such an uncertain status. Yes, I could go for the interview after lunch on Friday. Luckily, the day and the time were perfect for the company as well.

From first greeting the assistant personnel manager, the interview was nothing but positive. He asked if I would come back as soon as possible to meet the personnel manager.

A day or so later at the conclusion of another good meeting, this time with the personnel manager, he shared how the Urban League contact had begged them to "please let me send you this one more person. You will not be sorry."

Laughing, after he and I finally agreed on his job offer (salary my issue), he told me he was glad the Urban League rep convinced them to bring me in. So was I.

In a few weeks after a celebratory—congratulations—best wishes— farewell gathering in the offices at the State Employment Service, I was on board and warmly welcomed by my new employer.

My search for a position with career growth potential in private industry was over.

Chapter 34

The New Job

Describing my new employer,[20] I would say "we are a manufacturing/marketing company with a product line of liquid and powder detergents and bar soaps." Those were the consumer products produced in the St. Louis plant. At the time, the company's plants in other cities produced dentifrices and other personal products, and food products such as pancake mix, pancake syrup, and margarines. Each plant had state-of-the-art production lines. The U.S. Government's Standard Industrial Classifications (SIC) Index listed the company in the manufacturing category, a chemical company. The research center developed new products. Packaging design, marketing, and sales decisions were finalized in corporate. The company's strong sales strategy focused on supplying retail and commercial businesses, as well as the industrial sector.

My job was to help maintain a necessary workforce by administering company and personnel policy. I was the site personnel representative for hundreds of hourly and nonmanagement employees. Language in the union contract guided actions taken to handle needs related to hourly employees. The company's personnel policies manual guided me in giving assistance to employees not covered by the union contract and not in management, i.e., clerical and professional employees. I was extremely proud to be on the front line of responsibility for insuring the best people were hired, served, motivated, and retained to help the company meet and exceed its business goals in a very competitive industry.

From the beginning, I was given an office, a private office, but nary a window to the outside world. In fact, the personnel department was totally configured with inside offices, not even the personnel manager had an outside view. He and none of the staff cared. I certainly didn't. Without a doubt, my new position gave me the chance to make important contributions to the success of the department and to ultimately become a personnel manager somewhere. Then a position with the perk of a prestigious corner window office would follow.

I'm certain I brought a confident demeanor to my new job though hidden, not allowed any power over performance, was fear. I was afraid of being fired without warning for reasons I had no control over, like business restructuring or job elimination.

Once years ago my father's impromptu verbal challenge had me considering, "Would you rather be a big fish in a little pond or a little fish in a big pond?" My unspoken answer was "Neither, I want to be a big fish in a big pond." No matter, I kept my thinking to myself, Daddy had launched into a lecture that resulted in opening my mind to understand the comfort or discomfort resulting from the choices and decisions one makes. The challenge of greater opportunity appealed to me. That is how I viewed a career in the profit sector, an opportunity for greater challenge with commensurate reward.

Even though fear resided in my subconscious, I knew each day I held my position in private industry meant another day for me to learn new things, develop new contacts, and leave behind noteworthy contributions building my employer's business, all leading to a stronger resume to take someplace else when necessary. If and when I had to hear "I'm sorry we have to let you go," I would be better equipped than when I came. Such optimism enabled me to shrug away the cautious counsel of friends and relatives who cared about the single mom with two children quitting the known for the unknown.

An overriding truth of significant importance to me was Equal Employment Opportunity was the law of the land and companies were trying to comply. In the decades before, courageous people sacrificed, some dying, in the turmoil leading to enacting the law. Did I not have the courage to accept the chance before me? My obligation was to stay on the path others made possible and face my challenge in my time. Plus, other blacks, close personal friends were doing fine in positions they accepted with IBM and Ralston Purina. I could thrive with my company.

* * * * * * * * * *

I gave amused thought to the weirdness of me working for a company manufacturing and marketing detergents to consumers. Never did I pay attention to detergents. Mother cared about brands and had been faithful to a particular washing powder, Rinso. As an adult, caring for my family, I still had no preference and bought whatever was on sale when I shopped. Now here I was with a vested interest in the profitability of several brands, none of them my mother's lifetime choice. Soon though, my family members, far and near, adopted the same product preference—brands produced by "Marva's company."

* * * * * * * * * *

The first morning on the job, my big boss, the personnel manager, appeared in my doorway with an invite. "Got time to go for a walk?" he asked. "Come on," he added, "Let's give you a tour of the place. Once you've seen it you may not want to stay," offered in a serious tone. I couldn't see his face as I trailed from my office, following him to the personnel department entrance. When he opened the door and stepped aside to let me exit ahead of him, I saw he was smiling. I did too. He was tall, good looking, well built, athletic, and blond, about my age, I guessed. He was a serious man with a good sense of humor. He filled the walking tour with information about the place as we went throughout the entire facility. I was totally impressed with the view standing on the catwalk high in the ceiling above workers on the production floor.

I cherish remembering him tell me, when we returned to my office, that I should read the files, thoroughly, any file, active and archived, all the records, any correspondence, files concerning selecting and hiring, recruiting, benefits, employee activities, employee grievances, anything I could put my hands or eyes on so I could better understand and know what we did and my role. "If you have questions, ask! And," he advised, "if someone asks you a question you can't answer or may not be certain of, there is nothing wrong with saying, 'I'll get back to you.'" That specific piece of advice was like gold. I did add my own mental caution—"and I *will.*" He reminded me I had supervisory responsibility for the medical department, so I should read the general administrative files as well. I learned the plant doctor came in on certain days. Introducing me to the plant's industrial nurse, a black woman who had been in the job for several years, he told me I would find her to be very helpful. (She was all that.) I was encouraged to become familiar with the names of people in corporate personnel in New York, their jobs, and their interactions with us at our location. I felt free to be the best I could be for *our* company.

He took me to sit in with the plant scheduler, a fantastic outgoing personality responsible for assigning hourly workers their weekly shift and shift rotation. The scheduler, his office next door to mine, our offices sharing a thin wall, was as forthcoming with his insight and observations as our personnel manager had been.

The plant operated twenty-four hours; three shifts of hourly/union workers came and went starting and ending their shifts (8–4, 4–12, or 12–8). As Mr. Scheduler introduced me to the intricacies of his work and the configuration of job assignments, engineering, production, packaging, warehouse, cleaning, and more on the weekly schedule (a huge, handwritten document), we were interrupted by workers sauntering in, having taken break time to see their scheduler and plea for assignment to a certain job or shift.

Undergirded by the union contract, bid sheets and seniority lists aided and guided Mr. Scheduler in making up the schedule. Some employees came into the office to see him to carefully complain because they didn't get the shift they posted for. I soon learned why they were careful in approaching the scheduler, not wanting to upset him. Sufficiently unhappy, he would let loose, yelling, occasionally using office-unacceptable vocabulary, especially when the guy or gal's manner was also candid, meaning rough tones and a four letter word or two spewed forth expressing displeasure for not getting "my shift." They usually ratcheted down their approach knowing they would need him for a scheduling favor later. Some times Mr. Scheduler popped into my office warning me to "expect a blowout when so and so comes in on second shift and sees his hours for the next week. I did all I could to give him what he wanted, I couldn't, not with 'whomever' out with the flu." In some cases, that person had learned his fate before reporting to work. He had called a friend working on shift who saw the posting. Not surprised, he still stopped in to see Mr. Scheduler but used civility, which served him well when he needed a particular shift another time; his understanding manner might garner an available favor. It was a "you owe me one" visit. Mr. Scheduler remembered, and if he had a favor he could extend, he did.

My position description called for me to back up the scheduler just as his called for him to fill in for me if needed. I for one prayed for Mr. Scheduler's continuing good health so I would never have to do his job.

For me, it was amazing that in the emotion-filled hoopla surrounding the scheduler's work I never heard or sensed racism in the drama. Many minorities, but far more nonminorities worked in the plant. Yet the problems he (and I) resolved were not a factor of race or ethnicity.

Sitting in the scheduler's office that afternoon, observing interactions between hourly workers and an employee with power and not hesitant to use gruff, rough language with those earnestly seeking favor, provided a quick and revealing insight into the company's character. Supplementing the personnel manager's professional, relaxed, informative tour, and his encouragement for me to get involved and "read the files" led me to conclude I was in an honest environment.

At the end of that first day, I walked out of the building and made it down the walkway to the employee parking lot and my car. I slid behind the wheel of the Impala convertible bought just nine months earlier in an attempt to be more attractive to the husband I would lose. I drove home to our children in the house with the white-picket-fenced backyard that he had relinquished in the divorce settlement. For the first time in a very long time, I wasn't sad. I was pleased with me. I was in a good place.

Chapter 35

What Now?

"It could be just loose cables. I'll come by the plant and take a look under the hood. If you need a new battery, I'll install it so you won't have trouble driving home. Is that okay?" Of course it was okay. The new man paying attention to me seemed to like doing all he could to make my life easier. He softened the edges of my days like I'd forgotten was possible.

Our romance started one night, several months before, in the grocery store. I had worked late and came home to put a healthy meal on the table and then sat to hear about Farah and Darin's school day and after-school doings in the neighborhood. Being teenagers, I knew they carefully selected what was willingly shared with their mom. I religiously put in "face time," asking questions when contributions were scant. That night, while they cleaned up the kitchen and got ready for bed, I dashed off to the store with my grocery list.

Maybe eight thirty or closer to nine, I was shopping, finding what I needed, and moving on to another aisle when Curt and I pleasantly acknowledged each other. We were not strangers; he was the scoutmaster, and both our sons were active participants. A cordial greeting became conversation that evolved into him apologizing for being bold as he declared, "I need a date. Would you consider going to a class-reunion dinner with me?" That's why he was in the grocery store, he explained. Time was running out for returning the RSVP; he wanted to go, but not alone. He had forced himself out of a depressed stupor to "get up, get dressed, go find someone, and ask her to go with you!" His plaintive honesty appealed to me. Plus his dilemma was a near-perfect scenario for how I envisioned meeting someone appropriate to bring home to my kids. His outreach brought to life my expectation that when God wanted me to meet the right man, he would cross my path as I went about involved in day-to-day interests and obligations.

His class-reunion evening was a comfortable storybook time. I was proud to be with Curt, a handsome, unpretentious, charming, interesting conversationalist. I could tell he was just as proud to have me by his side. After that "I'm sorry, please I need someone to go with me" date, Curt and I enjoyed each other's company watching TV, eating popcorn at the movies, dating with other couples, talking, just being together.

The day Curt replaced the convertible's failing car battery, he also cooked dinner, and my family ate with him and his family at their house that evening. He was a dedicated single parent of three, two girls and a boy. Their mother had died in a tragic accident. It seemed they loved their father in the same proprietary way my children loved me. Not one of the five saw a reason to be more than polite, pleasant, and respectful with any member of the other family. The dinner was one of our ongoing and low-keyed attempts to forge a bond between our children.

* * * * * * * * * *

Major staff changes announced in personnel merely weeks after I joined the department, resulted in Mr. Personnel Manager being promoted to an executive management position in corporate. He relocated to work in New York City. The assistant personnel manager moved up to fill his spot, and they brought a man from another plant to be the new assistant, therefore, my new boss. Departing personnel manager told me I had been considered for the assistant spot. My experience was too weak; I hadn't been there long enough. I was surprised and flattered to learn I was considered.

A new boss can be challenging as you respect the strengths and weaknesses he/she brings. Adjusting to my boss wasn't difficult. The opportunities to be helpful to him in his new situation enhanced my self-confidence. Also, I grasped much from the labor relations background he brought, having been a union officer in his former location. Basically, months became a year and more, and each day I was content, growing professionally, handling staffing, counseling, and disciplinary issues, employee programs, and other activities.

Election Day, November 1974 and I came to work, early as usual but in an unhappy tizzy. It all started on my way to work soon after leaving home when I breezed into my customary voting place and discovered my name not listed in the registration book. A poll worker brusquely announced, "Your polling place was changed." In answer to my quick, frustration-filled question, he professed, "You were notified more than a month ago, by mail. Your new polling place is"—and he directed me to a school many blocks in the opposite direction from the plant. Muttering a vow to vote on the way home that evening, not wanting to risk being late to work, I headed to the plant.

Driving along, angry because my intent to vote had been disrupted, I fantasized about it being a conspiracy to keep as many voters as possible from exercising their right. In the seventies, voting rights activists gave considerable oversight to insure fairness at polling places. My thing was to stay personally alert for unfair actions and speak up. That morning I wasn't in a trusting frame of mind, particularly since I convinced myself I wasn't sent the change notice.

Well, no matter the unexpected interruption, it wouldn't stop me from voting. I'd make sure to do it after work that evening.

You should know that several days after Election Day I discovered a notice of the new polling place did come in the mail at home many weeks earlier. I didn't notice it. No wonder. My busy life was crammed with various new urgencies on the home front as well as in the work place. The daily activities of children—a fourteen-year-old and twelve going on thirteen-year-old—wouldn't be ignored. Curt shared our time, thankfully. The company had finalized union negotiations at the plant, and we were busy implementing new contract provisions. On several levels, my life was anxious, yet good. At home I rushed to devalue unsolicited mail. No surprise a small, unexpected, preprinted postcard informing me of my new polling place had been pushed aside for reading, later, when I had the time.

Anyway, that Election Day I hurried into the personnel department, not in a pleasant mood, sharing my "I couldn't vote" experience with everyone and no one in particular. "I've got to leave tonight in plenty of time to vote before the polls close," I declared. Then I realized my *former* personnel manager was walking toward me from his former office. What a surprise to see him! No one had said he was coming out from New York. But there he stood, waiting patiently, for me—to run out of breath, I guess.

He quietly motioned me to follow him into the personnel manager's office.

"Was he there to fire me?"

There was no reason I knew of to do so, but I had been around long enough to know a staff reduction could happen and be a surprise. If I was the one from our small staff chosen to be axed, they might send him to do the dirty work. He had hired me. Perhaps they wanted me to hear the bad news from someone they felt I trusted. As I consciously adopted a confident casual stride, I considered how to respond to his devastating words. Not with malice, for sure. Since I came on board, there had been a cutback or two in the company. I had survived more than two years in the dream job opportunity I never expected to last forever.

Working for the state, I felt insulated from arbitrary downsizing. Back then, nothing seemed as secure as a government job, whether you were black or white. Knowing that, I still made the decision to abandon the security of civil service and sign on for the more lucrative promise a career in private industry offered my qualifications. I was glad I did.

Grimly, shoulders straight, I followed the executive from corporate headquarters into the personnel manager's office. He shut the door.

Many minutes later I walked out in shock. There was a position vacancy in corporate. I was to leave for New York City that evening for meetings with several people. Flight arrangements and a hotel reservation had been made. I was flying to LaGuardia and would be in Manhattan that night.

In the office, I had participated in a conference call, speaking with a warm genuine sounding man, the executive in New York who had the vacancy on his staff. He briefed me on the aspects of the job. They were looking for a personnel manager for their headquarters facility. The person reported to him replacing the incumbent, another woman, who had been promoted. He said my former personnel manager, now with an office that was down the hall from him, had begged him not to make a selection decision until he met me. I was totally stunned. Would I come to New York right away to sit down with several others and possibly the head of corporate personnel? Mostly he wanted the two of us to learn more about each other.

As I rushed home to pack, make child and home care arrangements, my mind pondered in slow motion, over and over—what would I wear to look like I belonged in New York City? Without a doubt I would go. It was a chance to see the Big Apple and see Harlem, both on my life list of things I hoped to do. As soon as I got home, I called Curt. His words mirrored my shock. He agreed the only appropriate action open to me was to be on that flight and go to New York and gather all the information and stay open to fully consider the possible offer. He insisted on taking me to the airport.

In New York, the interview experience was fabulous. The man who could become my new boss was as genuine in person as he had sounded on the telephone. I had open and pleasant conversations with his peers, and his boss, the top personnel division executive. A couple of the executives recalled our having spoken with each other during one of their visits to the plant, which I remembered and was pleased they mentioned. It was my birthday week, and the employee choir, in rehearsal when we peeked into the auditorium on an abbreviated tour of the building, serenaded me with "Happy Birthday."

I was comfortable with all I learned about the scope of the responsibilities, my co-workers at every level, my staff reports, and the work environment. Still, I was glad to do as suggested and not give my decision until I went home and did as was suggested, "talk to family and friends. Think about it carefully before you make your decision."

Analyzing the offer, facing the important issues the offer raised considering it all, was nothing but agony. Surely they were amazed when they saw the telephone bill for my hotel room. They didn't want my answer right away; still, I was on the phone all night to family in Ohio sharing the good news and seeking different perspectives rationalizing the answers to the questions tormenting me. What if they wanted me on board only to enhance their affirmative action reporting? What if I got out there and, knowing no one, could not adjust to the isolation from family and friends and thrive with only long-distance social support? What if my children would have problems making new friends? Wasn't it obvious I should stay where I was—comfortable and confident about everything?

What if I rejected the opportunity in New York? The job title fulfilled my goal and there was great opportunity for even more responsibility. But was it wise to uproot my children for my goal? If I rejected the offer, would I be considered for promotion at the plant if either of the two personnel spots ahead of me opened again? Now, I was better qualified and had more labor relations experience. However, I also realized the possibility of being offered promotion to assistant personnel manager no longer sounded attractive to me. Need I worry about growing a future in personnel with them? I had good contacts through my membership in various personnel associations in St Louis. A personnel manager position might be even more available to me in another company.

I returned to St. Louis, continuing agonizing deliberation to make the best decision. The second day back from New York I came home from the plant to find a packet of information mailed to me by my original personnel manager who had recommended me for the position. He commuted to the office every day from his home in New Jersey. He had packaged real estate sections from newspapers circulated in his town and those towns near to him. The packet also included information about schools in the areas for my children. His handwritten note scribbled the amazing suggestion that if I choose to live in his neighborhood or nearby, I could be in his carpool and ride into the office every day with them. It was apparent I need not fret about being enticed away and then ignored.

"Don't let 'us' get in the way of your decision," Curt solemnly demanded. "We'll be just fine. You think you want the job, take it. We'll find a way to see each other. Every two or three weeks I'll come there or you come here or we meet at an interesting place in between. If after three months or so you're certain the move is what you want, I'll relocate. I can get transferred to New York. If you realize you don't like the work, the people or being on the east coast, come back to St. Louis."

My children wanted to move. "It'll be exciting." They hoped I would accept.

* * * * * * * * * *

I turned down the offer in a telephone call to my would-have-been boss. "My children are at an age where I should know family or friends can fill in for me if necessary. I can't risk work demands getting in the way of attention they may need. My sincere thanks and appreciation for the offer, but it's not a good time for our family. I have to say 'no thanks.'"

My would-have-been boss sounded sincerely disappointed. He was a proud grandfather still very much involved in his grown children's lives. I could hear the truth in his voice as he told me he understood my decision. Then he added their insight, a group opinion from his peers in corporate, "Marva's children are in a perfect place in their lives for this move. One is in the last year of middle school, the other in the first year of high school." They'll be in after-school activities. She will be home soon after they are." To know they had the discussion touched me.

Hanging up the telephone from saying no, a great weight came off my shoulders. It didn't stay off.

My children were disappointed we were not going to New York, or New Jersey. Plus, my regular work always exciting to me was all at once only boring. I was not happy looking forward to rolling out projects I had in the planning stage. I had, so to speak, "seen the lights of the big city." Something more challenging in every aspect had been offered to me. "What could I have been thinking?"

The plant nurse, a good friend, helped me work through where I had taken myself. Learning I had said no, she dragged me to the quiet of the empty executive conference room, and forced me to talk about all my issues and made me explore whether I made the best decision when I said no. She was great.

I realized I had made a mistake turning down a challenging career opportunity in corporate headquarters. And relocating to the New York area held the promise of positive new experiences for both me and my children.

Before we left the conference room, I placed a call to the man who wanted me to work for him. He answered, not his secretary. I was relieved to get to him so quickly. I asked if I should congratulate him on having been able to find someone for the position.

"No, I'm afraid not. We're going back to the drawing board."

Through the connection, it was my impression I clearly surprised him when he heard me say, "I've been rethinking the opportunity of working for you and those personal factors that affected my decision. I've changed my mind."

"Are you saying you would accept the job?"

As hard as I tried, I couldn't read the disbelief I heard in his tone. Was he disappointed or merely stunned that I called with a change of mind? It had been weeks ago when I told the busy executives no. Had my inconsistency shown him I wasn't as smart as he had judged me? I should know life is faster than that in New York. Negativity darted about in my head, but my voice answered his question with a breezy, "Yes, I would."

There was no doubt he was thrilled with my yes. Hurriedly he asked me to stay on line while he told the news to his boss, whose voice I heard next. He too was pleased and had picked up the telephone to thank me.

I flew back to New York for the salary negotiations and to discuss relocation benefits and procedures.

In Richmond Heights, our modest brick ranch and white picket-fenced backyard was put on the market—a For Sale sign on the front lawn. Curt, understanding and committed to "us," helped in every way possible, encouraging me, working alone and with me to get the house in condition recommended by the realty company.

I made several trips to New Jersey to look for a new house. Other locations had been considered, New York, any of the five boroughs, even Connecticut. New Jersey won out when I learned Route 80 west from New Jersey was essentially a direct shot to the farming community of my family home on the Pennsylvania/Ohio state line. Also, family friends, Marge and Earl and their three daughters who once lived across the street from us in Richmond Heights, had moved to Teaneck, New Jersey, several years ago. Earl's company relocated him to the east coast to work for IBM. They since moved on to an assignment in Paris, but having seen the pictures of their Teaneck home, interior and exterior, and hearing of the good schools in Teaneck, the town received priority focus as a perfect home site for my family. With my boss's help and the company's labor relations director's assistance, I found the right house for us in Teaneck. I was shepherded so thoroughly by those considerate executives I wouldn't allow myself to succumb to the mind-boggling anxiety that stressed me when I thought deeply about the big step I had taken for our family. And there was Curt.

* * * * * * * * * *

Our new home was a well-maintained two-story older building with full basement, attractively paneled except for the furnace room and the laundry room. The owner had a plumbing business, and the house and garage reflected such with his neatly organized shelving and storage systems, particularly in the garage. There was ample accommodation for me, my children, Angel, our dog, and my sister, Kathleen, who now had her own apartment in St. Louis.

When Farah and Darin were well into their elementary school routine and could go to the home of a good friend and neighbor after school, Kathleen moved out on her own. We were still an important part of each other's lives, visiting on weekend days, her doing overnights once in a while. As I started planning the family's move, I encouraged Kathleen to consider moving also. "Out there public transportation is very good. The house is big enough for you to stay with us until you find a job and get your own place," I offered.

She did not want to leave St. Louis. I was relieved because I knew I would worry about her deciding to live in New York City. By this time, our brother Jim and his wife and family had a home in St. Louis. They vowed to give Kathleen good attention.

The day arrived when moving company folk in their small vehicle appeared as scheduled and packed up our home. The next day an impressively huge moving van came. Everything we owned, including my Impala convertible, was loaded into the van. We watched (along with every kid in the neighborhood, it seemed) as the moving van was driven away, disappearing from sight. The next day Farah, Darin, and I boarded a Newark Airport bound TWA airliner with Angel sedated in a cage in the luggage area. The move from friends and family was complete.

My career continued from an office with a huge window in a skyscraper on Park Avenue in New York City. I was a personnel manager.

Chapter 36

Acclimating

We were the second black family on that block in Teaneck, and very few others lived on surrounding streets, all of which warranted my awareness. Racially transitioning neighborhoods in America were known to experience news-making violence, but I didn't worry. I prayed those living in the seventeen other single-family homes on my block were similarly nonchalant about accepting us. Teaneck's reputation for valuing diversity strengthened my faith we wouldn't have any problem. Privately I steeled myself to ignore For Sale signs should they sprout on lawns when warm weather came. It would be too depressing to think folk were running from my beautiful family. None of it happened. From the beginning, neighbors were welcoming and friendly or respectful, cordial strangers. Many years later, I was momentarily offended to learn erroneous information had circulated that my home was bought for me, a single black mother, through a welfare program.

Our move from Missouri took place in February 1975. Family from Ohio came several times that first spring. We had a good time introducing them to New York City, the boroughs, Harlem, the stadiums, museums, and Broadway and locating and exploring other tourist sites and amenities. Friends from the St. Louis area visited to share in helping us acclimate. Between hosting visitors, bouts of loneliness were tough, especially on the weekends.

Anticipating those weekends absent the interaction of family or old friends was sad though all had assured me they were only a long-distance telephone call away—hoping to hear from us. So call! We did. A couple times I placed telephone calls to Shirley in Kirkwood, Missouri, knowing no one was home. The continuing ring of the phone on an end table in a room so well known transported me from strange to familiar surroundings and contentment.

* * * * * * * * * *

Subtly a chameleon quickly changes colors melding into her environment for survival. How long would it take me to adjust and phase into my new environment? Handling the commuting process was my sole responsibility. How long would it take to build physical stamina to comfortably make the trek every day into mid-Manhattan? When would confidence kick in, and I would blend into the mosaic of strangers rushing on a path to where they needed to be? When would I, like the chameleon, match my environment?

Before we left St. Louis, among the first tasks I gave myself for succeeding on the east coast was buying fashionable, comfortable, business-appropriate shoes for the walking I knew the future held. No such shoe could be found in stores throughout St. Louis city and county, whatever the price range of their stock.

"Since no one else is providing the product, perhaps I should," I rhetorically considered, "You could cancel the relocation and stay in St. Louis, open shops selling attractive, comfortable footwear to career women and get rich." Instead I shelved the futile search for shoes and came east hoping for the best. There I discovered many lovely and comfortable styles.[21] I was in a market where the call for walking shoes flourished. NYC's pedestrian traffic crowded sidewalks block to block unlike St. Louis where walkways were virtually empty except for those going from parking spot to door. Obviously there was an insufficient market in St. Louis to support allocating valuable shelf space to attractive walking shoes.

* * * * * * * * * *

Daily commuters into Manhattan mostly left their cars home. If they drove in, the car was parked in a space or garage, and they proceeded to their destination, on foot or via taxi, bus, or subway. I walked, a lot!

I never seriously considered joining a carpool. Accessible and varied public transportation was my preferred mode of travel. Early mornings found me trudging the five blocks or so from my house to board a New Jersey transit bus. I could take the bus across the George Washington Bridge into the Port Authority Bus Station in uptown Manhattan. Then I marched downstairs to the subway tracks and got on the "A" Train to mid-Manhattan. However, my preferred route was the bus to the midtown Port Authority. It meandered east and then south through several New Jersey towns alongside the Hudson River and east into the Lincoln Tunnel. Exiting the tunnel, a few turns of the bus's big black wheels took us into mid-Manhattan's Port Authority Bus Terminal.

Once in the Port Authority, I might go downstairs—several flights downstairs—and board the subway that whisked me to within half a block of my building. It was a perfect thing to do in inclement weather.

Or I could depart my commuter bus and go down one level through the hustle and bustle of the main terminal floor and outside to Eighth Avenue. After a brisk saunter twenty or so blocks across town, I would be at my building. Other options included hopping a cab on Eighth Avenue, with several persons sharing, or boarding the cross town bus and hopping off a block or so from St. Patrick's Cathedral, within four or five blocks of my destination.

Mainly due to finding it easier to travel in advance of the crowd, whatever mode of transportation I used, I established a habit of getting to the office early.

* * * * * * * * * *

Curt had been one of the first visitors to us in New Jersey. He came for several days gaining assurance Farah, Darin, and I were secure; the house, grounds, and garage had no needs he couldn't correct. The four of us went sightseeing in New York, went to Coney Island, drove through surrounding New Jersey towns and neighborhoods and especially to those places such as the post office, schools, grocery stores, and malls and other shops we were likely to frequent on a regular basis. When Curt's visit ended, I was comforted feeling he knew as much about our new environment as we did.

Business related to relocation matters took me back to St. Louis several times. On one such visit, Curt and I faced the fact that I passionately wanted the relocation and my career change to succeed. Worse, I failed to evidence equal passion for our relationship. Communication was strained. Curt and I agreed to free each other from our commitment, and in fact, break up entirely. Melancholy would ever after cloud my trips to St. Louis.

* * * * * * * * * *

My children gave me no real problem in school or at home. On the job, I was able to project the impression career was my priority. Farah and Darin knew better. I had accepted the change to enrich *our* lives. I was grateful every day to trust they were doing their part while I did mine. We were a unit well aware of the importance of my work to our family. The three of us knew family came first.

Chapter 37

Because of My Father

Sunday, the day after Christmas in 1976 and my two children and I were well established in Teaneck, New Jersey. We were approaching two years in our new community. We were comfortable in the house my employer generously helped me purchase after our home in Missouri was put on the market for our relocation to the east coast. My two teenagers were out with friends. I was home, unhappy, and lonely.

I decided a glass wall surrounded me, a barricade to being the socially adept woman I yearned to be. When I was a kid in Zanesville, Ohio, my mind started building the wall subsequently fortified each time no was the answer to my request for permission to be with friends. My father's dogmatic proclivity to raise his children his way, especially his girls, kept us close to home and family. I learned how to have a good time alone, all by myself.

As a teenager, the restriction continued because we were black, the only black family in our farming community. Interaction with wonderful school friends was limited to the school day only. It was Daddy's tactic for insuring his children not face racial problems among strangers because we were black. I tolerated the restriction with minimal objection as I looked forward to social freedom after high school attending a historically black college in the South.

But a habit had taken root, and unfortunately I wouldn't shatter the class wall excluding me from having fun with friends. Matriculating at AM&N in Pine Bluff, Arkansas, because I was usually short of funds, I declined invites. I gave carefully planned excuses for not participating while vowing to myself, "one day I'll go to movies, shopping, parties, and dances." I was content keeping busy completing work-related goals, either volunteer campus activities or money-earning projects.

Now here I was a successful adult in the midst of Christmas season. I was depressed, close to tears because I couldn't look forward to a festive evening mingling with friends. I knew I was responsible for my unhappiness.

"Make your situation improve," I chastised me. "You can do it."

Thoughtfully questioning why the problem existed, I heard my mind say, "It's Daddy's fault you're adrift socially. His parenting strategy ruined your ability to overcome social shyness and encouraged you to drift happily into time-consuming personal pursuits all by yourself."

It was time to find a solution. I had an invitation to a cocktail party—the next night! But I didn't want to walk in without a male companion. "Now, in all honesty," I thought, "Why would I saddle my psyche with such an unsolvable burden? Just admit you don't want to be there."

I realized I was who I was because of past experiences. And it wasn't all bad, not at all. Quite honestly, I was living a wonderful life. And that too was Daddy's fault, in a good way. His planning, intentional parenting, and attention to achieving goals enabled me to achieve my cherished goals. I had a family to love, who loved me. I was a black woman employed as a corporate personnel manager, in a career I sorely wanted. Those realizations soothed my anxiety over what was missing in my life.

My parents raised four boys and four girls—now adults making our own choices, doing as we please. Not everyone followed Daddy's plan, but each, within his or her family and/or community, became a self-sufficient, caring, constructive human being.

All at once totally positive emotions broke through my morass. "Thank God for my dad," I thought. Maybe I thought I was socially adrift at this time because my career had taken me away from the comfort of family and old friends. But I was succeeding in the business world just as my father predicted would be an option for me and black folks in America. My father had to give up his Zanesville Black Stars baseball team, but I had achieved as he said I could. I was his Black Star girl. All at once I was filled with gratitude for him having been the goal-tending dad he was.

That night, alone with myself, pleased my children were having a good time with their friends, I lamented them not knowing how hard their grandfather worked as a parent to give me my future. They wouldn't know the sacrifices, the difficult challenges, and hard work he consistently faced, and the constant thinking and fearless negotiating he employed enabling me and them to live as we did and dare anticipate even better futures for them.

They were growing up in an America where black men were likely to be disparaged as patriarchs, rarely given good press. In fact, the man I married, their dad, was not participating in their lives. My father had been an involved parent, his priority—the well-being of his family. I started thinking about recording the stories I knew and the experiences I lived, documenting his leadership and what it meant to my own success. If I wrote it down my children could leisurely read about the qualities of Daddy and Mother's diligence that instilled strengths necessary to bring me and them through the not so easy times to the life we lived. In turn the children they might one day have would know about a black father they could be proud of. And, other black children could have knowledge of a black man who was not a public icon, but contributed so much good during his lifetime. I could write a book celebrating a black man who was an involved patriarch!

Sitting at the typewriter that evening, I forgot about being lonely. No longer did I envision an interested, interesting man, my date beside me at a cocktail party, us laughing, in exhilarating conversation. There was work to do. I would write a book.

Chapter 38

Accomplishments

Adjusting to working in corporate, the procedures and personalities wasn't difficult. There were brief distressing thoughts wondering how I was perceived by peers, subordinates, employees, vendors, anyone doing business with me. I worked through a period of self-questioning. Do they think I'm qualified? Do they think I'm in this job just because I'm black? Do they like working with me? As New York City's mayor, Ed Koch, in later years, profusely welcomed critique, I secretly challenged me, "how am I doin'?" The self-questioning was short lived. I was doing just fine.

As the only new gal or guy in corporate personnel, everyone could teach me something. By listening to co-workers at all levels, in all departments, asking questions of anyone, sitting in on meetings, speaking up to offer unexpressed perspective, hearing honest feedback, in no time all new-person insecurities vanished. I felt at home.

We were an intensely busy personnel function. My department handled staffing concerns, i.e., recruitment, selection, hiring (and terminating), counseling, and disciplining, for every department in corporate. We administered and monitored employee benefit plan provisions for each employee. The company was committed to being a socially responsible employer in the community. Our department developed and managed employee-driven activities such as the Blood Donor Drive, United Way Campaign, and U.S. Savings Bond Drive. Considering all the daily tasks involved in our work, the volumes of written and spoken communication, record keeping, evaluation, and tremendous unplanned employee and public contact, it's no wonder a day in the office exceeded eight hours. It was fast-paced work adding value to the business.

Promotion from the plant into corporate personnel afforded several opportunities for me to realize visible accomplishments beyond handling, streamlining, or improving routine tasks. I recall with pride achievements such as (a.) the development and establishment of a job posting program. Thanks to my director's unflappable support, we introduced the program and opened up the process for employees to be considered and chosen for promotional job opportunities outside their own department. (b.) I also set up a process for employees to purchase at discounted prices a broad range of the company's popular product line. This was the forerunner to a sophisticated company store eventually available to employees and retirees. (c.) Recruitment, placement, and retention of candidates and employees with the best of credentials from every sector of the population flourished under my watch.

Several years after coming into headquarters, I was given a lateral promotion—a change in title and responsibilities, as well as an increase in salary. I appreciated the recognition. The promotion also awakened and encouraged my serious attention to career-expanding opportunities available in other divisions.

The company's marketing function—creative, quantitative, and staffed with vibrant professionals—appealed to me. I realized I should attempt a career in the field when a marketing manager conferring with me on an unrelated matter had reason to casually remark "we round off at $50,000 projecting costs for most marketing projects." Our department budget provided no such largesse, and personnel, not a profit center, didn't have the lucrative salary ranges marketing worked with to highly compensate their staff.

Later, expressing official interest in an entry-level assistant brand manager position, I was shaken to get an immediate thumbs down. "What have you ever marketed?" I was asked while being gently dismissed as a viable candidate for personnel to recommend. I didn't hear a good reason for the early rejection, and I knew the hard qualifications of others interviewed, so it was convenient for me to surmise if I were not a black woman but a white male with my credentials, proven abilities, and interest, I would have gotten an interview. It was one of those incidents my father had warned I might face, and determined it was best to go pleasantly on my way, to "fight" another day for something more important to me and my family. That is what I did.

The experience reminded me of the time back in the plant when my request for approval to take a labor relations course at Washington University given on company time and at company expense (all of which was not unusual) was denied even with my moderate persistence. Then I thought if I had been a white male with my credentials and potential, I would not have been denied.

I held no grudge in either instance. Those were two times I let patience and understanding of the real world guide me to accept the imperfections of life I felt.

* * * * * * * * *

Some nine years after I arrived in New York, the company purchased the corporate property of a company that had moved its headquarters to Detroit. The beautiful grounds and building were located in a nearby suburban New Jersey community.

I was named to the management team selected to convert the building and restructure it for our company. Entire departments would be relocated from Manhattan to provide several functional support activities for headquarters.

My responsibility would be to lead in configuring and structuring the personnel function. If I accepted the charge, I was also agreeing to a change of work location from my headquarters office to be the on-site personnel manager of the new facility.

It was a confusing offer to consider. It was not a promotional opportunity, i.e., no increase in grade level. Plus, I did not relish leaving the hustle and bustle of Manhattan. After all, a big incentive for relocating my family those many years ago from Missouri was the opportunity to be in exciting Manhattan. Still, I could not ignore the elation that crept into my emotions as I considered the promise the exciting challenge offered.

Should I accept or reject the offer? If I said "no thanks," I would remain where I was (for how long, who knew?) and watch and hear the achievements of another that could have been mine. The assignment promised significantly broader business exposure with new experiences. Clearly, I was proud to have been tapped for the position. I accepted the offer.

What I did not ignore was the existence of the glass ceiling, a most appropriate word visual. The term, frequently explored in print and talk news media, invited discerning attention to the plight of women (and minorities) in management, elevated to within sight of (not into) the decision-making power circles in the business world. Very few women were hired for these highly compensated positions. They couldn't break through the invisible barricade keeping them down. Rarely did you hear of a woman promoted to bonus level or into a job level affording the prestige of being on the policy-setting team getting for themselves and their families the first-class perks conferred on top-level executives. Talented proven women *could* expect an in-grade promotion, salary increase, and a grander job title with opportunity to feed critical information to the powerful. It was with gratitude I accepted such an enhanced new position available to me although under the glass ceiling.

I appreciated the moderate increase in pay and anticipated an exciting future in our expanded organization. Managing a range of tasks structuring the company's newest facility, it was an appreciated dynamic time. Coordinating with facility and space planners, engineers, technology experts, furniture vendors, and others was exhilarating. We collaborated to configure the human resources department, cafeteria, and medical department and company store. Engineering, IT systems, financials, distribution, and other departments were completed, and on schedule, hundreds of employees and their operations moved from our Manhattan headquarters into fresh, modern, state-of-the art equipped offices in the suburbs of NYC.

I cautioned myself to remain career growth oriented, avoid becoming career comfortable as I proudly settled in, the only personnel executive in our company's newest business location. There was no indication my future was far from the promise implied with my new responsibility.

Chapter 39

Cautious Optimism

As we adjusted in our new work site, corporate was adjusting to a new vice president of human resources. He was, of course, also my new "big boss." Holding forth in the prestigious corner office on the HR floor in headquarters, he was generating mild hysteria among the staff. Everyone was concerned about the new and different perspective he brought to HR. No longer in the building, my distant but still close peers kept me apprised by telephone of every little concern.

This important new hire replaced the personnel executive who approved my promotion to corporate manager in the seventies. He had retired several months earlier. His position remained vacant for some time, which encouraged much internal companywide speculation about how the board of directors would fill the spot. Would one of the fine executives on board be elevated? Would someone be brought in from another company location for the job? Would an executive from a sister company in the United States or another part of the world be transferred to New York? The answer was, "none of the above." Our new vice president was hired "off the street," as is said when the individual hired is new to the company. His performance credentials were earned in other companies.

One or two incumbent directors had been disappointed at not being selected. After all, an internal vice-president vacancy doesn't occur that often for those in line, qualified for consideration. The guy who hired me, the boss I left when I took the position in the suburbs, decided to take early retirement. Managers were dealing with some insecurity about their own future. Who wouldn't survive the change at the top? It was known that a new leader from the outside brings a new broom to sweep out the old. Plus, it was not at all unusual for an executive new to a company to get creative with staff changes and make room for people he knew and trusted to come join his team. Who would be replaced?

I wasn't worried. I was in a brand new location, part of a fresh strategy for the company's operation, and everything was going great. It was too early for us to be disrupted. New VP's attention was elsewhere, I was certain. All I had to do was—maintain! I looked forward to meeting and knowing our new boss.

I did become somewhat concerned when several weeks had gone by, and telephone conversations with the folks in headquarters began to include the questions, "Have you met him yet? Has he been over there?" I had not met him and comfortably assumed he had not been to *my* building because I *had not* met him. Midmorning one day I picked up my telephone to hear, "What did you wear today?" A management peer in corporate continued to say VP was on his way over to me. I thought her question a strange one because everyone knew appropriate corporate dress was my style. Why was my appearance of concern? The question was worrisome.

To this day I do not recall anything significant about our first meeting, my new division leader and me. He impressed me as a confident, capable person. Perhaps, though, because of the warmer persona of his predecessor I was not drawn to the new VP's more gregarious attitude and blustery communication style. The difference was, in no sense of the word, a problem.

It was our next meeting I'll never forget because of how my life was affected by what I heard him proclaim to me as important in his future plans for personnel, i.e.

(a.) "A person of your high level is not needed here."

(b.) "I want you to come back to headquarters and be on my team with responsibility for headquarters and this place. A personnel supervisor for this facility will report to you."

(c.) "It will be your responsibility to prove both functions can be effectively merged as a corporate personnel operation."

(d.) "Your title will be manager, corporate headquarters personnel."

(e.) "You will have to spend a day or two each week out here."

Hearing it all, there was logical reason for me to be confident about my future in his organization.

My new VP's conversation ended when he stood up to give a charming but absolutely firm no to my suggestion I remain at that site through the end of the year, only weeks away.

"We need you now!" he said briskly, sternly. "Be in New York bright and early Monday morning." It was Friday.

I forced positive thoughts because I didn't trust in his fine words that did not match his body language or his lack of eye contact. I wouldn't let myself be consumed with worry. Perhaps if what he said was subterfuge, it was for good reason. My new VP wanted me nearby in headquarters so he could confirm, first hand, I legitimately qualified for a director's spot on his team. I might replace the great guy I had worked for, who retired soon after new VP came. Did I believe that? Not really. The thought resulted from the thinking necessary for my mind to weave a safety net of positive emotions and possibility enabling me to constructively respect new vice president's authority.

My former immediate boss in his last days with the company came out from Manhattan for a farewell visit. Early in our conversation behind the closed door of my office, I caught a sense of resignation that his best times in the company had passed. The future held nothing for him to look forward to. It was time to do something else with his life, thus his retirement decision.

"It seems it's going to be a significantly changed organization," I threw the words out. Hoping for any insight he had about my future in our "different" division, I added, "I know I'm not retirement eligible. It might be a time for me to take a look at opportunities in other companies."

He cautioned I should think it through, keeping in mind many find the grass is not always greener on the other side.

My mentor, classy, so professional, and such an executive gentleman, exited my office with parting words I translated as "Watch out."

My retiring former director's visit was weeks before the power of new VP walked directly into my world verbalizing promise while leaving me with a sense of foreboding.

I began to focus on the obvious problem for me right then. I was being removed from the position that fully utilized my knowledgeable, caring, confident management style. The reason for dislodging me suggested a hidden agenda. My father's teachings when I was in high school came to mind. His parental caution was to think through a problem and prepare myself to handle what I could see, and also be prepared for what was possible though not apparent. Discrimination might be the real issue, and Daddy said how I responded would be critical for my survival. Intelligent attention to the issue, not emotion, had to be my approach.

Eventually I knew survival was important to me. I wanted to continue a career with the company that had been so good to me. The new VP said I must return to my office in NYC, so that was going to happen. I had known only respect interacting with my employer. If respect continued, surviving would not be a problem.

Chapter 40

The Return

As soon as new VP departed our building, I rushed to my site boss, the director of the facility. I don't know why I was surprised he knew about the change and had not given one tiny hint of what was to befall me.

In a detached manner, he coolly placated me with, "Do the best you can. Get all your personal things together. Leave any business for your replacement to handle." There was no "congratulations on your new job," only his advice that said it all and gave credence to my skeptic reservations. I could not relax on laurels I must not have. I had to be a civil but conscientious participant in what was going on, whatever it was intended to accomplish. My future well-being was up to me.

My exit had to be organized. I couldn't sever my association with the employees, department managers, and all others I served by abruptly disappearing. Every ongoing project involved other departments and affected daily schedules of more than me. Contacts had to be made.

I vowed to do all I had the power and resources to accomplish. My objective was to insure my reputation was not tainted by the self-serving manipulations of anyone coming to manage my domain after me. I would leave no opportunity for anyone to negate or co-opt my production in the time I was in charge. I couldn't just go away, worrying my achievements (more likely to be conveyed as my lack of achievement) would be left to "their word against mine." I would document.

I worked day and night throughout the weekend until Sunday night. While packing what was business related to take back to Manhattan, I reviewed every file, making sure they were complete and in order. I was returning to a smaller office that couldn't accommodate all my personal artifacts, so some were packed for storage at home.

Thankfully, I realized if I distributed A Status of the Business Report, my future with the company might be better protected. I knew I had to do it, so I did. The report, directed to my immediate boss, detailed what had been accomplished in the setup of our new personnel function. It described how the office was maintained; referencing files, forms, and procedures we developed and used to serve the employees and the company. I also crafted a detailed report of the status of my unfinished projects and included a forecast of activities and objectives planned for attention in the coming year. I thanked my boss for his always supportive oversight. Though directed to him, several others were copied, including the new personnel VP, and his boss, the corporate VP, and the man coming out to replace me. Each would have documentation conveying my understanding of the scope of my responsibilities together with my future goals for human resources in that location. I took ownership of everything that had been done and quite possibly everything that might be done by those who came behind me.

At the end of that last Sunday, my office and projects were thoroughly organized as if the order to vacate had been long anticipated. In the dusky evening light, I backed my white two-door Mercury Cougar onto the oversized walkway to the building, as close as I could to the double doors that led to my personnel suite. Still working alone, I carried, lifted, and tugged the many stuffed boxes, loading everything into the limited space of the fancy car (red velvet upholstery) I had bought only months before to drive to and from work in suburbia. I anchored a bright and breezy note to the desk of my office assistant and left another for my replacement, on his desk.

In the morning, once in the company garage, there would be plenty of building service workers very pleased to make certain I would not have to lift another box or anything I packed in that car. In fact, I was honored to have received several calls from building service guys who had heard I was returning. Congratulating me and welcoming me, they volunteered, "We need you." Those guys would do everything possible to ease my return to the building.

That evening, though, my heart was heavy as I drove off the grounds, away from the sprawling building in the middle of the thick green grass carpeted landscape. I had lost my wonderful office suite in one of the most lucrative high-end business-zoned suburban enclaves across the Hudson from Manhattan. As I headed down the highway, my mood brightened. It was my son's birthday weekend. I had not taken time to give his birth milestone any attention. Now I could. It was a joy to be heading home to family.

* * * * * * * * * *

The next morning it was kind of neat leaving home early heading for New York City. I was actually excited driving down Route 4 and then across the George Washington Bridge.

I took the Eastside Drive into Harlem, then through Central Park, and into mid-Manhattan returning to the headquarters building that had been my home away from home for so many years.

The garage attendant and other building service staff fulfilled my expectations. They gathered around as I drove down the ramp and stopped at the end by the office. Their warm welcome helped me believe the new chapter I was beginning was a good one. Following my car to a parking space against the far wall, the guys converged on me again and insisted I not take out anything. "We'll get everything up to you right away."

"To your old office?" one of them asked.

"Yes, thank you," I said stepping into the elevator. Up I went to my office with a window, high in the skyscraper glass and stone edifice in corporate posh, mid-Manhattan.

Chapter 41

New Attitudes

That first morning I scarcely had time to flip on the light switch and scan the familiar small office when new VP sauntered in. He offered no "good morning" only abruptly ordered, "Fill the secretarial openings. Get applicants in here to interview."

The warm fuzzy exchanges moments ago with the garage staff were memories I struggled to secure for future reference. Pleasant times ahead might be elusive.

Thank God I was able to articulate an agreeable response to his secretarial recruitment directive, a task not usually a priority on the manager's plate. Shaking off negativity, since time with a VP is precious, I attempted to share a first step planned to begin overseeing the satellite office. "I'll give Art and Stacy a call shortly. No one will be in before eight."

"Don't worry about that office anymore," he ordered. "The nonexempt openings in here need to be filled." And he added, "Get the United Way campaign going! It is long overdue." Then he slipped in a bombshell pronouncement. "Your new boss will be here on December 11."

Uh Oh! So I was not being considered a candidate for the director's spot. Feeling crazy, but keeping a sane face, I threw down, quietly. "A new boss is coming?" Out went the positive spin I had crafted as reason for his abrupt change to my career path.

"I'm the best boss you could name," I actually challenged, trying to look into his face that wasn't looking at me.

He went on like I had not spoken. "He's a good guy, comes from (named a major company in the area) where he was a director. You'll learn a lot from him."

I'm thinking, "Why come here for another director's spot? What kind of problem did he have there?" Then, my mind mumbled, "He will learn just as much from me, without a doubt."

* * * * * * * * *

My new boss came on board eight days later. He was a tall guy whose appearance and manner met my expectations for a corporate executive—one I would choose *not* to work for. His swagger, tone of voice, disdain for others as he sauntered through the department implied he was in charge—of something. Yet as I struggle to describe him in one word, "pompous" comes quickly to mind.

Early his first morning, as we were introduced, he favored me with a cold facial expression, eyes partially open, averted, no direct gaze, and a weak smile, more of a grimace. A bit later, I invited him to come to the auditorium for the United Way kick-off campaign meeting I had organized as directed. I felt pushed aside with his reaction, i.e., eyes still not meeting mine, a negative shake of his head, a wave of his hand, and in a bland tone, saying dismissively, "have a good meeting."

Sensing the smile still on my face, I hastened its disappearance and pleasantly, solemnly, and gratuitously perhaps continued with, "I was looking forward to introducing my new boss to the team captains."

He walked on, turning his back to me, head weaving side to side in tiny motions that said, "Don't bother me," and then quickly extended a cheery greeting to grab a passing manager's attention.

"That's it," I confirmed to myself as I turned and walked in the opposite direction. "He's been told 'she's got to go'!"

If I was to survive, my work was cut out for me. I was not wanted.

At the end of the week, the new director entered my office saying he wanted us, the secretary and our receptionist (both reported to me), in the conference room for a meeting—*now*. I said, "Okay, they're not here, but I'll get them. We'll be right down."

"Don't worry about it," he waved that hand again and strolled down the hall. "Just come on down."

I grabbed a legal pad and hurried after him hoping my staff would show up soon and not be late for our first meeting with the new boss. We entered the room, me following him, and there sitting around the conference table were "my people" chatting with each other.

"Oh, there you are," I had to say nonchalantly or risk my face showing how stunned I was to see them. He had sent my reports to the conference room—but made it a point not to tell me.

After my initial discomfort, his meeting was somewhat of a blur of nonsense. I do recall he told us we were all on equal footing. My two subordinates let a momentary look of amazement come my way. I froze. I was their boss, we thought. I guess I was *not* their boss. Then as he concluded his meeting, he gave a deep chuckle and proclaimed, "The important thing to keep in mind is I'm here to have fun! Let's do it!"

I shivered, mentally.

I had to be smart—work through the turmoil at hand and reverse any strategy in place for derailing my career. Pleasant, respectful patience and hard work had to be the foundation of my response to their kind of leadership. But in no way would I turn into an Aunt Jemima or an Aunt Tomisina—smiling and serving, grinning and bearing. Neither was I about to fall on my knees in blind reverence to their misuse of power.

For me, equal opportunity became meaningful in a different way, one that helped me deal with the situation changing my business environment. It meant I had equal opportunity to confront them. It meant I could use our company's organization and experts on my behalf when necessary to protect my well-being. It was my right and responsibility to do so.

If the newly hired executives had declared war on me, so be it. To date, nothing illegal had happened. True, I felt mistreated, lied to, excluded—all I viewed as them purposefully disrespecting me. I devised a totally private plan, a new goal. I was hanging tough, not quitting. I would be a formidable opponent of their strategy.

Chapter 42

I Shall Overcome

I recalled my father's admonishment to be wary of camouflaged crap that could turn a pleasant prospect into the exact opposite, something terribly unpleasant. It was his parable-like caution to be alert for "the most delicious looking frosting to be hiding 'doo-doo' underneath" (Daddy never used that other word!). I was alert for more than was apparent.

What was the "real" reason new VP removed me from the HR manager's position? Hearing him say he "needed my expertise" in headquarters generated skepticism that I desperately tried to deflect. After all, he had been onboard a month or more before sharing his assessment that I was so competent he wanted me near him.

Whatever his reason I chose to latch onto the positive premise that he wanted me nearby because he was considering me for his director's vacancy. That was proven wrong, so what was the ultimate goal for uprooting me so abruptly? I was afraid.

Intellectually I determined I shouldn't confront him; I didn't have enough information. Truthfully, I didn't have the courage to confront him. All at once from my office high above Park Avenue, there was strong indication my career was on a smooth path—downhill. What to do?

As a black woman, I needed to keep proper perspective for what was important, i.e., recognize illegal actions against me by my employer resulting in harm to my employment status. I was protected by EEO laws. If I did not use those laws, the men, women, and children in the civil rights movement who battled for the better life blacks like me had gained would have suffered in vain. I vowed not to be a party to that. So going forward, my attitude and actions had to be based on fact, not how I felt. I would seek redress from the courts if necessary. To discourage emotion overriding fact, I copiously journaled troubling experiences noting my anxious thoughts.

* * * * * * * * * *

"Life is not fair," new VP volunteered one day. I saw no reason to respond. I didn't and just filed his four-word declaration in my brain—an important "take away," a learning from my powerful corporate executive. He had poked his head in my doorway while on the way to his office down the hall. I never mentioned "fair" or "fairness" in conversation with anyone. Thus, his statement telling me, "We're all subjected to unfairness," was taken by me as strong indication I was under the leadership of a workplace superior who was not pleased with the outcome of the '60s civil rights movement.

"Life is not fair" arbitrarily spoken to me that day suggested he would be deliberate in demonstrating how *lawfully* unfair they could be to me. Yet the information humbled me; it wakened me to realize having grown up black in a white-powered world, I had subconsciously ignored how rampantly unfair human beings are to each other no matter race, gender, etc. Not withstanding that truth, I knew my circumstances were different. Civil rights activists whose persistence enabled me to have a corporate management career hadn't sacrificed in vain. The laws their brilliance, pain, and suffering brought about wouldn't be ignored.

* * * * * * * * * *

I had to be careful and wise. I may have been his only black manager, but I was not the only manager subjected to change, change that so far had not affected my livelihood and status in company records. It was important that I take every undesirable experience one incident at a time. I invited positive thought to prevail. I was open for career-beneficial opportunities on my new VP's team.

I devised a survival plan, the foundation being I would not quit. I wouldn't run because I was miserable or because they were unkind. Others had suffered to get me there; I could suffer to persevere. We black managers new in the corporate world were charting different territory. Just because the law enabled us to file for legal redress, it wasn't the only option. My predicament would be addressed to my satisfaction by challenging the bad actors among the powerful white men in suits who challenged me in "our" company.

It was clear I preferred anticipating the defeat of my adversaries on their playing field rather than getting a few dollars in a legal settlement. After all my father had taught, "money does not guarantee happiness." Plus, the burial of any management malfeasance in thick manila folders filled with wordy depositions and wordy responses eventually hidden in law offices of government and private industry would only help the perpetrators, not the brothers and sisters coming behind me.

The demoralizing workplace tactics bordering on illegal must cease. That was my objective. Throughout the years, I used my expertise to help employees correct unacceptable behavior that hindered their own advancement or threatened their continued employment. When it was the manager at fault in the interaction with the employee, I worked with the manager to improve his/her people-handling technique and get better results from staff. Now, my skills had to be effectively used on my behalf. As a long-term, experienced, personnel executive, if anyone could meet the challenge, I could.

Chapter 43

And Then

It was obvious to everyone in headquarters I was persona non grata. The big bosses didn't initiate conversation with me as had been my customary experience; would-be peers and others were careful not to be friendly when bosses were around. I was engaged in a conflict that would endure for five years.

My responsibilities were diminished.

I was excluded from management meetings.

My office was moved several times, always to a more undesirable location.

I was assigned different managers to report to.

I was demoted.

I was not given a raise in salary, again, and again, and again and...

I was given an unsatisfactory performance review.

I was told to leave if I was unhappy.

I got through it all by counseling myself, willing thoughts for my opponents to act on. "If you want to fill my job category with a new body, more personally attractive to you, just move me along in *this* organization. Keep me, use my expertise, my work ethic, and promote me. Worst case scenario—let me go. Respect me with direct action, honesty. Tell me I am fired. State your reason for terminating my employment. All my best thinking cannot come up with a lawful legitimate reason to be relieved of my employment, so without a doubt, I will file a charge of unlawful discrimination against you and the company I've been proud to highly regard. I do have evidence of your unlawful tactics detrimental my employment situation."

After only a few months, working under the new management, it was clear I had come face to face with discriminating tactics because of my color and my physical appearance. I was never slim and svelte but didn't let being overweight impede my confidence and my performance. Privately, being overweight concerned me. In fact many, many years ago when I was asked to go to New York to interview for the job in corporate a first thought was, "haven't they been told how fat I am?"

Whenever discussion of weight surfaces, I tell folk it's a good thing dieting was a routine habit of mine since I was twelve years old. Otherwise my physical health would not be as good as it is. Thanks to several dieting regimens I learned much about nutrition and exercise which I incorporated into my daily living.

Though I never got a handle on controlling emotional factors that engender weight gain, I maintained a healthy, positive attitude about who I was.

Frequently, humor, always private humor, managed to relieve any harmful anxiety I might harbor about being an overweight person. Here's an example. It's a note I recently discovered among many others I've jotted recording personal observations to one day become part of some great literary work with my byline.

I was driving across the George Washington Bridge to my corporate headquarters office in mid-Manhattan. It was a morning when the traffic was stop and go, proceeding as if all was well, then stopping without warning. All at once, a huge eighteen wheeler in the lane beside me was forced to come to an abrupt halt. The semi-trailer groaned and lurched. For a split second I imagined it toppling over, smashing my vehicle and me in it. Then I had to laugh. It was a Pepperidge Farm Bread truck. Bread to me was like liquor to an alcoholic. It was a comfort. It was a necessity. I loved bread, especially Pepperidge Farm. Practically any night of the week you could find me in a daze-like state at my kitchen counter buttering and eating soft white bread, unwinding after a long stress-filled day at the office. How prophetic, I thought. I've done it—gone to my great reward, killed by a truckload of bread. I never dreamed it would be an external hit that caused my demise!

* * * * * * * * * *

The day finally came when without reservation I could accept the reality that my body image was unacceptable, in more than one way, to those with power to change my life. A trusted corporate colleague, department head and mature long service man, told me one of the executives watching my approach from down the length of the hall was heard to say, "Look at that, fat and black, I hate it!" The man who told me said I could rely on him to testify to the occurrence if I ever needed it and so would the person who heard it firsthand. Armed with such information, I had to accept the mistreatment I experienced was perpetrated with malice aforethought based upon non-performance-related motivation and it would not be ignored.

As a charter beneficiary of equal opportunity legislation gained with a nonviolent civil rights movement that took the lives of many including four little girls[22] in a Birmingham, Alabama, Sunday school; a young husband and father[23] in Jackson, Mississippi; the lives of three young men[24] near Philadelphia, Mississippi; and a Detroit housewife[25] in Selma, Alabama, I had to fight. Additionally, individuals and families from all walks of life suffered the loss of property, physical and emotional well-being, and livelihoods. Before all this personal mayhem, the doors to leadership opportunity in America's business

191

sector were essentially closed to black folk. Then those doors opened. I was "inside" and could expect every titan of industry and their underlings to respect the laws written to protect me and others from unfair employment practices. Hearing the words spoken with despicable malice about me, i.e., "fat and black," fortified my resolve to antagonize and overcome without filing a charge, unless, in their zeal, I was fired.

I was to be sorely tested when I heard the ultimate insult for a person who came to the company as an affirmative action candidate.

"You have never been a satisfactory manager. You were brought into corporate and used, because you are black. Shame on them for using you."

I heard this blatantly unlawful diatribe in a one on one meeting behind closed doors. The moment the words fell menacingly on my ears I realized it was planned to make me crazy angry. Apparently, someone thought I would finally rush to file a charge of discrimination. Instead it convinced me they actually thought I was stupid. The words hurt a lot, but there were no witnesses. It was not a winning scenario, for me. In a daze, I returned to my office. "What now?" I worried.

Chapter 44

I Seek Help

In private, I cried incessantly. I lay awake at night, wide-eyed, forcing my brain to come up with "next steps." Eventually I prayed, and then fell asleep.

Worried about maintaining good health, and having no one to confide in, for the first time in my life I went to a psychiatrist. He was a young black man with offices not far from my home. It was pure relief to talk to a person who listened with an interest in helping. My new therapist recommended I see a lawyer.

"You would never have to work another day in your life." His forthright observation in our initial session stunned me.

Before inviting the psychiatrist into my conflict, my most helpful communication was talking into a tape recorder going home whether on the bus or jostling about on the subway or while driving home through Central Park and up the Harlem River Drive or on the West Side Highway route. Communication with self wasn't enough. Reluctantly I shared incidents with my son and daughter. My reluctance was because I wanted my children to remain as proud of me as they had always been. The day came when they actually refused to listen. "We don't want to hear anymore. It's not healthy, Mom! Quit and go get a lawyer!"

I told the psychiatrist why I did not want to file a charge of discrimination. I was the only black manager in personnel; their affirmative action plan continued to pass review with flying colors. My boss's actions were possibly legal, just plain old mistreatment. New VP was a challenging kind of guy. Once he violently jerked the telephone wire from the wall in the office of a white manager, a blond young man who was humorously known to engage in loud, long-winded, expressive conversations.

The therapist encouraged me to see a lawyer to give me peace of mind on my situation. He recommended one.

I made an appointment and kept it.

"I'll take the case," said the extremely thin black man, punctuating his declaration by quickly reclining in his impressive leather executive chair. We were in his legal firm eight floors above the hustle and bustle of afternoon traffic in downtown Newark, New Jersey. He encouraged me to sign with him that evening.

"I'll get back to you," I said.

What if he was motivated by our "brother/sisterhood"?

I needed to know if my situation would be similarly viewed by a lawyer, not black.

"Yes, I'll be glad to help," said the white attorney from his office deep inside one of the many corridors of the richly paneled prestigious Manhattan law firm. This was a major firm, not on retainer with my company's legal department. He wanted the case.

"I'll get back to you," I said.

Both lawyers said I should report the problem to the Commission on Equal Employment Opportunity. I did that.

"That is why my son turned down the job offer from Drexel," said the EEO counselor in the depressed décor of her government-funded office. "It's not worth it, what they do to us. The money is good, but life is short and has enough other problems to deal with," she sighed. The intake counselor shifted her body, impressing me with a nervous effort to reclaim control of escaping empathy. She obviously wanted to handle the task at hand without compromising an unbiased official duty. After all, she had an obligation to maintain the professionalism required of her position in the United States Department of Labor's Equal Opportunity office. Hearing what I reported, it was apparent she was having a difficult time doing so.

I completed the forms documenting the unfair actions I felt occurred, making a claim of discrimination due to my color. "I believe if I were of the Caucasian race, I would not be subjected to the above treatment."

They typed my handwritten submission onto the appropriate form and mailed it to my home for signature. I did not sign it. I stored the official report in my house hidden from sight. I didn't want to stumble upon the typed paragraphs. The words brought too much distress to my soul. Having made the EEOC report, had the conversations in the EEO offices, the results were in from my self-imposed field research to determine if (1) I "had a case" or (2) I was inadvertently relying on my blackness to rescue me after becoming an inept, self-centered, whining roadblock to the progress of my employer's business.

The reactions of the two lawyers, the psychiatrist, plus the Equal Employment Opportunity officials gave me confidence and strengthened my resolve to take on my oppressors on their playing field. My complaints were legitimate. For the time being, I had all I needed to proceed as planned.

Going forward, I would respect what I had observed in my years managing personnel issues in a big company. To seek any form of legal redress, outside of the company, would make it a totally adversarial contest, the company versus me. I didn't want that. *All* employees of the company would appear to be against me, even sympathetic managers who had not hesitated to saunter into my office, casually shut my door, plop down in one of my side chairs, and unabashedly begin a discussion encouraging me to "be tough, be strong." I was certain the battle would be mine alone. I would not file a charge against the company, for the time being.

My intention was to be more positive doing whatever work I was assigned, while I insisted on fair treatment. When it was not forthcoming, I would report the incident to the next level of authority. If warranted, I would even go to corporate legal to convey disregard for policy, procedure, and the law. All of the above I had done with good results for employees who came to personnel claiming discrimination. I had to do it for me. In the meantime, I would be like "dripping water torture" to the enemy. Only if they were stupid enough to fire me would I get a lawyer, and a good one!

And when the storm I planned to encourage touched on making me crazy, I would call in and stay home in bed. I had vacation days. I had sick leave time. I was fully aware of how employees could spend both categories of personal time, legitimately. I knew the company's established practice for supervisors granting unplanned time off.

I was energized with the opportunity I had to force necessary change in the actions of management by means other than a lawsuit. After all, I'd never known of a legal settlement that provided long-term appeasement to an individual plaintiff. Big companies won, if only due to stonewalling the person they had mistreated, wearing them down, driving them to run for legal help, and then handing the case over to law firms on their payrolls to work out a settlement. Settlements were never made public, and the aggrieved plaintiff's planned career was forever off track.

I knew of too many people emotionally broken after challenging big business through legal action. I contacted the husband of a close acquaintance who sat down with me in their home and talked about his own situation.

He had progressed in corporate America only to become an unemployed business professional with great credentials and, I found, a broken spirit. He had worked for a major company and suffered blatant unyielding discrimination. He filed a charge and settled out of court, "to get on with my life." It had been several years before he had success in securing a career opportunity. When he did navigate the interview and the employment process and was hired by a firm he was proud to join, he was let go within a few months, for a reason having nothing to do with his demeanor or the quality of his work. His new employer said he was let go due to staff reduction. He believed it was because they discovered he had filed a charge against a former employer.

I was going to stay in the fight to regain fair treatment from my employer.

Regular visits with the psychiatrist had to continue. I needed someone to talk to, in confidence. After all, I still contemplated suicide—not because I wanted to be dead but because my life had become mournfully humiliating, painful, close to unbearable.

1987

I was demoted to professional level, given business cards for everyone, my family and the world, to know I was no longer a manager. I was a supervisor, in the lowest supervisory grade level. They recorded in their records the demotion was predicated on their evaluation of my work and "department restructuring."

I asked for and was given an appointment with the company's top officer.

The meeting went well. Mr. CEO was, of course, aware of what fueled my unrest from the perspective of my bosses. I remember hearing him say, "They claim you make errors, do not keep up with work or do what they ask you to do, and they cannot rely on you to give results in a timely way." I sensed a sympathetic tone to his voice even as I cringed from the pit of my stomach hearing him cite those unacceptable performance critiques point by point.

I answered, disagreeing with the report he reiterated. Because of a tremendous workload in personnel, everyone constantly revised priorities as we went along. No one could escape that reality. I tried to emphasize how I was demoralized by their day-to-day actions, the lack of a raise in years, the drastic change in my duties, and my unwarranted demotion. Without hesitation, I blatantly though not emotionally charged they were discriminating against me because I was black.

Throughout our conversation, he listened. He responded without promising to neither tar and feather my enemies nor even dispense lashes with a wet noodle. In no way did he say he was on my side, nor did he say he was appalled with the actions of my superiors. However, his unwavering gaze, unemotional statements inviting my agreement to recognize change calls on all of us to give our best attention to how we handle ourselves, assured me he was hopeful I would "hang in there." Exiting his office, I felt my situation would improve. After all, someone at his level wouldn't take the time for a face-to-face meeting with an employee if he hadn't concluded that employee's grievance seemed to require adjudication.

It was several long weeks before there was solid evidence my talk with the CEO did some good. They gave me a salary increase. Though not a traditional increase, the one time, lump sum payment of several thousand dollars brightened my outlook. The additional money, although included in documents for tax purposes, didn't change my salary base and thus did not improve salary-driven benefits. My monthly paycheck remained the same as it had been for so many years. It was discouraging, yet receiving the one-time payment offered a glimmer of light in miserable darkness.

Chapter 45

The End Begins

Time moved slowly Monday through Friday, me tolerating obnoxious authority at the office, trying desperately to hide the agony of knowing I was not wanted. I wasn't threatened with termination, but neither was their unsatisfactory review rescinded and pulled from my file. Established past practice called for management to terminate me for my failure to meet requirements and improve my performance. Frightened, more for the damaged pride I was sure I wouldn't be able to hide once they fired me, I kept thinking about next steps after being called in and the deed done. A month passed, and another. I wasn't being fired. Why not? When? Work days passed slower than sap dripping from Ohio's sugar maples on a January day. Weekend's relief away from the threatening office environment was short lived. Sunday night dread for the week ahead came fast as lightning.

Then, one day, my boss, in one of his silly unprofessional moments blurted out, "You won't be fired. You might quit, but you won't be fired." It was confirmation; their game—officiously jabbing and jousting keeping me unsettled, miserable—continued. No way would I quit. It was sickening, though. What must I do?

In my strategizing, I could stop worrying about losing a regular paycheck and the health benefits my continued employment gave me. Halleluiah! Still, I couldn't luxuriate in the comfort of such security. Them continuing to "beat up" on me, which his words implied, couldn't be allowed. I had to inflict return pressure to effect improvement in my status. Most importantly, I must not become nor appear to be a "yassuh boss" person.

Silently, I agonized about my apparent complacency as I peacefully handled the relatively menial tasks pushed down to me, e.g., working in the company store, enrolling newly hired casual and temporary employees, gathering data for others to discuss at meetings where I was excluded. I knew I must not surrender as it surely seemed I had.

"Dear God," my soul implored, "give me the strength and courage to continue this battle for fair treatment."

Then, they helped me—or at least one of my bosses did.

I had stepped into immediate boss's office to apprise him of a possible problem. An immigrant from Iran being hired for temporary work had disappeared from my office after being unable to produce appropriate INS documents. My boss listened, I thought, only to respond with off-the-cuff rambling about how unsuited I was to business and how better suited I was to social work. And then it happened. I heard him tell me point blank, "Resign and I will see that the company gives you a good package of termination benefits, including training to make a career change. How would you like a fully paid program so you can become a social worker?" Continuing to talk about what was on his mind, brusquely dismissing my attempt to discuss the business at hand, he insisted promoting how such a termination package could improve my life.

Cursing him out would have given me the greatest pleasure as I recalled my father listing teacher, nurse, and social worker among the professional careers white folks allowed black women to access. From high school, my goal had been to take a different path. I represented a new generation and vowed to succeed as a manager for a profit-making business. That I had done. Now this white man, in my age group, who grew up knowing black women were seldom hired for office work, except to clean up after him and the others, here in the '80s was telling me I was out of place and should be a social worker. I only said, "I enjoy the challenge of the business world and was known as a fine business woman until you showed up."

He laughed.

I continued, "Just take the unsatisfactory review from my file. Give me a decent raise and reinstate me to a management position."

Inside I was seething. What was he doing? I was so upset over his enthusiasm for maneuvering me to (1) resign and (2) become a social worker. I could hardly breathe and felt the whites of my eyes getting hot. "Tears please don't spill out," I willed.

More of a problem was his totally inappropriate attempt to rid the company of me, a female employee fifty years old, and a black person. Why did he do that? What should I do? It was such an obvious infraction of company rules. Yet as he rambled, my lips continued speaking its mantra, "I want a raise, a promotion, and the unsatisfactory review pulled and torn up." My brain labored over why he brazenly defied company policy.

It was a summer Friday. Standing up, I told him I was on summer hours, which meant I had worked extended hours Monday through Thursday to be able to leave at noon on Friday. It was almost 1:00 p.m., and I pretended I had made a commitment and had to be on my way. As I exited his office, he jovially yelled, "Think about it!"

Somehow managing to safely drive home, I went directly down to the cool dark of my basement. Absolutely depressed, I tried to understand why such a faux pas was made by a personnel executive. What was his agenda? Was I being baited, to do what? We had been alone. He could deny all he said. How must I, an employee protected by employment law related to my age, race, and gender, handle myself having been handed a loaded gun couched in an executive saying our employer would make it worthwhile for me to quit my job.

Back at work Monday morning, I was so tense it was difficult holding a constructive demeanor until I was to meet a co-worker for lunch. Once we settled at our table, I heard myself begging, "Don't say a word about what I am about to tell you." I had utmost confidence in Shirley, a demur lady, thoughtful with a precise manner, and poured out what had happened the past Friday. Shirley, a Brit, had worked in the United States for many years and managed a function in another division. "What are you going to do about it?" she asked in a low but urgent tone. "He can't make such an illegal workplace proposition and get away with it." She suggested I go to the top legal guy. Of course, that was the answer to my dilemma. I put my lunch tray away, jumped in the elevator, and very soon found myself in conversation with the general counsel.

The general counsel, hearing my story, was charmingly astounded, at times humorously astounded. His interest in my perspective on the underlying problem gave me a good feeling. The two of us were shaking our heads in disbelief as I left to go down to my office. He said he would speak with the perpetrator's boss, New VP.

Back in the sanctuary of my office, door closed, on bended knees, I prayed. I asked God for the right words, the right body language, and the right attitude to survive what I knew would be an explosive meeting with New VP.

Bang! Bang! Bang! "Open that door!"

"Just a minute," my words particularly quiet against New VP's incessant pounding, his commanding yell.

"Get down to my office, *now!*" he ordered.

As soon as I stepped across the threshold into his office, he motioned me to a chair, which I took, making a conscious effort to sort of melt into the contours of its completely padded frame. Feeling anything but respectful of the company I was in, I slouched in the chair—legs extended like a man might relax. I closed hands across my stomach and twiddled my thumbs. My eyes tilted toward New VP's eyes, while never holding my head up to look at him. God must have told me to assume the pose. Such thoroughly unattractive disrespect was absolutely foreign to me!

"Why did you go to (yelled the lawyer's last name)?" I heard VP screaming, "Why didn't you come to me?"

"You've told me to my face I wasn't qualified to be a manager," I quietly responded. "You said the company knew it but used me because I was black. I don't trust you."

"Why don't you go up to 125th street if you are so unhappy?"

Aware he referred to the Federal Office Building in Harlem, where I could file a charge against the company, I grasped the opportunity to take ownership of the entitlement I was confident was mine. "Why should I involve people outside the company?" I challenged him. "I'm part of the company. I'd rather let the company's legal staff protect me, help me resolve any problem you think 125th street should hear."

He had summoned my immediate boss who joined us. The culprit, embarrassed and livid, glared at me. Defending his actions, he claimed he was not encouraging me to leave the company, he was only "blueskying" (translated— "brainstorming") possibilities I may not have considered. He apologized for any discomfort his words may have caused. "That was not my intention," the man said, too easily.

New VP, after more streaming screaming, and cursing, ordered the two of us back to work. Adding with increased verbal force, clearly directed at both my boss and me, "stop this nonsense!"

I wished.

Chapter 46

Onward

Not many weeks later, New VP cordially beckoned me to follow him to his office. "Have a seat," he graciously invited, lowering himself into the side chair opposite the one his gesture indicated I should take. It was another Friday afternoon of a week that had not been free of hysteria. My immediate superior and others in the chain of command ruling my work life had ordered me to work the Dr. Martin Luther King, Jr., holiday that past Monday. Nine co-workers, including my three bosses, were off for the day, but "you are needed," a proclamation I challenged but had to accept. I saw it as another power play to antagonize me. Now seated holding my legal pad and pencil ready, I respectfully waited for words of importance.

Without preamble to prepare my wary ears, but in cordial tone, strange for him with me, conveying words absent even a hint of cruelty, I heard him say, "I want you to take charge of a long-ignored personnel need I'm now able to address. I want you to make it work."

What was this "new game"—"battle plan" he introduced so harmlessly? I choose to hold an expressionless demeanor. I said not one word. He continued and I heard words such as.

"Personnel will announce a new function dedicated to serving the company's more than five thousand retired employees. This company has first rate benefit coverage for retirees, but there's no central system for supporting their use of the plans—medical, dental, retirement pay issues, death and survivor benefits, or communicating important benefit change information. I spoke about this when I first came on board. Retirees must have a focal point for questions and problem resolution and eliminate the possibility their concern is pushed back, low priority on someone's desk. I'm pleased to say I've selected you to be my retired employees service manager. You'll provide assistance to the company's retirees throughout the world."

I suggested being a director of the new corporate-wide activity. "No," he thoughtfully responded, "you'll not be a director."

Actually, I made the suggestion just to hold onto a combative attitude. After all, the man knew I didn't trust him. A smile from him in my direction quickly became a sneer. My guard remained in place. As he dealt with me implying I should be named a director, my brain cells had more time to work feverishly and determine the whole truth in what I had heard. It was true when he first arrived in our company he *had* suggested retiree issues be handled centrally as a corporate personnel function. (A downside was the plant locations worked diligently to take care of their respective retirees, and it was a responsibility they preferred to keep.) So now, what closed-door strategizing birthed his plan to evolve into uplifting news for me? The dark side was perhaps he intended I would prove to be inept and he could finally be rid of me.

"You will report to a different director," he informed me. It would be Anthony, a congenial man, about my age. He prided himself on having worked his way up the corporate ladder earning his undergraduate and graduate degrees through the company's tuition reimbursement benefit plan. There would be no problem. I respected him; he would respect me.

New VP continued, somberly running through tasks I should immediately address.

"Set up a toll-fee telephone number available twenty-four hours for retirees to call the company with their problems. As soon as the eight hundred number is operational, write a letter introducing personnel's new service and send it to all retirees. You'll handle their calls. As soon as possible, produce and mail a retiree newsletter to everyone, on a regular basis. Later you will help design and conduct retirement benefit information meetings for retirees in our plant cities."

He expressed future plans for expanding the new function to include active employees within five to ten years of retirement eligibility. Meetings would help them understand retirement benefit provisions and savings plan options. The preplanning retirement programs would also cover healthcare issues, Social Security, and discussions on retirement's effect on lifestyle.

No, I wouldn't have dedicated office support but could feel free to seek help from others in the division and elsewhere as needed. I asked for a computer. He said no. I knew I would continue to petition for staff and a computer. The volume of work generated by the varied activity would prove both necessary.

As I left his office, I heard him call my name. I turned. He was smiling. I heard him say, "Now you can go throw out all that crap you've been saving."

Hopefully, I thought, as I smiled wryly. If only I could cease adding to the stored evidence of their ongoing malicious treatment. I had documented everything. After being threatened with "no one knows *what* you do every day," I added more paper to my files. No longer did I scrap and discard telephone messages. I scribbled the action I took on the pink note, which I stashed safely away to be dumped on a table in a court of law the day I needed evidence to prove my employee worth. Yes, I yearned to once again have a career I could build without feeling I must be prepared to defend every decision before a judge.

* * * * * * * * * *

Soon system technicians set me up with a computer and printer in my new office. A second telephone, dedicated to responding to retirees, was installed on my executive desk. Some long months and several memos later, I was approved to hire a part-time assistant.

* * * * * * * * * *

Maybe a year later, New VP left the company. We gathered to congratulate him on his retirement.

His replacement came on board. Replacement VP, a younger, calmer, available though busy executive was hired, again from outside the company.

New Director (my old boss, who kept trying to hasten my departure) also left the company.

* * * * * * * * * *

After replacement VP's arrival, my job category was raised to bonus eligible level. It was a major moment learning of the eligibility and then getting my first bonus check. Bonuses had never been discussed in my presence. I didn't even think about who might receive them. Before my troubles began, at performance review time, I always campaigned for a performance rating that gave me the highest salary increase possible. Receiving a bonus, it was Christmas all over again. At once I understood why the director's homes I visited had lovely modern furnishings and window treatments throughout. They had a big check to spend every year. Their homes resembled new furniture displays showcased in the best furniture stores.

"This is more of what it is all about for them," I thought as my mind raced back, several years prior to the classy company-paid event I attended when Mr. Gilson retired.

* * * * * * * * * *

It was a warm May evening, perfect for a retirement celebration. I entered the softly masculine and exquisite decor of the Pan Am Building's Sky Club fifty-six floors above the pavement. A magnificent view from the room's magnificent windows drew my eyes across the Manhattan skyline, beyond the twin towers of the World Trade Center even into Miss Liberty's view of New Jersey. I remember feeling privileged to be there. It was a fantastically glamorous New York experience. "I love the beauty, the wonder life promises in moments like this!" I gushed to myself. "This is what my struggle is all about, the struggle for opportunity to achieve! I want to know the best life has to offer. This is why I must survive and continue making it in New York!" I reminded me.

The retiring executive being recognized, Cliff Gilson, with the company for almost forty years chose to take "early retirement," and New VP decided this warranted a celebration, nonparallel. The invitation we each received was engraved. RSVPs were required with yes the only acceptable answer. It was a Friday evening cocktail party, five to seven. All corporate personnel staff from the lowest clerical category up, plus all plant personnel managers from around the country, and the directors' wives were expected to attend. The directors and their wives were going to join New VP and his wife for dinner with Cliff and his wife immediately following the cocktail party.

As we arrived, hors d'oeuvres in simple though elegant trays carried by crisply attired silent waiters made their way to each of us. The bartender was standing ready to pour and mix and help us ease into relaxation. Drink in hand, munching shrimp dipped in sauce, I took in the just above eye-level view of the towering peak of the Chrysler Building appearing next door in the sky with us. In the time it takes to snap your thumb and index finger, a group of stressed-out people became a party.

The room filled with soft music and chatter. Smiling ladies and gentlemen all mingled in twos, threes, and larger but still cozy numbers. Outbursts of tastefully raucous laughter implied there were one or two comedians in our midst. Some conversations looked serious; perhaps a player was intent on gathering the very latest information to possibly move a business project or personal career along. It was the best kind of inclusive exposure for one wanting to progress in Corporate America.

"America, the land of opportunity," I plaintively mused listening to the honoree express gratitude reminiscing gratefully over his years of service and experience with the company. I could not keep my mind from comparing his life of opportunity to what was *not* available to people of color in the same years he progressed in his world. I shook off the negativity. After all, change had come for blacks. "We must believe," my mind cautioned, "our preparation and hard work can at last provide a higher quality of life and result in great improvement for our families, just as those who went before us smoothed our way." A worry visited my mind that too many of us might become complacent, we who had achieved positions of responsibility with salaries for necessities as well as for luxuries. We must not. My generation and those following us must continue seeking change for the better where vestiges of racial discrimination impeded justice and personal, political, social, and economic well-being for blacks.

Scanning the room, I shuddered for the shameful evidence of tokenism in our division's hiring practices. Only two minorities, a young lady and me, were among the almost forty or so employees present. It was the late eighties, and not one black man mingled with us at the invitation only, company-paid social gathering. The sobering realization instilled my resolve that evening to go from that shiny place and confidently use skill and patience to regain my management status with the company.

That evening hobnobbing like business royalty at the top of the Pan Am Building helped me stay the course to overcome my dilemma.

Now years later receiving my first bonus check, a five-figure amount, I vowed to make greater contributions to the business and gain higher rewards.

* * * * * * * * * *

A year or so after the pleasant shock of achieving bonus eligible status, the replacement VP summoned me to his office. I was asked to accept a new, expanded position in his organization. He wanted me to return to the suburbs and take charge of personnel activity at the satellite facility I had started up. And he wanted me to relocate my retirement services department to the facility.

I returned to an office suite in the same building, a space much larger than I had been forced to vacate six or seven years earlier. HR, human resources, as was now the nomenclature, had offices in the front of the building with fabulous huge windows. My staff grew.

The work load was tremendous and challenges seemed never ending. Handling the facility's staffing needs, maintaining personnel files, delivery of benefit information to employees, managing employee activity and employee counseling, and resolving management and supervisor issues was ongoing. Retirement tasks included the retiree newsletter, which informed and entertained retirees. The company's retiree database was cleaned up—address and contact information validated. Provisions in the many and varied retiree benefit plans were structured for easy reference. Retirement benefit information sessions held on the east and west coasts and in the Midwest were well attended as were retirement preplanning meetings held throughout the country for active employees. Any stress related to my department's broad and heavy workload was minimized knowing those we served, employees and retirees, appreciated our accomplishments.

Business Travel

I wanted to travel for my employer. The first eight or nine years after I moved to the east coast and corporate, several times a year my secretary coordinated with the travel department to secure airplane tickets and make hotel reservations for me. I attended personnel seminars or participated in meetings of groups doing business with the company. I treasured the times I packed my bags and went on the road for a few days.

Strangers, before meeting on a trip, sometimes become good friends. For any business traveler, only business details are included in the travel report submitted at the conclusion of the trip. Personal activities after business is done for the day are a private matter. Such a diversion is reported on the following pages, with the names of people, places, and various other particulars changed to protect whatever might best be shielded from public scrutiny. The reported emotions—anxiety, insecurity, fear, joy, contentment, resignation, and hope for the future—can be read as real.

Chapter 47

A Diversion

His fingers barely touched her skin as the note slid into her hand. Yet for Maggie Cason, the moment led to the Summer Conference for Personnel Executives becoming an unforgettable chapter in her life. "Anson," he had scrawled on the hotel's tiny stationery, "522-2561, Rm 935 Eden Roc."

Moments ago, his presence registered with Maggie as she stepped into the hospitality suite. Maybe it was his height. It didn't matter. She was deep into her "why did I come to this party?" attitude. She valued the expense subsidized escape from routine that business trips meant, but the push to tie up loose ends at office and home wiped her out. Maggie wanted to return to the relaxing solitude of her hotel room. The midmorning flight to Miami had given ample time to unpack, see colleagues at the coffee shop, then freshen up, and now meet and greet at hospitality hour. A good night's sleep was foremost on her mind. Getting up early and leisurely preparing for the day and her first session was her goal. Still she noticed him.

The man was tall—like a Celtic, shoulders broad—like a cowboy. He was impeccably dressed in a pale grey double-breasted suit, white shirt, and early-tomato-red tie. His black hair, natural style, neatly trimmed, framed a square Oprah-brown face punctuated with heavy eyebrows and a healthy mustache running the length of his wide mouth.

He stood with several guys midcenter the ballroom in the beachfront high-rise hotel—all attentive to an obviously secure young woman in a green cocktail dress. Maggie's eyes lingered on him until, without any intention, his persona vaulted into her subconscious. She shook her head dismissively. Maggie had no plans for him. She moved on. He was just there.

For Maggie, any sort of party, no matter her determination to "relax and enjoy," invariably suffered forward. Cocktail hours were an unwelcome challenge, a concoction of rituals she inadequately handled until the bartender's "Harvey's with a twist, please" soothed the panic in her midsection.

Maggie had to get to the bar. Gracefully slipping past and through clusters of mingling folk, excusing herself for any distracting intrusion, nodding "hi" to familiar faces, a smile for others—when (there is no truer way to tell it) *their eyes met*, for a microsecond. Her mind shivered. His glance was not casual. It clearly conveyed she was on his mind, a realization easy for her to accept because he was on hers. Admitting the fact, frightening because connecting with the strange man in a room full of strangers introduced a sensuous fantasy she had no experience controlling, she stopped putting one sandaled foot in front of the other. Maggie stood perfectly still, willing visible interest in the people sharing the space she occupied at the moment. She must join their conversation and hopefully camouflage a real proclivity to *run*.

They were several women analyzing the revelation of one that a hotel maid offered to arrange social companionship for her, "anytime, day or night." Wow! Maid service could mean more than the luxury of a turned down bed. A chocolate man, or whatever, could accompany the expected foil wrapped chocolate kiss. "At last," they laughed, "here is solid evidence women in management are getting some sort of treatment equal to their male counterparts!"

After a few moments, having regained a semblance of her internal composure and doing her best not to turn in the direction of the one man in the room still on her mind, Maggie sauntered toward the bar for her Harvey's. What luck, there was Pamela, her traveling buddy! Latching onto Pam, the two of them got the attention of the bartender. Drinks in hand, Maggie carefully maneuvered them away from the source of her emotional turmoil.

In a few minutes, though, he was standing at her side, a clear plastic cocktail tumbler in his right hand.

He greeted Rich, who had joined the two women. They'd met Rich earlier that afternoon.

Looking down at Maggie, the Celtic-tall dark brown man spoke, quietly, like he was in a church and the pastor was delivering his sermon. "Hello there," he said. Maggie sensed a momentary suspension in the rhythm of the breath entering and exiting her body insuring her heart continue its beating. During the pause, perceived or real, Rick had started introductions. That was when Maggie would learn he was Anson, Rick's friend. Anson was told she and Pam were conference presenters, leading discussions on "Avoiding Legal Action by Employees Terminated Due to Restructuring and Downsizing."

Anson was in Miami searching for real estate suitable for his company's expansion plans. Rich represented the financial consulting firm on the search team.

While responding to Pamela's interest in zoning, access to waterways, and distribution arteries, in general, Anson managed to slip Maggie the note paper inscribed with his name and hotel numbers.

She noticed him writing as they talked. So that was what he was doing. How crass. How lowlife! Well, he was way off base about her! No way would she call or come to see him, a perfect stranger. Yes, he had appealed to her; perhaps, Maggie realized, on the same crude level he was attracted to her. But her upbringing had ingrained the wherewithal not to succumb to basic instincts. Maggie, embarrassed, held onto the note as Anson talked about multiuse property issues resolved on their recent trip to Texas. She would trash the scrap of paper with illicit implications at the first opportunity.

Listening to the conversation, Maggie couldn't deny Anson and Rich were interesting and fun. The two of them shared many business travel assignments and were longtime friends. All four were having a relaxed good time comparing business experiences and expectations, laughing a lot. She wouldn't let the faux pas of the note passing infringe on an evening that had evolved into an enjoyable escape into the business world of professional black men, knowledgeable gentlemen.

Then Anson looked down directly into her face and abruptly changing the subject asked, "Where are you from?"

"Connecticut," Maggie said, "Stamford, Connecticut."

He knew people from Stamford. She knew the same families. The scope of their conversation expanded. They were strangers with personal and honorable connections.

Shortly, they were alone, standing together, not touching—talking and looking out the magnificent floor-to-ceiling windowed wall of the room, no longer filled with people. Anson and Maggie were high above the lights of Miami Beach and the Atlantic Ocean directly below them gently rising and falling. Moonlit waves pushed and pulled at the wide beach, empty, that late hour, of everyone. She sipped her same drink. He continued to hold his half-full cocktail tumbler. The scrap of paper, his note, ignored, never discussed, had become a part of her hand. She was comfortable with the handsome, soft-talking stranger.

Later, saying goodnight at the elevator, he surprised her, his lips finding hers for an absolutely wonderful kiss—just wet enough, warm, seeking. She was thrilled. She was scared.

Perhaps he was oblivious to the elevator's arrival. Maggie, hearing its chime, sensed an opportunity to save herself from the emotional upheaval she was beginning to crave. As the elevator doors were closing, she slipped from his arms and darted inside. The doors had accomplished the necessary. They took control, putting distance between her and irresistible, dangerous risk.

As she prepared for bed, Maggie caught herself wistfully recalling an evening like no other she had known. "I was wise to escape his need," she thought. "That is certainly all it was." She was pleased with how she had handled herself.

Maggie wondered if Pam had been pursued in the same fashion by Rich. After all, gaining the adoration of romance-starved women must be usual for them on the road constantly. Well, she knew she was too sensible and in control to fall for such a come-on. She smiled, and then catching herself somewhat melancholy, she sighed. Too bad she had to be so straitlaced. Anson was like what her dreams were made of. Remembering his gentle and genuine interest in her, she slept very well.

The next morning Maggie and Pam met as planned for an early breakfast. Maggie had charge of the morning session. Materials for Pam's afternoon meeting were expected and had to be tracked down. Hopefully Pam would locate all in house, in time.

Having returned to her business sensibilities, it was unsettling to learn from Pam's chatter that Rich was surprised about Anson's attention to "your friend, Maggie." Apparently, Anson, always outgoing and charming to the women they met, didn't take up with "any one lovely lady, no matter how much or how little they appeared interested in him. For sure, he has your friend on his mind." Pam said all this, supposedly reiterating Rich's very own words. Maggie did not trust herself to say one thing; a warm sensation moved the length of her body, from her forehead down through her knees.

She had not said anything to Pam about her evening with Anson after Pam and Rich left them to go get hamburgers. It was unusual for Maggie not to regale Pam with the particulars, especially since all of it now confused her sense of self. She and Pam were mutual confidants, customarily dissecting important details about their significant encounters with men met while conducting business or new in their private, personal lives. Across the table, Pam shared, effusive and forthcoming, without reservation while Maggie didn't offer one thing about Anson and his effect on her.

"It could help me put it all in perspective if I told Pam how I ran from Anson," she thought, "left him at the elevator with no explanation, no hint I would be rude, actually childish!" Now here she was thinking about him again as if it there was merit to the whole thing. "What if I mishandled our few harmless hours together? What if our time together had been as memorable, as promising for him as I was afraid to admit it was for me? Will I ever grow up?" Maggie thought.

Pam rambled on, Maggie half listening, if that, when she heard Pam's loud whisper, "I *said*, don't look now, but here comes Anson." By this time, Anson was pulling an extra chair from the next table, asking to join them.

There was nothing insecure about the man. Without hesitation, he was asking for another place setting, ordering breakfast, beckoning the young fellow at the newspaper stand to bring him a paper, taking charge of what he wanted.

Only he and Pam talked. Still, Maggie didn't see it a bit strange that she contributed nothing to the conversation. She was lost in thought wondering which spirits had put her and Anson in the same room one more time, spirits for good, or the ones for evil. She came out of her trance when Pam stood up to leave, mumbling something about catching up with her later.

Then Anson was holding her hand—not really holding her hand, just sort of caressing her hand. He was apologizing for kissing her the night before. "But," he said, "I want to kiss you again. It is all I can do to keep from doing so right this moment. Lady, do you know I couldn't sleep? All night I worried about how long it would take me to find you in the morning. I will not do anything to hurt you. I think I understand why you ran. I'm surprised myself, and I hope you'll accept my apology. You are a very special lady. I want to know more about you. I want you to know more about me."

Maggie had work to do; otherwise, she wouldn't have left his side for one single moment. As it was, she assured him she would meet him after lunch on the terrace at the hotel where they parted the night before.

The next four days were filled with sunshine, sand, cool hideaways, rumpled sheets in midday, dinners at dusk, music under the stars. Business had to be handled, but they returned to one another as soon as they could.

He was a widower raising two daughters. His wife's sudden death several years before still hurt him terribly. Yes, Maggie had been correct. He did have a need. It was a need to move forward in his life and to master letting go of the tragic past. It was a need to once again bond with a loving woman.

Maggie opened up to him about her life. She was alone, a cherished husband no longer hers, belonged to another. She had loved him deeply and couldn't discard memories of their passionate claim to be forever the soul mate of the other. She eventually accepted her loss, but having known his love, their love, she was blessed to have experienced real love. She decided that would be sufficient for her earthly journey. Shielding her heart from fresh hurt, Maggie admitted to the stranger so easy to talk to that she made it through her days finding passion in building a career doing what she could to be of help to others and disregarding the possibility of romance. She didn't tell him how that resolve was thoroughly weakened having met him. She needed what Anson offered, and accepting his gift of sensitive caring, unselfish consideration, and generous attention, she returned the same to him. They were in tune, a healthy merge of emotion and reality. Drawn so inexplicably to each other before anyone could expect to know enough about one another to be simply friends, they embraced the moments they had. It was a bond as strong apart or coupled in a crowd, or alone together in each other's arms. Not keeping to themselves, they shared their togetherness with others.

As beautiful days and nights passed from them, Anson began to project a solemn resigned manner that led to brief, only brief, reference to the inevitability of their parting. He didn't believe in long-distance romance. "Too much loneliness, too much hurt. I couldn't bear the pain," he said.

She truly cared about the romantic man she found. Unfortunately he wasn't hopelessly romantic. Maggie learned she was hopelessly romantic and could not envision their romance fading away to merely a wonderful memory.

Her flight was to leave for LaGuardia on Thursday morning. The reality was she had to get on that plane. Having rebooked his return flight to be at the gate with her, he would fly to Boston the same afternoon.

Their farewell time seated in the midst of passengers in the airline's boarding section was cozy and quiet. It was as if the two of them relied already on memories made the preceding four days to give comfort that moment and forward. Light conversation was absent talk of the future, of seeing each other again. Anson was too skittish on that subject, and for Maggie, their remaining time with each other in the same space, feeling the pressure of her body touching his, was too precious to contaminate with confusion brought on by words.

When he held her in his arms at the gate, she didn't cry. Miserably, Maggie had at last accepted "them" being over. But it was important he never see her devastation. There would be no tears. As her face touched his, she thought she would break apart. The memories of his strong body lying against hers or her hand enclosed in his as they walked and talked together or simply watching him come to her from across a room were all so vivid. As Maggie looked into that distinctive face she would never again stroke, she smiled. "It was fun," she said. "Take care."

The tears hiding behind her eyes were almost unbearably hot as she turned and walked away. The pain deep in her throat was unbelievable. She had believed Anson Hadley Phillips would never let her disappear, nor would she have to accept this parting as their last—their knowing each other, only a diversion.

The gate attendant took the boarding pass from the packet Maggie aimlessly directed to his outstretched hand.

"Here," he said handing her a scrap of paper that had fallen to his desktop. Taking it, Maggie made her way morosely down the ramp then stopped in her tracks.

"Anson," the firm scrawl of dark blue ink painted in the middle of the paper, "(617) 482-6193. Please call me tonight."

Chapter 48

In Charge

Finding happiness is a personal conclusion; accepting beauty and joy in life is a personal decision. Together with your own action, or lack of action, others dampen your parade when you let them. There are those who help you break through troubling times to achieve goals, if you let them. Confidence and courage are two basic ingredients you bring to the mix for a life that pleases. All of this I believe. Plus, giving up is shortsighted, wimpy, easy. Having faith in yourself and a higher power keeps confidence and courage poised to engender the good your heart desires. Being prepared is the catalyst.

Personally and professionally, whenever I have a role in improving a situation or an individual's condition in life, I'm happy. It's understood failure to take care of me and my surroundings compromises my ability to be helpful to others. I also believe no one is perfect, so a span of laziness, selfishness, resentment, impatience, or other negative personal attribute is understandable and that I work to overcome after the briefest indulgence. Being of some good to others is my goal. It has been since hearing my father's theory that helping others could bring more personal satisfaction than accumulating hordes of money. At night, as I lay down to go to sleep, I ask myself, "What good did you do today?"

Looking back, when new VP initially named me to structure and manage a retiree focused function for human relations, I was not happy. Although it seemed the screws torturing my attempt to regain a respected career had been loosened, a dark thought invaded my brain. The management function I was assigned would serve ex-employees, those no longer contributing to the company's profit-making goals. How essential could that be to the company, for how long? Was I being set up for my demise? Were my adversaries relishing making me, the black woman they couldn't get rid of, an in-house social worker, positioned to be eliminated soon? Maybe so, but I chose a business development perspective. I decided they had freed me to engage in a different kind of battle. I would both systematically and empathetically address the problems and inefficiencies retirees experienced over the years in using the benefits costly for the company to provide. My new responsibility could contribute to a fiscally improved result for us as a company. I decided I would be happy with my new challenge.

A brochure in my office mail that spring described a Retiree Relations Seminar for business leaders being held in Detroit, Michigan, at the General Motors Building.[26] My spirits lifted seeing boldly presented on a glossy promotional folder the implication private industry perceived a balance sheet driven necessity to harness the haphazard approach in which companies delivered company-paid benefits to retirees. "Of course you should go," my boss encouraged. I boarded a 7:00 a.m. flight from Newark Airport on a Friday morning in June to attend the one-day seminar sponsored by the Council of Communication Management.

When I returned that evening, my motivation was strong for the work I was doing. I had enjoyed one full day in a place I never before visited. Looking across the Detroit River to the Canadian shoreline impressed me. And to this day, I smile remembering my amazement seeing from the taxicab window, a giant tire monument near the highway heading into the city. The drive-by close-up view of Tiger Stadium, home[27] of the Detroit Tigers Baseball Team prompted the ever-recurring pensive wish my baseball-loving father was alive to know where life had taken his daughter. Most importantly among the two dozen or so participants in the seminar, I was one of only several currently managing a retiree service. My hands-on experience was well received in our fact-finding, idea-, and needs-sharing discussion. I departed Detroit with a strengthened self-confidence in what I was charged to do.

* * * * * * * * * *

Several consecutive Friday evenings or so during a month, I was off on a business trip to lead an information-packed seminar, developed by me and various experts. It was a hectic time. While others left the building, meeting friends for dinner and a night out or heading home to relax with family or have self time, I hopped in a cab or limo. The driver grabbed and deposited the heavy bags and briefcases in the trunk, and the presentation team was off to LaGuardia Airport in New York or to New Jersey and Newark Airport. The destination might be Chicago, St. Louis, or Los Angeles areas or Amtrak to Baltimore. Arriving, picking up the rental car, one of us behind the wheel, we found our way to the hotel convenient for driving to our meeting site the next morning (unless it was planned for one of the hotel's spacious conference rooms).

Some were precisely planned one-day ventures. I would board an early morning flight out of Newark to either Chicago or St. Louis, rent a car, and drive to where I participated in a morning session or a luncheon meeting. And information shared, questions asked and answered, and a conversation-filled sit-down lunch completed, I returned to the airport for the flight and limo service home by ten that night—a strenuous day of worthwhile contacts and accomplishment.

Interest in health maintenance organizations as a possible option for retiree health plan coverage found us involved in intense travel to all parts of Florida. Important information had to be shared with as many retired employees as possible living in the Sunshine State. We were up and down, in and out of the sky, and then driving overland to reach retiree groups for luncheon meetings in the announced destinations.

We took care of business and enjoyed ourselves doing so. Once we flew into Tampa/St. Petersburg airport, daringly rented an available red convertible, and enjoyed the beautiful weather driving from one session to another. Driving over the Sunshine Skyway Bridge to Sarasota, we couldn't resist slowing down to lift our bodies from our seats and scream into the wind and over the sun dazzled water "I'm king of the world!" mimicking the movie actor who stood on the front of the ocean liner depicting the Titanic.

A flight from Tampa to Palm Beach for appointments in the south of Florida was uneventful except for my anticipation of disaster. I knew the flight path was over the Everglades, alligator territory.

At the terminal we proceeded to a ground-level gate to board the flight. Briskly approaching the desk, I asked the agent to confirm I had a window seat as I pushed my papers onto the counter. Not looking at me or the ticket, she drolly answered, "They're all window seats." Any satisfaction with her response was short lived. In fact, I was puzzled, not satisfied. "Great, I would have a coveted window seat, but how could that be?" I'm thinking.

Soon the waiting room doors opened inviting us onto the tarmac to board the plane. Off I shuffled in the midst of a line of passengers headed toward the smallest airplane I had ever approached in my travels. I was actually too frightened to board, I thought. But I did. Climbing the step/door combination entry to the plane, I conjured up a picture of this toy plane dropping from the sky spilling each of us into the open mouths of alligators, waiting patiently in the everglade swamp for their evening meal. Our bodies would be their succulent reward. On this day, their fortune would be my misfortune. No one else appeared terrified; I kept my cool.

This was also my introduction to flying in other than a large jet.

Staring down the aisle, I saw only window seats, against each side of the plane—a single row of seats, maybe ten per side. The tiny plane, in height as well as width, made each of us, all full-sized adults, bend from the waist to walk to our seats. To reach an assigned seat far down the aisle, we had to quickly choreograph knee bends to accompany our bent waists in order to negotiate our bodies over a hump in the middle of the floor, no doubt caused by the sculpted-out luggage-storing space down below. Once we were airborne, the flight was perfect.

My business travel had exposed me to the small plane known as a puddle jumper, an experience I would never have chosen. Thus, years later, spending my own money, I was prepared to carry on, almost nonchalantly while vacationing on a far distant continent when a puddle jumper was the only travel mode available for a connecting flight.

Several times I extended my planned time away on business to stay and travel just a bit farther, spending personal time and money to be a tourist. One memorable business trip my traveling partners headed home after our meetings in Anaheim, California. It was my first time in the state. Yet I drove up the Pacific Coast Highway toward Venice Beach to look for my brother. Larry had been lost to the family for some time. Several days later when the plane circled out over the Pacific returning me to the East, I had been to Disneyland, the Crystal Cathedral, the length of Venice Beach, and thanks to Larry's guidance, went to Rodeo Drive, the Hollywood Bowl, and the San Fernando Valley.

* * * * * * * * * *

Eventually business travel became so demanding I no longer looked forward to being away from the office or away from home. I recall the first time I realized travel had become a routine known too well. It was a Friday afternoon. For a change, no preretirement seminars or benefits information meetings were scheduled for that early summer weekend. I drove straight home, parked my Thunderbird in the garage, and walked directly to the lounge chair on the lawn, carrying purse, briefcase, and all. I adjusted the cushion, looking to lazily savor the pleasant afternoon weather prior to the sun starting its descent.

High above, a 747 lazily made its way across the sky toward the northeast. "Let's see," I mused, as I settled down and kicked off my shoes, "by now, the cabin attendant is handing out snacks—pretzels, no doubt, and drinks. They'll have dinner later." For an instant I missed not being part of the familiar scene—for a fleeting second only. The joy of comfortably reclining at home, in my backyard, was paramount. What a privilege to contentedly consider two full days and nights ahead totally mine to fill as I chose. What a blessing to anticipate Monday morning, returning to the rewarding challenges waiting for closure in the department I managed. I smiled. I had absolutely no reason for melancholy.

Epilogue

Loretta Spann said, "If you are unhappy and it's in your power to change the situation, then do it. There's nothing you can do about it? Then leave it in God's hands and move on." I was talking on the telephone one evening to Mrs. Spann, a favorite best friend. Our frequent conversations, face to face or by phone, found the two of us exploring a variety of subjects. She said she liked that about our friendship. We shared perspective on current news, world and community issues, or activities in our church, Galilee United Methodist. I enjoyed hearing her cherished memories from childhood, college, and throughout a life of service and fun. Mrs. Spann was a 1930 graduate of Clark College in Atlanta, Georgia. She had worked in Harlem as a teacher before becoming a social worker, eventually a supervisor. My father's guiding words included the suggestion I surround myself with people I could learn from. I didn't base friendships on that criterion; however, I've found something of value can be gleaned from just about everyone. You have to be open for the good; listen and observe to recognize wisdom in word and ways. Never did I have to search for Mrs. Spann's positive influences. This particular day I lamented missing my daughter and her family, whom I had not seen for a number of weeks. It was understandable. Their home was miles from mine, and she and her teenagers juggled a hectic schedule. Still, Mrs. Spann's quiet reminder brought relief to the sadness in my soul. I drifted to sleep that night, mind clear. I could do something about my unhappiness! The next day I would drive the two hundred-mile round trip and spend time with them. I did and we had a glorious day. Mrs. Spann died a year or so after sharing her wisdom on dealing with unhappiness. She was ninety-seven years old. Many times throughout my life I've done as Mrs. Spann advised—given constructive energy to what was possible, not wasteful attention to what I could not affect.

Those many years ago, compensating for good friends deeply missed in the move from Missouri to New Jersey, I made new friends by joining first the church, and then the NAACP. Becoming a member of the civil rights organization, I also fulfilled a goal of mine impossible in the '60s and '70s for those who worked in civil service. Employed in private industry, I could join but hadn't found time to get involved. A summer Sunday in 1976 our family visited Galilee United Methodist Church in neighboring Englewood, NJ. Galilee would become my church home. There Rev. Walter Scott Taylor, Galilee's pastor from 1952 until his death in 1984, was an outspoken positive force in the community. The first (and only) black mayor of Englewood, Rev. Taylor was also a member and avid NAACP supporter. He stressed the importance of everyone working with the NAACP to advocate for justice denied black people. In the Bergen County Branch, I served as treasurer and was elated the night I was elected a director of the New Jersey State Organization.

While my personal happiness diminished as I weathered the daily struggle to hold onto a business career, the church was constant, reminding me God through his Son Jesus Christ was on my side. Sunday sermons, Bible lessons, regular prayer, and gracious fellowship fortified me week after week. Christian service repaired damaged self-esteem. Chairing the Council on Ministries, responding to a suggestion of Rev. Taylor's successor, interim pastor, Rev. Dennis Fletcher, I developed a church newsletter. Evenings and weekends I lost myself in the many aspects of producing *The Communicator* for our congregation. Then there was the mission work of the organized unit of United Methodist Women that I joined and whose members, one after the other, seemed to make "me" their mission. My telephone would ring after arriving home late from the office. "How are you? Yes, I know you've had a busy day, but are you eating a good dinner? Got tuna fish? Got lettuce? It's not too late. Fix a salad." Working in Galilee, chairing, co-chairing events such as Church Anniversary, Every Member Canvas, Women's Day, and participating in Galilee's activities strengthened me spiritually, thus personally.

My children provided the warmest bright glow in my life. Farah and Darin were never "squeaking wheels" overtly needing my attention so a worry was, "did I give them enough time?" "Your job," I told them, "is to go to school every day and learn all you can from each teacher, even the ones you don't like. My job is to go to work every day and do and be the best I can so we will have the money for living a good life. You do your job. I'll do mine. We might be a broken family, but that doesn't keep us from being a great family."

If my children let sickle-cell disease hinder their approach to experiencing the best from life's opportunities, I didn't know it. They were active in school, had extracurricular interests, kept good grades, and great friends. From preteen years, I watched them assume remarkable responsibility for dealing with sickle-cell anemia. Always attentive to how medical personnel in the emergency room and elsewhere took care of them, Farah and Darin knew what was being done and why. A technician, nurse, or doctor not as experienced with the protocol need not fear; my girl or boy spoke up with a question or observation. It was amazing when I realized those kids could complete their own medical claim forms. They took ownership of what had to be done. My devastation exceeded theirs when they were hospitalized with no assurance the intravenous fluids, blood transfusions, and medications would send them home vibrant once again. They rolled with the punches, weak but upbeat. Even as children they kept a positive outlook, managing each crisis, enjoying their lives when they were well. Great credit goes to Coach Neville, their elementary school physical education teacher in Richmond Heights, Missouri's West Richmond School. He pushed them to achieve physically, do what they could when they were able. Sickle cell shouldn't be an excuse. Farah and Darin went on to college after graduating from Teaneck High School. Darin was released from the hospital just hours before marching with his class. To this mom, he didn't appear strong enough to make it to the stage. What a comfort to see the ambulance in place that afternoon (as usual, stationed to administer assistance if needed by any in a large crowd on the field). Farah graduated from Cornell University. She had been Dean of Pledges for her sorority, Alpha Kappa Alpha. An actress in high school productions, she continued in college. Particularly memorable was driving up to Ithaca to see her perform in *For Colored Girls Who Considered Suicide When the Rainbow Was Enuf.* And I still remember her call to my office—her thrilled exuberance telling about her midnight induction into Cornell's prestigious Quill and Dagger Honorary Society. Darin's study at the University of Maryland was cut short due to illness and emergency surgery. He resumed study as soon as he could at Florida AM&N in Jacksonville.

My children married, and each has two wonderful children. Treasured grandchildren, Jai and Will, are the daughter and son of Farah and their devoted father, William Dungey. My treasured granddaughters, Jasmine and Sydney, are the children of Darin and Patricia Carter Stith. For my daughter and son, in spite of the incurable genetic disease that shadows them, family and careers are their focus.

Farah with her children
Will and Jai Dungey

Darin and Tricia with their children
Jasmine and Sydney

What a blessing to be able to
celebrate retirement.

I retired in 1998 after more than twenty-six years of service with the company. The New Year was only weeks old when I had presented my director a letter of intent to retire midyear. It was just several months following my sixtieth birthday. I had revisited Daddy's question posed my first summer home from college. "How much money do you think you'll need to be content?" More than four decades later my answer led me to know, as a retiree, I would have financial resources sufficient for the lifestyle comfortable for me. And becoming a director with the company was not in the cards for me, a discouraging reality. Not uncommonly, experience and ability remained on the sidelines as younger folk were named to such vacancies. A change to using my talents in another venue the remaining years of my life promised greater personal happiness than continuing to plod along, noncompetitive in the competitive arena that is the corporate environment. Yes, my retirement income could fund a life of creative independence.

After a retirement date was agreed upon (I was pleased to be asked to stay three months longer than intended), an assistant returned from a meeting in corporate and asked where I wanted my retirement luncheon held. "No place," I said. "I don't want a luncheon." She looked stricken, like she would have to deal with me being difficult by choosing to leave absent the requisite hoopla. "I want a retirement dinner at The Carlyle," I assuredly continued.

"The Carlyle Hotel in New York?" she asked incredulously.

"Yes," I answered. "If I that's not possible, then I don't want anything."

"The Carlyle wouldn't have a room for that?" her statement posed as a question she seemed relieved to suggest.

"They can do it. I talked to them, and they have rooms for large groups. Anyway, I'm sure we wouldn't be more than fifty."

You see, my direct reports numbered six. The invitation list might also consist of corporate HR folk working closely with us and certain local facility staff along with peers and higher level persons from other divisions. My two children would round out the possible invitees. I could invite Farah and Darin because I hadn't remarried. Generally a spouse was the only family member invited to share in the company-paid event. In fact, I had been asked which of my children would be my guest.

"It has to be both of them," was my reply. They agreed.

I wouldn't push for my daughter-in-law, Patricia, to be included since Farah, divorced from William, would be attending without a man at her side. She was dating, but I didn't want to suggest her guy be included either. He was a well-known former NFL great, and I intended to be *the* celebrity that night. I was glad "my other daughter, Tricia" accepted my heartfelt apology and cheerfully planned a fun time at home with my three grandchildren. (Sydney, the fourth grandchild to bless my life, was born a year and a half after I retired.)

The balmy evening of the event Darin arranged for a limousine to chauffeur us to and from Teaneck and The Carlyle on Manhattan's upper east side. My director, apologizing for not thinking of providing the amenity himself, insisted Darin forward the bill to him for our company to handle.

For me, it was a fabulous night. I remember the Carlyle's staff, minorities mostly, hosting and serving us in the cozy banquet room, seemed so proud to see a black woman, actually black family, so well respected—for them to graciously accommodate. My observation was confirmed when upon leaving, a waiter courteously almost apologetically approached.

"Excuse me ma'am," he said. "I want to wish you a happy and healthy retirement. I hope you enjoy your train trip across the country." (Conversation had included joyous attention to my plan to leisurely travel by train across northern America to the Seattle area where my cousin Helen and her daughter Sara lived and then return to New Jersey by train through the Southern states.) If I had not worked through the hysteria that surfaced to threaten my career almost fifteen years prior, neither those gentlemen nor I would have experienced the first-class celebration on my behalf that wonderful night at The Carlyle.

My ability to retire when I did was a golden opportunity because our company, like many in the 1990s determined downsizing made good business sense. In 1997, the announcement was made of the enhanced Voluntary Retirement Plan available to those eligible by age and service to retire. Only employees eligible received the packet giving the employee expected company-provided retirement pay and the enhancement of a one-time payment of up to two years' current salary. Along with many others throughout the company, I received the packet. The information confirmed we could look forward to automatically receiving one year's salary. Dollars equating a second year's salary would be added to the amount if you signed a prepared document forever releasing the company from legal liability with regard to your employment experience with the company. I shuddered at the thought of affixing my signature to any paper excusing an employer from violating employment law. I was certain the release must reference laws or some feature of the laws gained in the civil rights movement by people who sacrificed livelihood, health, comfort, security, and life to open doors for my career. I couldn't sign the release. Farah and Darin counseled me to make certain I wouldn't be sorry later, not to have the year's salary. Thinking they considered I could accept the money and give it to them, I suggested perhaps I should. "You could get new cars," I offered. Darin's quick response, Farah agreeing, was all I needed to hear. "Mom, new cars are soon old cars, needing to be replaced. You would remember you took the buyout. If that is what you don't want to do, don't. You're the one that has to live with your decision." The following was included in the letter I submitted to my director.

"This letter is sent to let you know I am not signing the Agreement and General Release.

This Release, as you know, includes (along with a number of other stipulations) an agreement that the Company is released from liability related to laws based upon several Civil Rights Acts. I cannot be a party to such an agreement.

Young men, women and even children died, during my lifetime in the struggle that produced those Civil Rights laws. Although I had no direct participation in the effort, I remember clearly the pain, humiliation and hope my family and I experienced reading, listening to and discussing the news each day brought. Those who died were innocent, dedicated citizens brutally killed. In addition, many others were seriously injured, maimed and emotionally destroyed.

Due, in great part, to their courageous sacrifice, I had the business career I dreamed of. If I sign an Agreement and General Release giving up legal rights fought for and finally won in my lifetime, I would have trouble sleeping. Actually, I am forever grateful for the sacrifices that proved my father absolutely right when he told me, his little girl, "keep studying, be prepared; there will be opportunities for you."

Since corporate America invited me to access management opportunities those many years ago, the glass ceiling for minorities and for women has been gradually yet resoundingly shattered. At one point after regaining my lost managerial status, I reported to a dynamic director who was a young black woman. For many years my son has managed a large department in the major company that employs him. My daughter's career has included many years as a vice president. Black men and women serve as CEOs of major businesses, and many others are ascending the corporate ladder in positions of increasing responsibility, poised to become top officers in industry.

The campaign and election of the black candidate, Barack Obama, inaugurated the forty-fourth president of the United States of America on January 20, 2009, has been cathartic. The nation has been energized with a "we can" spirit, i.e., purpose and quality attention reversing an unacceptable status quo is possible and will happen.

What a blessing to savor the election and the inauguration and especially to feel the exhilaration of the many who never dreamed they would live to see a black person elected president of our country. I suppose having been brought up listening to my father's optimism about the improvement of the condition of blacks in America; I could not say I didn't think it would happen in my lifetime. Why not? In 1967, the city of Cleveland, Ohio, elected Carl Stokes as mayor, the first black mayor of a major city. Hundreds of blacks have been elected since that time to the office of mayor, serving in practically every major city and others as well. And in 1990, voters in Virginia elected Douglas Wilder to govern their state. Governor Wilder became the first black governor of any state in our nation. He had been elected lieutenant governor in 1985. I was thrilled to attend Governor Wilder's inauguration and festivities in January 1991. As President Obama took his oath, Massachusetts was concluding the first year with a black man, Deval Patrick, serving as governor of their commonwealth.

Our nation's historic and major accomplishment in electing President Obama instilled much of the world population with a "they will" belief—reactions around the globe, refreshingly implying America is a world leader poised to respect all peoples with constructive attention to the universal concerns of the economy, the environment, immigration, and dispensing with violence to resolve deep-seated issues.

Still, in our country there's work to be done to address the discouraging impact of racial disparity that continues to exist. I say the gains realized in America because of the civil rights movement, more than historical fact, must always evolve and continue to help improve the lives of those who are in need. I believe individuals who have "made it" due to the civil rights movement, especially the men and women in positions of influence and power, can help eradicate pervasive racial disparity in the business sector and in our communities by sharing experiences that inform and strengthen another's personal resolve to succeed.

Endnotes

1. Branch Normal College, founded in 1873, a branch of the Normal Department of the Arkansas Industrial University. Ten Bachelor of Arts degrees were conferred between 1882 and 1885. From 1886 through 1927, the school operated as a junior college. A teaching certificate was the only degree awarded until 1930. During the span of its existence, there have been three name changes: from Branch Normal College to Arkansas Agricultural, Mechanical and Normal College (Arkansas AM& N) to the current name, the University of Arkansas at Pine Bluff (source www.uapb.edu).

2. Civilian Conservation Corps was a public works program of work opportunity for young men and adults during the Great Depression, which started in 1929 (source www.cccalumni.org).

3. Works Progress Administration (WPA), Roosevelt's major work relief program, would employ more than 8.5 million people to build bridges, roads, public buildings, parks, and airports (source http://www.pbs.org/wgbh/amex/dustbowl/peopleevents/pandeAMEX10html).

4. Kate Smith—Kathryn Elizabeth Smith was born May 1, 1907, in the nation's capital. From an early age she loved to sing and dance. She performed in theaters and at nightclubs and was discovered by a New York City show producer in 1926. She had the most popular radio variety hour, *The Kate Smith Hour*, which aired weekly from 1937–1945. She entered television with a Monday through Friday afternoon variety show, *The Kate Smith Hour*, in 1950, the beginning of an extensive television career. She recorded, appeared, and starred in movies, on concert stages, and a number of other venues including in the '70s for the Philadelphia Flyers hockey team and as Grand Marshall of the 1976 Tournament of Roses Parade. Kate Smith's theme song was "When the Moon Comes over the Mountain." Irving Berlin regarded the song she made most famous, "God Bless America," as his most important composition. Kate predicted the song would still be sung long after all of us are gone—it surely will. The last song she sang was that Irving Berlin anthem on a bicentennial special just

before July 4, 1976. She died in Raleigh, NC, June 17, 1986 (source http://katesmith.org).

5. Three of my brothers would serve in the military; Jim in the U.S. Air Force, Larry in the U.S. Navy, and Roy in the U.S. Army. A brother-in-law cherished his service in the U.S. Marines.

6. Satchel Paige (July 7, 1906–June 8, 1982), born Leroy Robert Paige, was a legendary storyteller and one of the most entertaining pitchers in baseball history. A tall, lanky fireballer, he was arguably the Negro League's hardest thrower, most colorful character, and greatest gate attraction. In the 1930s, the well-traveled pitcher barnstormed around the continent baffling hitters. In 1948, on his forty-second birthday, his contract was sold to the Cleveland Indians, becoming the oldest player to make his major league debut and helping the Indians win the American League pennant. On August 20, 1948, Satchel Paige pitched the Indians to a 1–0 victory over the Chicago White Sox in front of 78,382 fans, a night-game attendance record that still stands. Satchel Paige was elected to the Hall of Fame by Committee on Negro Leagues in 1971 (source: the national Baseball Hall of Fame Web site www.baseballhalloffame.org).

7. Negro League—African-Americans began to play baseball in the late 1800s on military teams, college teams, and company teams. They eventually found their way to professional teams with white players. However, racism and racist laws would force them from these teams by 1900. Thus black players formed their own units, "barnstorming" around the country to play anyone who would challenge them. In 1920 an organized league structure was formed under the guidance of Andrew "Rube" Foster—a former player, manager, and owner for the Chicago American Giants. In a meeting held at the Paseo YMCA in Kansas City, Mo., Foster and a few other Midwestern team owners joined to form the Negro National League. Soon, rival leagues formed in Eastern and Southern states, bringing the thrills and innovative play of black baseball to major urban centers and rural countrysides in the United States, Canada, and Latin America. The Leagues maintained a high level of professional skill and became centerpieces for economic development in many black communities. In 1947 Jackie Robinson became the first African-American in the modern era to play on a Major League roster. The historic event in

baseball and civil rights prompted the decline of the Negro League. The best black players were now recruited for the Major Leagues, and black fans followed. The last Negro League teams folded in the early 1960s (source: Negro Leagues Baseball Museum Web site www.nlbm.com).

8. Jesse Owens—James Cleveland Owens, born in 1913, was a record-breaking track star in high school. The African-American athlete entered Ohio State University and excelled, breaking track records there as well. At the end of his sophomore year, he entered the 1936 Olympics being held in Nazi Germany. Hitler was going to prove to the world that the German "Aryan" people were the dominant race. However, Jesse Owens won four gold medals, i.e., the 100-meter dash, the 200-meter dash, the broad jump, and was a key member of the 400-meter relay team that won the gold. He also won the cheers of the German fans. Notably, he was the first American in the history of Olympic Track and Field to win four gold medals in a single Olympics. Despite his success, in America he was not offered any endorsement deals because he was black. To provide for his family, he left school to run professionally. For a while, he was a runner-for-hire racing against anything from people, to horses, to motorcycles. The Negro Baseball league often hired him to race against thoroughbred horses in an exhibition before every game. Jesse Owens was an articulate and enjoyable lecturer who took numerous public-speaking engagements. He was so well liked he started his own public relations firm. In 1976, President Gerald R. Ford awarded him the highest honor a civilian of the United States can receive, the Medal of Freedom. Jesse Owens overcame segregation, racism, and bigotry to prove to the world that African-Americans belonged in the world of athletics. On March 31, 1980, Jesse Owens died in Tucson, Arizona, from complications due to cancer. His family operates the Jesse Owens Foundation, striving to provide financial assistance and support to deserving young individuals that otherwise would not have the opportunity to pursue their goals (source www.jesseowens.com).

9. Larry Doby—Lawrence Eugene Doby (December 13, 1923–June 18, 2003) the first African-American player in the American League. He was a power-hitting center fielder and a key member of Cleveland's

pennant winners in 1948 and 1954. Before joining the Indians in 1947, he starred with the Negro National League's Newark Eagles for four seasons, leading them to a championship in 1946. During his lifetime, he was a nine time all-star (seven times with the Indians and twice with the Eagles); Doby led the American League twice in homers. His lifetime statistics include a batting average .283, Games 1533, AB 5348, Runs 960, HRs 253, SBs 47, RBI 970. Larry Doby was elected to the Hall of Fame by Veterans Committee in 1998 (source www.baseballhalloffame.org).

10. Pymatuning Lake—Before the glaciers swept across Northwestern Pennsylvania, the Pymatuning was a lake. But the great ice movements gouging out hills, filling the valleys, etc., reduced the lake to a swamp. Man reversed the works of the Ice Age and, to the joy of hunters, sportsmen, and naturalists, created a lake from the once great bog. Just north of Hartstown, Pa., the Shenango River originates. It flows northward to the present upper lake (the refuge area), across the spillway into the main lake, turning sharply south in both Ohio and Pennsylvania toward Espyville, Pa., and Andover, Ohio, and then southeast to Jamestown, Pa., and the current dam. The upper lake was impounded in December 1933. The lower lake was closed some weeks later. The upper reservoir tract was set aside as a game refuge in 1935. The Pymatuning was dammed primarily for water conservation and flood control in the Shenango and Ohio River valleys. It comprises twenty-five thousand acres, of which seventeen thousand acres are water and eight thousand acres are land. The lake is sixteen miles long with seventy miles of shoreline and is the largest body of water in the state of Pennsylvania. It lies partly in Ohio and has a capacity of 67,275,000,000 gallons and a maximum depth of thirty-five feet. The name Pymatuning is of Indian origin and means "Crooked-mouth man's dwelling place," the term "crooked-mouth" referring to an ancient Red Man who was not famous for truth telling (source www.pymatuning.com).

11. New Deal—In 1932, Franklin Delano Roosevelt was elected overwhelmingly on a campaign promising a New Deal for the American people—he worked quickly to deliver the New Deal, an unprecedented number of reforms addressing the catastrophic effects of the Great Depression. The Works Progress Administration

(WPA) would employ more than 8.5 million people to build bridges, roads, public buildings, parks, and airports (source http://www.pbs. org/wgbh/amex/dustbowl/peopleevents/pandeAMEX09.html).

12. Milk Snake—Eastern milk snakes are commonly encountered throughout Ohio in a variety of habitats. Their frequent occurrence in rodent-infested barns led to the fallacy that they milk cows by night, hence the name milk snake. Like other members of the king snake group, milk snakes feed primarily upon mice and other small rodents, as well as smaller snakes. They should be considered an asset, worthy of protection on anyone's property (source www.dnr. state.oh.us).

13. Gabriel Heater—New York's Library of American Broadcasting (on 7-20-2005) picked Gabriel Heater, radio newsman, as one of five posthumous honorees at the year's annual event in September. He was one of a total of fifteen broadcasting "giants" honored in 2005 (source www.broadcastingcable.com)

14. Lowell Thomas (1892–1981)—Lowell Thomas pioneered radio journalism with a career that spanned fifty years. He brought news and a sense of adventure into America's living rooms. During World War II, Thomas broadcast accounts of the war, often from a mobile truck behind front lines. Between his standard opening, "Good Evening, everybody," and his closing, "So long until tomorrow," people knew they were hearing a solid, objective voice of authority. Lowell Thomas was inducted into the Radio Hall of Fame in 1989 (source www.museum.tv).

15. *Amos 'n' Andy*—the story of two black characters—the modest, pragmatic Amos and the blustery, self-confident Andy—created by two white actors, Freeman Gosden and Charles Correll. In the '30s, *Amos 'n' Andy* became a national phenomenon, a comedy serial with nearly forty million listeners. Movie theaters were forced to stop their features each night to pipe in the fifteen-minute show for their audience. Although *Amos 'n' Andy's* dialect humor caused much controversy among African-Americans, the show's appeal during its prime was not restricted to any single race. *Amos 'n' Andy* was inducted into the Radio Hall of Fame in 1988 (source www. radiohof.org)

16. Bill Veeck—William Louis Veeck Jr. (1914–1986) elected to the National Baseball Hall of Fame by veterans Committee in 1991. Bill Veeck consistently broke attendance records with pennant-winning teams, outrageous door prizes, enthusiastic fan participation, and ingenious promotional schemes. He introduced the concept of honoring fans, Bat Day, fireworks, exploding scoreboards and player names on backs of uniforms. He signed the American League's first black player—Larry Doby in 1947—and the oldest rookie—forty-three-year-old Satchel Paige in 1948 (source www. baseballhalloffame.org).

17. Academic Achievement: I was our Class Salutatorian. My father would not let me give the Salutatorian's message at graduation. He said it would be an embarrassing contradiction for me to stand before everyone grandly expounding on the magnificent future before our class knowing there wasn't a person in the room who would hire me, a black person, for a meaningful job, if they had one. Significantly, a week after graduation, the son of the local business icon (owner of a major new car dealership in Youngstown) came to our house and congratulated my father on "your daughter's accomplishments." "I know she is going away to college in the fall. I would like to hire her to babysit my children this summer." Of course, Daddy said "no" and unfortunately, forever after, I had to hear his observation that the man, if I had been white, not black, would have offered me a job in business, not babysitting.

18. Emmett Till—Emmett wasn't a civil rights activist. He wasn't politically active. But the national media attention surrounding his death and the trial and acquittal of his alleged killers had an impact that no one ever could have imagined. The Emmett Till case became one of the key incidents of 1955, the explosive year that launched the modern civil rights movement (source www.jimcrowhistory.org).

19. Dick and Jane—the children's book characters who taught children from the 1930s through the 1960s how to read. They were the creation of Zerna Sharp, a consultant for publisher Scott Foresman. The rest of the family included Sally, Spot the dog, Puff the kitten, and Father and Mother, smart, gracious, a model mother, wife, and homemaker. By the late '60s, Dick and Jane's days were numbered.

Educators wanted children's books reflecting all kinds of kids, not just white, middle-class ones (source www.mediahistory.umn.edu).

20. In an effort to avoid the least presumption of invasion of privacy or conflict regarding any preference for confidentiality, I have not included the employer's name nor have I given the actual names of co-workers and others. The story is true.

21. In 1980 during an eleven-day transit strike, footwear became more comfortable. Sturdy sneakers worn to get us where busses and subways refused to go until worker demands were met continued to be a popular walking shoe of choice after the strike ended. Once at work, women and men changed into office appropriate footwear. The transit strike spawned a welcome and healthy foot fashion that continues.

22. September 15, 1963—Carol Denise McNair, age 11; Cynthia Wesley, Addie Mae Collins and Carole Robertson, all age 14

23. June 21,1964—Andrew Goodman, 20, Michael Schwerner, 24, and James Chaney, 21

24. June 12, 1963—Medgar Evers

25. March 25, 1965—Violet Liuzzo

26. In 2002, the building was renovated by the State of Michigan and renamed Cadillac Place.

27. Since 2000, Comerica Park has been the home field of the Detroit Tigers. Demolition of Tiger Stadium began in 2008.

LaVergne, TN USA
17 March 2010
176366LV00004B/1/P